**52 READY-TO-USE
GAMING PROGRAMS FOR LIBRARIES**

ALA Editions purchases fund advocacy, awareness, and accreditation programs for library professionals worldwide.

52 READY-TO-USE GAMING PROGRAMS for Libraries

edited by **Ellyssa Kroski**

ALA Editions

CHICAGO | 2020

ELLYSSA KROSKI is the director of information technology and marketing at the New York Law Institute and an award-winning editor and author of more than sixty books. She is a librarian, an adjunct faculty member at Drexel University and San Jose State University, and an international conference speaker. She was named the winner of the 2017 Library Hi Tech Award from the ALA/LITA for her long-term contributions in the area of library and information science technology and its application. She can be found at amazon.com/author/ellyssa.

© 2020 by the American Library Association

Extensive effort has gone into ensuring the reliability of the information in this book; however, the publisher makes no warranty, express or implied, with respect to the material contained herein.

ISBN: 978-0-8389-4734-0 (paper)

Library of Congress Cataloging-in-Publication Data
Names: Kroski, Ellyssa, editor.
Title: 52 ready-to-use gaming programs for libraries / edited by Ellyssa Kroski.
Other titles: Fifty-two ready-to-use gaming programs for libraries
Description: Chicago : ALA Editions, 2020. | Includes bibliographical references and index. | Summary: "Ellyssa Kroski has gathered 52 creative programming ideas from public, school, and academic libraries. Most will hit your core gaming audience of teens, but you'll also find plenty of options for adults, tweens, and kids"— Provided by publisher.
Identifiers: LCCN 2019056401 | ISBN 9780838947340 (paperback)
Subjects: LCSH: Libraries—Activity programs. | Libraries—Special collections—Games.
Classification: LCC Z716.33 .A137 2020 | DDC 025.5—dc23
LC record available at https://lccn.loc.gov/2019056401

Book design by Alejandra Diaz in the Tisa Pro and Woodford Bourne typefaces.

⊚ This paper meets the requirements of ANSI/NISO Z39.48-1992 (Permanence of Paper).

Printed in the United States of America
24 23 22 21 20   5 4 3 2 1

Contents

Preface **xi**
Acknowledgments **xiii**

PART I | Tabletop Game Programs

1 Beyond Dungeons & Dragons: Building a Roleplaying Program **3**
ROBERT TAYLOR AND DANIELLE COSTELLO

2 How to Start Tabletop Gaming Programs at Your Library, for Absolute Beginners **15**
MARK HALVORSEN AND JAMES TYNER

3 Brush & Shield: Paint & Take Miniature Day at the Public Library **21**
MARK HALVORSEN

4 Recurring Game Events for Older Adults **29**
MARK HALVORSEN

5 How to Develop Socioeconomic Literacies with the Landlord Game **37**
RANDAL SEAN HARRISON

6 Hero's Handbook: Steps for Creating a Pathfinder RPG Beginner's Program **43**
DELANEY BULLINGER AND ALLISON RAND

7 Dewey and Dragons: Dungeons & Dragons at the Library **49**
JAMEY RORIE

8 How to Build a Circulating Board Game Collection for a Commuter Campus **55**
TIFFANIE FORD-BAXTER, DANIEL PALODICHUK, AND JENNIFER SELGA

CONTENTS

9 | Developing Science Literacy through Science-Themed Board Games **59**
BRYCE VAN ROSS AND TIFFANIE FORD-BAXTER

10 | Call of Cthulhu: Hosting Roleplaying Events in the World of H. P. Lovecraft **65**
MICHAEL FURLONG

11 | How to Host a Large-Scale Board Games Event for New Student Orientation **73**
ANNETTE M. VADNAIS

12 | Not So Trivial Pursuit: Board Game Creation in Your Library **79**
KRISTEN CINAR

13 | How to Organize a Tabletop Gaming Convention **85**
TIFFANY POLFER AND JAMES TYNER

14 | Play Your Cards Right: An Information Literacy Card Game for Undergrads **93**
MARTHA ATTRIDGE BUFTON, COLIN HARKNESS, AND RYAN TUCCI

15 | Advanced D&G (Donations and Grants): Building Your Game Library without Breaking Your Budget **97**
MATTHEW MORRISON

16 | RPG Writing Workshop: Lead Patrons in Writing Their Own Games **103**
CHRISTOPHER BUSSMAN AND SHEA'LA FINCH

17 | How to Highlight Locally Designed Board Games in Your Library **115**
MAGGIE BLOCK

PART II | Video Game Programs

18 | Exam Cram: Providing Video Games for Final Exam Study Breaks **121**
KYLE NEILL AND BRAD CASSELBERRY

CONTENTS

19 | How to Start a Kerbal Space Program Club **127**
JACQUELINE LOCKWOOD

20 | Game and Learn: How to Create a Library Augmented Reality Tour **133**
YINGQI TANG AND CHARLCIE VANN

21 | Level Up! Library Orientation with a Phone-Based Exploration Game **137**
BETH JANE TOREN

22 | Smash Your Programming Goals with a Super Smash Bros. Ultimate Tournament **147**
SARAH PROSSER

23 | Get the Most out of VR **153**
HALEY T. LEE

24 | How to Create and Sustain a Gamer's Club Even if You Are Not a Gamer **159**
MAYA BERRY

25 | How to Create an Arcade Program in the Library **163**
NICHOLAS DEASE

26 | How to Create a Video Game Recreational League **171**
LEAH CANNER

27 | Culper Spies: Choose Your Own Adventure Online Gamification **179**
KRISTEN CINAR

28 | Hosting Pokémon GO PVP Tournaments in Your Library **183**
EMILY BURKOT

29 | Building a Video Game Collection for Programming (And Keeping It Current!) **189**
EMILY BURKOT

30 | It's Locked: Combining Video Games with Real-Life STEM Challenges **195**
SELENIA PAZ

31 | How to Explore STEM Programming through VR **201**
ZACHARY STIER

32 | Teach Young Patrons Cybersecurity Using Minecraft **207**
CHRIS MARKMAN

PART III | Live Action Game Programs

33 | How to Run a Vampire LARP in the Library **215**
ERROL LOGAN

34 | How to Run an Instagram Scavenger Hunt
for New Student Orientation **221**
SUSAN M. HANSEN

35 | How to Create a Life-Sized Game of Life **225**
LINDSEY TOMSU

36 | How to Organize an Escape Room for Faculty **235**
MAYA BERRY AND MELISSA WRIGHT

37 | Live Video Games: Library Battle Royale **245**
SARAH AMAZING

38 | Hunger Games Survival Challenge **249**
SARAH AMAZING

39 | How to Create a Live Clue Game **255**
JONATHAN DOLCE

40 | Scavenger Hunt: Zombie Tag **267**
KARLENE TURA CLARK

41 | How to Create a Mini-Golf Mini-Tour **277**
KAITLYN MAY, MARY ATWELL, AND EMILY HAMPTON HAYNES

42 | Spy Hunt: A Library Research Scavenger Hunt **281**
KRISTEN CINAR

43 | How to Run a Fandom LARP **287**
ELIZABETH R. STRAUSS

CONTENTS

44 | Anything Bingo **293**
ELIZABETH R. STRAUSS

45 | Stop the Mad Librarian: A Library Orientation Escape Room **297**
SUSAN M. HANSEN

46 | How to Run a Library Research Gamification Program **307**
LISA NJOKU

47 | Laser Tag in the Stacks **313**
STEVEN WADE, JULIE HORNICK, RANDALL M. MACDONALD, AND MARINA MORGAN

48 | Save Lewis the Librarian! An Information Literacy Escape Room **317**
RUTH CHO

49 | How to Run a History Mystery Program for Teens **327**
RUTH COVINGTON

50 | How to Create Life-Sized Board Games **335**
LINDSEY TOMSU

51 | Just Try to Escape Your Training! Using Escape Rooms to Develop a Cohesive Student Worker Team **345**
MELANIE BOPP

52 | The Amazing Race: STEAM to the Finish Line **357**
SANDRA CALEMME MCCARTHY AND MAUREEN PERAULT

Index **361**

PREFACE

GAMES AND GAMING events of all types are actively being used in libraries as a vehicle to pass along valuable STEM (science, technology, engineering, and math) information literacy, and critical-thinking skills. Game-based learning activities are a potent tool to support curriculum, engage the library community through play, and provide an avenue for developing social literacies. Plus, they are just plain fun! *52 Ready-to-Use Gaming Programs for Libraries* is a one-stop handbook for how to plan, organize, and run all types of gaming activities in libraries. Programs range from tabletop gaming activities, such as Dungeons & Dragons, to family game nights; trivia events; large-scale board game events; classic and modern video games; games encompassing new technologies, such as social media, augmented reality (AR), and virtual reality (VR); and even live action games such as LARPs and escape rooms.

Each program walks the reader through step-by-step instructions for how to prepare and host these events, including a materials and equipment list, budget, and recommendations for age ranges and the most appropriate types of libraries in which to run it. We offer programs that range in cost, topic, and difficulty level in this book; there is something for every size and type of library. The authors of these gaming programs are knowledgeable professionals from the library field, offering real-world programming ideas for public, school, and academic libraries.

ACKNOWLEDGMENTS

I WOULD LIKE to heartily thank all the gaming librarians who shared their time and expertise within this book. It was a pleasure to work with all of you.

PART I
Tabletop Game Programs

Beyond Dungeons & Dragons
Building a Roleplaying Program

ROBERT TAYLOR
Acquisitions & Cataloging Librarian

DANIELLE COSTELLO
Library Technical Assistant

Valdosta State University

THIS IS AN effective program for the librarian under a time crunch and on a budget. In this chapter we will lead you through the process of developing a roleplaying game (RPG) program. The chapter begins with tips for selecting a rulebook/rule set and then moves into a step-by-step method for developing individual RPG sessions. These steps can be repeatedly used regardless of which rulebook you choose to run. We've provided a chart with a slight variety of rulebooks to help jumpstart your program.

Age Range	Type of Library Best Suited For	Cost Estimate
Tweens (ages 8–12) Young Adults (ages 13–18) Adults	Public Libraries Academic Libraries	$0–$100 (Cost will vary depending on the game rule set and required materials.)

OVERVIEW

This program aims to lower the bar of entry for librarians who are interested in RPG programs. The RPG rule sets in the chart included in this chapter were selected to show a diversity of playing styles. Some rules are easy to learn. Other rules do not require a Game Master (also known as a GM) to facilitate the game. Some rules include interesting and unique mechanics or settings designed to give you an introduction to the variety of RPG styles that exist. All the RPGs selected in this book do not require expensive components, are relatively cheap to purchase, and do not require time-consuming character-creation sessions. These games can generally be learned quickly and should be played in either one one-to-three-hour-long session or two to three sessions of similar length.

For this chapter, we've divided the RPGs into two very broad main categories: those that require a GM and those that are GM-less. GM-less games usually focus on collective storytelling with rules that specify who wins (if there is a winner) and what the winning conditions are. The bulk of time required to prepare for this type of game involves reading and reviewing the rules and creating reminder sheets (crib sheets), if necessary. Some GM-less games, such as Fiasco, feature very short rulebooks that do not require any preparation.

Other games, such as Silent Memories, require a GM, and you'll need some time to prepare for the game. Silent Memories is also an example of a game that can last longer than one to two hours. When choosing a game of this type, consider how many sessions you need to invest in the game and how much time should pass between sessions. If you are running a game with a large number of players, you should also try to include a colleague or friend in the session to help with playtesting and to answer questions during game night.

NECESSARY EQUIPMENT AND MATERIALS

Possible RPG program items needed include
- a pencil
- paper
- index cards
- sets of six-sided dice (D6)
- sets of seven polyhedral dice (seven die in each set)
- a deck of standard playing cards
- a Jenga tower

CHAPTER 1 | **Beyond Dungeons & Dragons**

Table 1.1 | Board games

Title	Publisher	Cost Print/PDF	Theme	Additional Materials	Notes
Archives of the Sky	Aaron A. Reed	$24.95/$10	Science Fiction	index cards, tokens, pencils	GM-less
Alas for the Awful Sea	Storybrewers Roleplaying	$30/$20	Historical High Seas	dice, pencil, paper	GM
Amazing Tales	Studio 2 Publishing	$19/$5.95	Open	polyhedral dice	GM
Blades in the Dark	Evil Hat Productions	$30/$20	Horror Fantasy Heist	dice, pencil, paper	GM
Dialect: A Game about Language and How It Dies	Thorny Games	$10/$29	Language Play	none	GM
Dread	The Impossible Dream	$24/$12	Horror	Jenga tower	GM
Dungeon World	Sage Kobold Productions	$25/$10	Fantasy	polyhedral dice	GM
Eden	Less than Three Games	$20/$10	Worldbuilding	paper and pencils	GM-less
ExSpelled	AndHeGames	$17/$7	Fantasy	colored pencils, crayons, scissors, glue	GM-less
Extraordinary Adventures of Baron Munchausen	Fantasy Flight	$24.95/$9.95	Storytelling/Boasting	tokens	GM-less
Fate Core	Evil Hat Productions	$25/$5*	Open	dice	GM
Fiasco	Bully Pulpit Games	$25/$12	Heist	D6	GM-less
Flatpack: Fix the Future	Machine Age Productions	NA/$3.50	Post-apocalyptic	pencils, D4, 2D6, D8	GM-less
Golden Sky Stories	Indie Press Revolution	$20/$10	Fantasy	paper, pencils, tokens	GM
Hillfolk	Pelgrane Press	$29.95	Iron Age Drama	playing cards, poker chips or beads, tokens, index cards, paper, pencils	GM
Honey Heist	Gshowitt	Free*	BEAR	3D6, 1D8, paper, pencils	GM
If Not Us, Then Who?	Riley Hopkins	NA/$15	Super-powered Teen Heroes	deck of playing cards	GM-less
Kids on Bikes	Renegade Game Studios	$25/NA	Supernatural Mystery	polyhedral dice	GM
No Thank You, Evil	Monte Cook Games	$39.99/$19.99	Fantastical	everything contained in box	GM
Noirlandia	Make Big Things	$19.99	Noir	dice, index cards, pen, corkboard, string	GM-less
Ryuutama	Kotodama Heavy Industries	$35/$14	Fantasy Exploration	polyhedral dice, pencils, paper	GM
Silent Memories	Morning Skye Studio	Free*	Science Fiction	Jenga tower, paper, pencils	GM
Ten Candles	Cavalry Games	$28/$10	Horror	D6	GM
The Quiet Year (PDF)	Buried without Ceremony	$25/$6	Community Building	deck of playing cards	GM-less
Tiny Dungeon 2e	Gallant Knight Games	$24.99/$17.99	Fantasy	index cards, D6, pencils	GM

*Pay what you like

STEP-BY-STEP INSTRUCTIONS

Preparation

Developing Your Program

- Consider your library's program needs.
  - Look for themed RPGs that can be applied to a season of the year or to library events.
    - » For example, Blades in the Dark could be run during Halloween because of its horror theme. Honey Heist, on the other hand, has a much more lighthearted theme and could be used as a springtime game.
    - » If you are showcasing an author or series, you can use a themed rule set within the same genre. Then, you can incorporate elements of one of the books into the game. For the examples included in this chapter, I used the John Carpenter movie *The Thing* as loose inspiration for a game of Silent Memories.
  - If you want to host a one-night event but don't have time to plan a complex story, select an RPG in which the story is created during play or in which minimal preparation is required.
    - » The Extraordinary Adventures of Baron Munchausen is an example of such an RPG. This game puts the work on the players by requiring each to boast about their most ridiculous and fantastical exploits.
    - » Many such RPGs, such as Dread, contain modules or premade adventures that you can use.
- Consider your patrons.
  - RPGs can vary widely in theme and tone; consider the type of patrons you want to reach and choose accordingly.
    - » For example, Ten Candles is not appropriate for a younger age group. However, Amazing Tales was specifically designed for children.
  - When preparing marketing materials, be clear as to what themes and mechanics are used in the game.
  - If you have patrons who want to commit to a multisession game, choose an RPG that gives you more freedom in world-building such as Fate Core.
- Most importantly, choose rulebooks that are fun for you to run!

Pregame Preparation

- Send out a consent opt-in form to the players (this is optional).
    - Read *Consent in Gaming* from Monte Cook Games for information on appropriate consent forms and other methods of keeping the game fun for everyone.
- If you decide not to use the consent opt-in form, be sure to find out player expectations and boundaries ahead of time. This will ensure you don't put triggering information in your story.
    - Check out our Additional Resources section on how to deal with potentially triggering scenarios that may happen during your game.
- Read your chosen rule set.
    - Print out any character sheets and gather needed materials.
    - Note player and GM actions. These will be useful later when you prepare a crib sheet.
- Create your story (optional—dependent on your rule set).
    - Tips for story creation:
        » Find your favorite book or movie that fits the theme of the game you've chosen.
        » Isolate some of the major and minor encounters.
            o Try to isolate one large event for the climax of the story. The rest of the encounters should drive the story or add to the theme.
            o Don't overthink your story. Flexibility is key. Even if you do not get to use an event or story hook, you can save it for a later game.
        » Create a few non-playable characters (NPCs) for players to interact with. You can also use the NPCs to help move the story if players get stuck or wander too far.
        » Create some simple puzzles or ciphers for your players to solve.
        » Include visual aids such as maps.
        » Prepare some alternative ways to guide players when they deviate too far.
            o Include breadcrumbs (details) that invest the players in the story and lead them to the events you want them to experience.

- Consider the size of your group. If many people are playing, you may need assistance managing all players and events in the game. Grab a friend or colleague ahead of time to help you during game night.
  - If possible, playtest your story with your friends/colleagues.
- Create a crib sheet: This is a simplified version of the rules and orders of action for you and the players to refer to.
  - Isolate some of the core rules from the rule set.
  - Try to keep the length of your crib sheet at one to two pages.
  - The trick is to only include rules you may need to reference often while you are learning the game.
    - » For example, you may want to include what actions a player can take on their turn and in which order, or the different phases of each round in the game.

EXAMPLE: We chose to create a one-to-two-hour-long game session using Silent Memories, a sci-fi horror RPG. The game requires paper, pencils, and a Jenga tower. In the game, three to five players wake up early from cryostasis. The players have no memories of who they are or why they are on the ship. The lights go out, and the players must start the ship and find out what happened. During the game, each time a player wants to take an action that could be considered risky, the GM decides how risky the action is. The player is then instructed to pull one to three blocks from the Jenga tower. Regardless of whether the pulls are successful or not, the player's memory is jogged, and they receive a memory from the GM. I decided to use the movie *The Thing*, as inspiration for the main story, with some adjustments to fit the space environment. The specific elements the players isolated were the use of blood to transmit the infection and the feeling of isolation from the outside world. I spent about three hours typing the story and the memories for the game. I also spent some time looking for a spaceship layout to help the players visualize the area and to assist me in preparing encounters for different rooms. I typed informational cues to help them remember what each room should contain. The total preparation time took me about five hours.

Program Instructions

Game Night
- Arrive early (thirty to sixty minutes before the start of the game).
- Make sure everyone is comfortable and address any accessibility issues.
- Distribute materials around the table.
- Introduce yourself and establish game-play boundaries with the players.
    - Emphasize that the game is collaborative in nature.
    - Introduce your chosen mechanic for dealing with potentially uncomfortable situations (X-card, Lines and Veils, etc.).
        » Inform the group of any boundaries previously requested by the players before the start of the game.

> **EXAMPLE:** We began the game by setting up the Jenga tower and explaining the rules of the game to the group. We also emphasized that while this game is cooperative in the beginning, the person who learns *The Truth* could potentially be a traitor. Silent Memories does not require a crib sheet because the game is almost completely driven by the players' actions. So, we typed a description of each available character role (Commander, Medical Officer, Engineer, Technician, and Generalist) and cut them into slips. The character roles were numbered on the back. The players then randomly chose a small slip of paper with a number on it. The person who drew the slip with the number one on it received the Commander role. As each player *woke up*, they received their character role and then *remembered* their name.

Character Creation
- If using premade character sheets, allow the players to choose their characters. If creating characters from scratch, begin the process laid out in the rulebook.

Play and Troubleshooting
- Explain the rules and hand out crib sheets to all players if needed.
- Set up the story by introducing your world and beginning scenario.
- Be prepared to deal with different play styles.

- Every player is going to come to the game with a different goal in mind.
- It is nearly impossible to anticipate what types of players will come to your table; so, there is only so much pregame preparation you can accomplish.
- Be prepared to mediate if issues arise and give every player an opportunity to be heard.

Story Conflicts

- If some of your details don't add up, don't stress! Get creative and find a way to weave them together.

- Alternatively, put the power of description in the hands of the players. Have the players describe the rooms to you and build on the foundation they provide.

- If you have non-engagement/a stalled story:
    - If the players get stalled, try to jumpstart some ideas by describing things in the room that may be important. You could also give leading hints.
        » If the players are stalled and arguing, do not be afraid to step in and move them forward. For example, an NPC can toss them out of the bar while they're arguing, or a strange noise might suddenly echo through the halls of the darkened spaceship they are trapped on, spurring the players to action.
    - Be sure to make time for each player to have a turn to speak and to take appropriate actions during the game.
    - Some players may not be familiar with roleplaying. Introduce an NPC and then roleplay as that character in the game to get people started.

> **EXAMPLE:** The story for one particular evening involved gratuitous amounts of blood and damage to the ship. As a result, the players caught on quickly that something might be wrong with the blood. Some of the memories and events sowed false suspicions toward certain players. These memories added additional flavor to the game and helped the players get into character. It also took the heat off the person who tumbled the tower and learned *The*

> *Truth*. In this particular game, the person who learned *The Truth* discovered that she was in fact the Traitor and had to infect everyone in the game to win. The players had the chance to create an antidote for the infection using salt, metal shavings, and whiskey. I put in different opportunities for the players to discover these items and have them on their person. During the game, the players spent a lot of time debating which actions to take. After allowing the discussion to continue for a few minutes, I directly asked the Commander what actions they would be taking and pushed her to take the lead in the group. At other times I grabbed an hourglass from a separate board game and put pressure on the players to make a decision. If the hourglass ran out, I would advance the story while they argued. However, before that could happen, the Commander always seized control to advance the game.

Decompression

- Build in five to twenty minutes for players to discuss the game afterward. This is also a great way to get immediate feedback.
    - Try to ensure that everyone leaves the table in a positive frame of mind. If the game play involved negative themes, give players the opportunity to discuss among themselves how they felt about the game.

> **EXAMPLE:** The Traitor in the game used trickery to convince the players that she was taking an action that would save the group. Instead, the Traitor infected the group, thus ending the game. After the game was over, the group took about five to ten minutes to discuss what happened and provide constructive feedback for me. The players also needed time to decompress from the story. They did not expect the Traitor to be capable of deceiving them in such a way. Despite the fact that everyone knew they were playing a game, their anger toward that character bled into their feelings for the person who ran her. They had given her more trust than her character in the game had earned. At the end of the game, the group took some time

> to talk about their feelings regarding that moment of betrayal and to laugh about how they were tricked. The Traitor also needed to talk about the game, desiring reassurance that the players didn't take the betrayal personally. I also learned that the group enjoyed the story but wanted something more in-depth for the next game.

ADDITIONAL RESOURCES

GM Resources

Davids, Matt. *The No-Prep Gamemaster: Or How I Learned to Stop Worrying and Love Random Tables*. DiceGeeks, 2019.

Guides from Dancing Lights Press: https://dancinglightspress.com.

Laws, Robin D. *Robin's Laws of Good Game Mastering*. Austin, TX: Steve Jackson Games, 2002.

Shea, Michael E. *Return of the Lazy Dungeon Master*. Independently published, 2018.

Game Safety

Reynolds, Sean K., and Shanna Germain. *Consent in Gaming*. Monte Cook Games, LLC, 2019.

Shaw, Kienna, and Lauren Bryant-Monk. "TTRPG Safety Toolkit." 2019. https://drive.google.com/drive/folders/114jRmhzBpdqkAlhm veis0nmW73qkAZCj.

Player Resources

D'Amato, J. *The Ultimate RPG Character Backstory Guide*. Avon, MA: Adams Media, 2018.

D'Amato, J. *The Ultimate RPG Gameplay Guide: Role-Play the Best Campaign Ever—No Matter the Game!* Avon, MA: Adams Media, 2019.

Helpful Websites

RPG Geek: https://rpggeek.com
ALA Roundtable: www.ala.org/rt/gamert/role-playing-games
ALA Games Round Table Facebook Group: League of Librarian Gamers: www.facebook.com/groups/LeagueOfLibrarianGamers

Awards

Diana Jones Awards: www.dianajonesaward.org
ENnie Awards: www.ennie-awards.com/blog
Origins Award, Best Roleplaying Game: www.originsawards.net/origins-award-winners
IGND: Indie Groundbreaker Awards: www.igdnonline.com/groundbreakers

Events

ALA International Games Week: https://games.ala.org/international-games-week

RECOMMENDED NEXT PROJECTS

- Review the included chart for RPG rule sets to start your program and for additional resources on story creation, game safety, and much more.
- If you have a group that really loves a particular rule set, such as the set used in Fate Core, look for additional premade adventures from the publisher and fans!

How to Start Tabletop Gaming Programs at Your Library, for Absolute Beginners

MARK HALVORSEN
Adult Programming Librarian

JAMES TYNER
Adult Services Librarian

Fresno County Public Library

CREATE A CASUAL recurring tabletop game night in your public library. Learn how to plan, prepare, and run an engaging event. This will facilitate confidence in participants who are new to all types of interactive tabletop games and introduce professionals to the concept.

Age Range	Type of Library Best Suited For	Cost Estimate
Adults	Public Libraries	$0–$200

Cost Considerations

Tangible games are required for this program; variety and expenditures depend on the intent of the program, anticipated attendance, and interest. Your library's capacity for donations and the inclusion of patron-driven materials may significantly reduce costs as well. Be sure to factor proper storage and transportation of your supplies into your budget. The price range listed in this book is meant to reflect minimum start-up costs and is not meant to

PART I | **Tabletop Game Programs**

FIGURE 2.1
Preston and Gabe enjoying game night in Fresno, California

limit potential. The optimal method for you may be to determine your maximum budget, request donations, and assess as your program progresses. As a result, these events will vary from zero cost to ongoing.

OVERVIEW

This chapter seeks to inspire public library staff to create a casual and entertaining game night at their branch for adults to enjoy. Librarians can offer a selection of tabletop games, paired with staff members or volunteers prepared to demonstrate and assist patrons in participation. Attendees should be encouraged to bring their favorite game options, further enhancing the evening and increasing the engagement level for everyone.

During game nights, expect attendees to show up at different times. Have staff members prepared to greet and assess their interest, demonstrate available games, or help incorporate them into sessions that are already in progress. The program should conclude with patrons feeling entertained, more confident in gaming, and eager to return to future events.

Deciding Program Length

Initially this program should run at least two hours to accommodate both longer games as well as people who wish to play multiple shorter sessions, try different experiences, and so on. It is recommended that this program be offered as a recurring event that takes place at least once a month, as word will spread and participation should increase over time.

Staffing and Event Capacity

During the first session, you should have one librarian on hand and ideally one volunteer or additional staff person. This allows one to engage directly in the game and show others how to play using demonstrations that they have practiced. A different member of the library staff may fill in a seat to keep the game flowing, gauge interest and time, greet later attendees, and offer them other game options based on what is available. This may include starting new games at another table. Alternatively, they can gauge when it may be beneficial to integrate new players into another active game.

Also, expect some alpha gamers to participate; these gamers may show up with friends who wish to start up their own table, thereby using additional library space to enjoy their game. In addition, regulars will begin to consistently participate. So, it is crucial that you ensure you will have enough game facilitators if the crowd begins to grow.

Your library capacity will be limited by physical space, game supplies, and your number of volunteers. Your institution's capacity may vary greatly from that of others, with space being the most critical factor. Assess and determine if you will have an open-door approach or free registration, based on your specific situation. Keep in mind noise levels, room temperature, and the privacy of all patrons present in the branch. Consider your system's online registration options, as well as apps or event management websites, such as Warhorn.net, which provide alternatives for more experienced gamers.

NECESSARY EQUIPMENT AND MATERIALS

Game Type Examples

- dice games: Yahtzee, Zombie Dice, etc.
- card games: Love Letter, Exploding Kittens, etc.

- board games: Settlers of Catan, Splendor, Ticket to Ride
- interactive or app-based party games: Dixit, One Night Ultimate Werewolf
- co-op (cooperative games): Forbidden Island, Pandemic, Shadows over Camelot
- miniature games: X-Wing, Blood Red Skies

Miscellaneous Supplies Recommended

- pencils and paper
- a binder or file folder for printed game-rule clarifications, errata, FAQs, etc.

Recommended but Optional Materials

- name tags
- neoprene mats or felt dice-rolling boxes
- card sleeves
- board game bands (for holding lids tight)
- plastic bins for storage and ease of transport
- extra dice (a variety)

STEP-BY-STEP INSTRUCTIONS

Preparation

- Assess crowd potential and reserve space.
- Determine your best approach. Two recommended approaches are:
  - Choose a minimal amount of games with multiple presentations of each.
  - Choose a wide selection of games with several choices left up to the player.
- Secure the games. Explore purchase and donation options.
- Recruit volunteers, staff, and Game Masters (GMs).
- Learn the game, play it with staff, and watch videos.
- Explore marketing venues such as flyers, social media, or community groups.

Program Instructions

- Pre-set up your games and demo stations, create displays, prepare materials, set up tables, and put out signs.
- Prep volunteers; answer any questions they may have.
- Greet patrons and assess their interest and experience. Introduce prepared volunteers and offer options to players.
- Group patrons together and start the games when possible. Fill open games first and then start new tables if more people/groups come.
- Ask your staff to roam and survey the room. Your staff should answer questions, clarify rules, obtain materials that game facilitators may need, and remind everyone of time constraints.
- Offer a warning approximately fifteen minutes before the program ends to allow players to finish up. Promote the next session.
- Take surveys, assess the contents of games, clean up and take down your materials, and thank all volunteers present.

RECOMMENDED NEXT PROJECTS

Once you have hosted a series of successful game nights, it may be optimal to assess your audience. How did the events adapt and evolve over time? Consider the specific predominant ages, as well as the type of games most eagerly engaged in. Did patrons voice requests for different types of programs or attend other events? Did certain groups attend with more frequency? You can use the answers to these questions to explore opportunities to design programs for specific patron demographics. Examples include tabletop events for older adults or game nights for the LGBTQ+ community.

Brush & Shield
Paint & Take Miniature Day at the Public Library

MARK HALVORSEN
Adult Programming Librarian

Fresno County Public Library

THIS PROGRAM INVOLVES providing a session of artistic expression through guided miniature painting at your library. In this chapter, we offer guidance in planning, preparing, and hosting your own Figure Paint & Take event. Library staff can assist attendees in painting their first plastic fantasy, science fiction, or historical models, which participants can later bring home and display. Designed for everyone new to the hobby, the following detailed guidelines and tips can open a world of imagination in your programming schedule.

Age Range	Type of Library Best Suited For	Cost Estimate
Young Adults (ages 13–18) Adults	Public Libraries	$0–$125

Cost Considerations

Supplies for this program will vary, with the most significant factor being your maximum number of attendees. Due to the average cost of supplies involved, it is recommended to limit the number of participants based on available materials and staff members. Online preregistration or a sign-up list at your branch will help gauge costs prior to the session. The theme and depth of the process will either contribute to or minimize your expenditures. Some supplies will need to be replenished such as miniatures used and depleted paints. Items such as palettes and brushes tend to have a longer expectancy than other paint supplies.

FIGURE 3.1
Painting in the library provides a relaxing and unique experience.

OVERVIEW

During a Figure Paint & Take event, your patrons have the opportunity to learn basic miniature painting techniques in a friendly, supportive atmosphere. Your featured miniatures can be based on a theme designed by the programming librarian. Intended for beginners, staff provide guidance in a casual atmosphere in this program, taking patrons through the various stages of the process. Participants can ultimately take their figure home as a keepsake from the event, thereby enhancing motivation to attend future hobby programs.

Miniature painting is a wonderfully versatile activity and well-suited to several approaches, depending on your situation and programming needs. A thorough activity takes about an hour and a half, if all steps are included. Drop-in activity stations, which involve participants spending ten to fifteen minutes on a few basic techniques, are also a viable option. In essence timeframes can be extended or shortened based on how much work and detail are planned for the project. The sequence of directed steps below will offer flexibility for your game leads based on their time, skill level, budget, and role in the event.

Ideally, schedule one person, be it a volunteer or system staff member, for every four participants. Examples of support these game leads can provide include answering questions, cleaning brushes, and guiding the sequence of painting steps. Staff should paint along with the participants when possible to foster confidence and allow active visual examples of the stages in the process. Staff can busy themselves changing water, cleaning brushes, assisting with thinning paint, and responding to needs for guidance. A limited-size group is again stressed for several reasons when running a full-length workshop. The pace of progress will vary with large crowds; so, expect to manage patrons at various stages. Eye strain and fatigue can impact the experience for participants as well. For activity tables, a first-come basis while supplies last is typically sufficient for smaller groups, and painting goals are set at several steps at most. The cost of the materials will necessitate a maximum attendee capacity for many public libraries.

In addition, this is a hands-on approach for beginners that requires assistance from staff or volunteers who have practiced the process. This adds to utilized staff hours, unless volunteers are used exclusively or librarians have prior experience in the event. Keep in mind, however, that you can learn the basics of this process rather quickly!

NECESSARY EQUIPMENT AND MATERIALS

- brushes—synthetic sable, not plastic bristle
- brush cleanser (Bristle Magic, etc.)
- Acrylic paints, preferably miniature-specific—avoid inexpensive, generic craft paint.

Suggested Options

- Several basecoat colors for cloth, skin, uniforms, etc.—keep in mind various skin tones for the inclusion of different cultures.
- Shades and washes—these can be purchased specifically. Some brands that offer these items include Games Workshop, Army Painter, etc. Alternatively, basecoat colors can be diluted with a mixing medium.
- Metallic paint will be necessary for any genre selected. Good choices include silver or other shades of metallic paint.
- Lighter shades of basecoat colors are ideal when teaching highlighting or dry brushing.
- water and cups
- plastic white palettes

- Miniatures in the range of twenty-eight to thirty-two millimeters—select only a few poses. Avoid too many options. Also, refrain from using highly detailed, *busy* minis that can be time-consuming and frustrating to complete. Examples include a basic goblin with a sword x 8 (this indicates an encounter with eight goblins) or a dwarf with an axe and shield x 8 for a group of ten participants and three staff. Leave extras for problematic situations.
- Attempt to acquire figures that are already primed and ready for the workshop so that the paint adheres properly. Examples include the excellent D&D and Pathfinder miniatures range by Wizkids. The Reaper Bones line is also affordable, but applying primer first is suggested with these miniatures.
- If necessary, a thin rattle-can primer spray can be applied outside of the library well in advance to coat the figures. You can spray a thin but thorough coat of primer in black, gray, or white, according to your need.
- washing station (plastic sink bin, etc.)
- paper towels
- proper lighting
- cut-up cardboard or disposable white tablecloths (avoid newspaper, as it is messy and distracting)
- smocks (optional)—or encourage your patrons to wear old clothing.
- Nitrile examination gloves (optional)
- Box art such as a picture—or you can bring in a sample painted miniature for group reference.

STEP-BY-STEP INSTRUCTIONS

Preparation

- Determine an appropriate theme, with a holiday relevance if desired. Examples include World War II infantry (Veterans Day), fantasy ranges (Bilbo Baggins's birthday), science fiction (Star Wars, May the 4th), etc.
- Determine the scope of desired time for the process, such as a full hour or just enough time for a fun, quick sampling.
- Seek donations if necessary. You can write to companies, visit game shops, and ask local players on Facebook and other social media outlets to donate their extras. Their generosity may surprise you.

- Recruit volunteers. This event is best suited for either library staff with some model-painting experience or those willing to engage with their community. Visit some friendly game stores and seek out enthusiasts on social media to secure appropriate hobbyists who would love to assist and grow their passion. Someone on your staff should have some experience prior to the event date, however, to alleviate the risk of volunteers not showing up.
- Research and purchase miniatures. Preassembled figures are recommended.
- Assess the cost of other materials and work on acquiring them. If you need assistance, tap any connections previously made at local hobby groups/stores for supportive advice.
- Ensure that lighting is at least adequate for this event. Small lamps are ideal, if available.
- Establish your selected format for preregistration if your program offering is not an activity table event.
- Once space is reserved and the proper time identified, create flyers and begin assertive promotion of the event online and within library branches. Flyers should specifically state the determined age range, unless the program is for the enjoyment of everyone. Be prepared to reinforce any requirements for the program at the door. In addition, encourage old clothing to be worn to the event.
- Make a detailed checklist of materials and inventory.
- Monitor your branch or online preregistration lists; send out reminder e-mails or call.
- Set up signage and book displays based on your selected theme and prepare a reserved room at least one hour in advance. Have attendees enter all at once to avoid distraction as you get your volunteers settled and discuss any relevant adjustments.

Additional Preparation: Painting Practice

Gather your team before the event and learn the process. Ensure that you are familiar with the application of shading, highlights, and dry brushing. Support from enthusiasts at your local hobby stores or game clubs can be invaluable. In addition, you can practice by using techniques demonstrated in appropriate YouTube videos. Google terms such as "How to dry brush miniatures" for helpful tips. Stating the type of figure you will be using in

your project in your search parameters, such as "how to dry brush fur cloaks" or "painting goblin skin," may yield better results. Games Workshop, a popular company, posts numerous tutorials on YouTube that cover a variety of techniques. In addition:
- Thin the paints on the palettes to be used by your patrons and adhere as necessary to the adage of "two thin coats."
- Gently clean brushes between coats, especially any brushes used for metallic paints, and change the water regularly.
- Keep a reference sheet available to allow for independent work (start with a skin shade for the faces, then select a color for the uniforms, etc.).

Program Instructions

- Greet patrons and let them know everyone will begin together as a group. Then, pair up attendees with staff and volunteers as evenly as possible. Assess each patron's exposure to this hobby and adjust your groups accordingly. Seek a balance of experience, if possible.
- Welcome the group, share names, and then display a completed miniature or box art. Smile and be patient and encouraging—any paint job can make monochromatic plastic look better, so make it fun!
- Suggestions for steps: Demonstrate how to basecoat a prepared model using colors of the group's choosing. Then wash/shade the model with diluted or pre-mixed paint to give the miniature depth. Then, either drybrush the highlights on or brush them on with a slightly brighter color if conducting a full program.
- Do not *fix* or touch up miniatures; encourage group members to paint over the mistake or let them know they are doing fine.
- Demonstrate thinning the paint and the first application at the beginning of the session. Have attendees follow along and suggest tips as they proceed.
- Begin the process, starting with basic techniques: how to thin paint, proper brush strokes, etc., based on necessity.
- Enjoy the step-by-step process with your group. Include such steps as shading, dry brushing, etc., along the way, based on the overall skill level of the group and the time allotted for the event.
- To avoid hassle, staff can simply clean brushes for the crowd as needed throughout the project.

- Keep close track of the time as the event progresses so that everyone can take home as complete a miniature as possible.
- Remind them that their practice project does not need to be complete; the event is simply meant to be an enjoyable process. Ask if they might enjoy more such events in the future.
- Thank everyone and survey them verbally to assess their interest in your next projects. Pass out library cards and promote any relevant events, online resources they can explore, etc.
- Clean up thoroughly after completion of the event, give the brushes a good final wash, and store all the materials used.

RECOMMENDED NEXT PROJECTS

Painting and modeling can be cathartic and pleasantly addictive. Such activities provide numerous opportunities for future recurring programs and special events once adults, teens, and caregivers have enjoyed the fun of the initial experience.

A program such as a Paint & Take for beginners segues nicely into self-directed modeling/hobby nights for groups at your branch. Many enjoy these types of hobbies at home, but creating a welcoming space where such activities can be shared with friends can harness significant new foot traffic at your public library and at others.

Future events may require people to bring their own supplies, but that's not a cause for worry. We needn't provide everything; a welcoming table in a comfortable room works wonders. Word will spread, new library cards can be distributed, and circulation numbers will increase as you introduce attendees to what the library now has to offer.

An introduction to gaming session is also an attractive option. Reach out to local wargaming clubs and ask them to feature demos. Alternatively, you can begin a D&D Roleplaying Game Day with assistance from the local RPG community.

Cross-promotion for larger events, themed holidays, branch grand openings, and so on is also ideal when combined with arts and crafts. A fantasy author discussion, a history lecturer from a university, and so on can bring in a crowd, which you can capitalize on by offering a painting class prior to that event or afterward during the reception. The possibilities are endless—just like our imaginations!

Recurring Game Events for Older Adults

MARK HALVORSEN
Adult Programming Librarian

Fresno County Public Library

CONSIDER ESTABLISHING A regularly scheduled tabletop game program in your library for older adults. This chapter includes materials selection, setup, and facilitation-style guidelines that emphasize the unique needs of seniors. A Game Day for Older Adults event can promote camaraderie, cognitive stimulation, meaningful teamwork, healthy competition, and the opportunity for consistent future library engagement.

This chapter includes game types and other important facets of event design that are designed to be player-friendly and considerate of those with limited dexterity, vision, hearing, or mobility.

Age Range	Type of Library Best Suited For	Cost Estimate
Adults	Public Libraries	$0–$150

Cost Considerations

Boxed physical games suited for this event can be purchased, acquired through donation, or brought in by the attendees. Your gaming variety can be less than offered at gaming events marketed to younger adults; a

PART I | Tabletop Game Programs

few recommended staples, which are presented later in this chapter, should suffice when you begin.

Requesting products and encouraging others to include their favorites from home can considerably offset costs. Variety and expenditures depend on the intent of the program, anticipated attendance, and interest. Smaller local games stores and toy shops may prove more likely to offer discounts for libraries than corporations, as they don't demand you overcome as much red tape. Be aware of your library's solicitation policies if they ask for recognition, flyers, or logo visibility in return. Lastly, common classic games can be found at thrift stores for a steal but be wary of missing contents. Simply putting up a sign at the branch requesting games for a program should help you harness acquisitions. Encourage participants to bring selections from their collection, which helps ensure that interest is retained and can foster a sense of ownership.

FIGURE 4.1
Ronna Silberman mixes dominoes at The Cards & Boneyards Game Day.

OVERVIEW

During an older adult game session, staff and volunteers present several tables of readied games and possibly a display of other options for variety. Attendees tend to be a bit more prompt than younger crowds, who often arrive sporadically throughout an event. Staff should initiate the start of a new game table if people show up too late to join existing ones. This also affords librarians the opportunity to cross-promote during the event and meaningfully interact with the crowd.

The recommended length of the program is two to two and a half hours. Senior patrons often take their time getting settled and engaging in socializing but usually stay the full duration of the stated event length. Your chance of success will increase if the event is recurring, so consider having it take place at least once a month. Flyers that advertise in large print the specific dates spanning a period of time, such as an event that occurs quarterly, are crucial due to less likelihood of senior adults using online calendars. An end time should be specifically stated, and ideally the event should conclude in daylight hours. Consistency in start time and duration is key, once a successful approach has been established. Develop a routine for older patrons to rely on and look forward to.

Staffing needs will vary; provide one librarian and perhaps an additional facilitator if a large crowd of ten or more is anticipated. Expect to answer questions, help with name tags, encourage grouping, and offer alternatives for those not interested or compatible with the dominant game being played. Questions are common for those new to the concept of open gaming. Friendly staff who can encourage someone to feel comfortable if they arrive alone help ensure a welcoming atmosphere. Retaining attendees depends more on the social climate than what specific game is being played. With that said, staff should take note of what is being enjoyed, as the need for additional copies of games, rather than variety, is more common for older patrons. Experienced and enthusiastic players can be highly valuable in making the day a success, as they may provide additional game copies, teach rules, lead tables, encourage new experiences, and often eventually become volunteers. Identify such patrons, thank them, and strongly consider everyone's suggestions.

Event Capacity

Event capacity varies with the typical factors: room space, staff availability, and the quantity of materials needed. It is important to ensure that a high number of people will not be forced to use one set of a game. For example, if the Dominoes table has exceeded six players, consider encouraging another table to begin play in the room. A high number of players creates long wait times between turns and can spurn confusion or conflict. Beyond such nuances, the size of your groups will largely depend on the factors listed above. Having a sign-up or registration process can help assess the special needs of and proper room selection for your Game Day for Older Adults events.

It is highly recommended that any event attendance notifications or flyers you use designate that this event is specifically for ages eighteen and over. Those wishing to bring grandchildren and the like may spark the need for event runners to discuss appropriate boundary-setting, but the point is for seniors to have a time and place of their own for unique camaraderie and social interaction. Younger children and other unexpected minors can prove highly distracting to a group seeking relaxation and company within their age group. Refer those who wish to bring children to event options for families within your branches.

While some younger adults may arrive to such events, seniors are the ones who typically come back. With that said, expect some patrons to attend with their adult children—which is perfectly fine and can become an immensely meaningful experience.

NECESSARY EQUIPMENT AND MATERIALS

Recommended Game Categories and Examples

- Favorites such as Dominoes—preferably with the pieces for the common and popular Mexican Train version. Your version of the game should be easy to read with eye-friendly colored dots. Several packs of playing cards for game versatility are also a must.
- Dice game options such as Yahtzee, Bunko, etc.—ensure you have scorepads/paper and a way to roll the dice quietly. Felt-lined rolling boxes, neoprene mats, etc., will work nicely. Ensure you have a dice cup for those who may have difficulty rolling due to joint pain, hand tremors, etc.
- Other board games—the key here is to avoid small-print cards if a game requires reading, and selections should not demand familiarity with more complex rules systems. Tsuro: The Game of the Path is an excellent choice as are others that are not *text-dependent*. If Scrabble is offered, ensure you have a large print official players dictionary.
- Providing options for participants with limited hearing or mobility is strongly encouraged. The game Happy Salmon comes to mind because play and answers can be vocally or silently demonstrated. This game includes options for those with limited mobility and speech printed in its rules. Be cognizant of similar accommodations as you evaluate entertainment products for your events.
- Cooperative games, such as Forbidden Island, may be an ideal choice, as all participants work together to accomplish a goal, usually before the time runs out. This concept will probably be new to older adults, so be sure and demonstrate carefully how to play and select games that are appealing in theme.

Use with Prudence

- dexterity games in which certain patrons may be at a disadvantage

Avoid These Game Types

- highly competitive games in which a player maybe eliminated early and find the experience discouraging
- app-based auditory games that require perfect hearing, technical skill with smartphones, and fast mental processing

Miscellaneous

- scratch paper, Yahtzee Score Pads, and pencils with erasers
- A folder to be used as a rules guide, with printed instructions and clarifications in large font for games as needed—examples include a quick reference page for several varieties of Dominoes, basic rules for Bridge or Scrabble, etc. This is important, as rules booklets that are included in games are often printed in small font.
- Bottled water and Kleenex, if your budget permits—patrons love to bring their own snacks, but be cognizant of your policy regarding outside food.
- A sign-in sheet to acquire phone numbers, e-mails, and perhaps note any special accommodations—reminder calls help provide a friendly touch for this age range.

Atmosphere

- Additional illumination, such as portable lamps, may be needed, depending on your room circumstances. Tape down extension cords thoroughly if utilized.
- Keep the gaming space at a moderate temperature. Make notations in your print advertising if the environment cannot easily be modified, such as "a sweater or layers are encouraged."
- Name tags also encourage friendship, bonding, and a welcoming atmosphere.
- Background music is not recommended. Those who are hard of hearing may find it distracting or difficult to participate due to the extra sensory impact.

STEP-BY-STEP INSTRUCTIONS

Preparation

- Decide what types of games you will offer and if multiple copies will be necessary, based on budget and expected crowd size. Be sure not to provide an overwhelming number of options for older patrons. Instead, obtain games that people find interesting and somewhat familiar and that are age-appropriate. Once you decide on an approach, begin your acquisition(s).
- Keep in mind that you wish to attract an older age group when purchasing your games. Card games, such as Rummy, and classics, such as Scrabble and Yahtzee, etc., are familiar to older patrons. Keep appealing choices on hand. More fiddly board games may be highly entertaining but can be reserved for your standard game night.
- Ask patrons, as well as current volunteers or staff, which games they own or would suggest for the event. For more advice, visit your friendly local store or peruse numerous lists and reviews online, such as what can be found on the popular website BoardGameGeek.com. Evaluate your volunteers to determine their game literacy and if they may be willing to demonstrate some of their favorites.
- Put out a call for donations—both in your branch and your community. Assess purchase options that offer discounts, free shipping, etc. Acquire your items well in advance of the event date so your flyer won't need any last-minute modifications.
- Designate a time favorable to your age range, preferably in daylight. Also, use a contained, quiet space (your participants may get loud while enjoying your program!). Reserve dates and a room. Start with perhaps a three-month commitment to your event and use the time to build your audience and assess the event's true potential.
- Develop flyers with potentially catchy titles that offer a clear message. Images of playing cards, Dominoes, etc., help viewers connect with the concept. Create flyers and continue to market the event assertively and creatively. Along with window postings and handbills a patron can grab, go out into local neighborhoods when time permits. Conducting outreach at nearby retirement communities, for example, can lead to a senior citizens' event coordinator providing organized transportation for an entire group.

- Designate specific volunteers and staff for the event. One librarian or event coordinator is recommended to establish relationships, which are conducive to future program ideas.
- Begin the marketing process; design flyers in large print that offer clear information about the program. Flyers should specifically mention, "This event is for ages eighteen and older."
- Conduct outreach specifically to the senior populace in your community. Distribute flyers at retirement homes, more subdued cafes, local crafts stores, and so on. Submit announcements in advance to free online or print publications for older adults. Definitely cross promote with enthusiasm at all your other events. Ensure that all branch staff are aware of the program, as "hand-selling" the event flyer is quite helpful in generating an initial crowd. Well in advance of the event, ensure you know how to play the games that will be included. Enjoy practicing with branch staff and volunteers as time permits and utilize *how to play* videos on YouTube, Facebook Groups, etc., to ensure a smooth experience for everyone. Print and collect anything necessary for your rules guide.

Program Instructions

- Table game stations should be designed so wheelchairs, walkers, etc., can be conveniently integrated.
- Set up games if applicable, create displays, and get your materials ready. Prep the demo stations and tables and put out signs. Prep volunteers and answer questions.
- Print a handy rule guide on how to play popular types of Dominoes. Use a rule guide that specifically states the amount and type of Dominoes to use based on the number of players, such as the specifics required for the popular Mexican Train format. Prepare for any other featured games as well (print rules in a larger, easily read font for activities such as Rummy or UNO. Check to see if the card packs for the games are already opened and ready to play, etc.).
- Greet patrons and assess their interest and experience. Distribute name tags. A warm welcome to the branch and introductions around the room are nice touches.

- When the event starts, demonstrate enthusiasm and don't be afraid to admit you are learning as well—this creates an empathic bond with shy or hesitant newcomers to tabletop play. When running games, foster new experiences with a statement such as "This is the first time for some of us with Forbidden Island—let's enjoy it and learn together!"
- Introduce prepared volunteers and offer options to players.
- Group patrons and start the games. Fill open games first and then start new games if more people/groups come.
- Have staff roam and survey the room. Their duties should include answering questions, clarifying rules, and reminding everyone of time constraints.
- Provide ample notice of the time remaining prior to cleanup; promote the next session.
- Devote some table space or shelf for purses, coats, etc.
- Provide ample seating, including space at the table for wheelchairs and patrons with other special needs.
- Direct attendees to a sign-in sheet and provide name tags.
- Survey all the elements of the room, assess the contents of the games, clean up and take down your materials, and thank everyone. Meet with volunteers/staff to gauge how things went.

RECOMMENDED NEXT PROJECTS

Initiate conversations about other library resources with your event attendees over time. Once you establish a rapport, ensure participants have library cards and can explore their other interests. After enjoying game days at your library, older patrons may be open to exploring programs that may require a bit more vulnerability, such as a support group in which feelings are shared, book club where they can voice their opinions, or a Tai Chi class that promotes physical activity.

How to Develop Socioeconomic Literacies with the Landlord Game

RANDAL SEAN HARRISON
Emerging Technologies Librarian

Hesburgh Library, University of Notre Dame

THE LANDLORD GAME is a multiplayer, turn-based board game for four to six players (patrons). It is an educational or *serious* board game that simulates the struggle of socioeconomic class mobility. At the start of play, each player is assigned a socioeconomic class. As players move around the board, they increasingly find that, after running through the gamut of roles from Owner to Manager to Employee to Unemployed, it becomes increasingly difficult to avoid bankruptcy. By effecting real-world economic disparities at the start of the game, the Landlord Game aims to help players challenge reductive ideologies such as social Darwinism and provoke thought and discussion around the systemic nature of poverty. The game mechanic of rule creation aims to help students imagine political activism as a means of increasing social justice. The game offers a socioeconomic sandbox, where players may have fun safely exploring these concepts, even as they productively challenge their own thinking.

Age Range	Type of Library Best Suited For	Cost Estimate
Young Adults (ages 13–18) Adults	Public Libraries Academic Libraries School Libraries	$40–$100 per game

FIGURE 5.1
Students playing the Landlord Game

Cost Considerations

If downloading and printing the game yourself, materials will cost approximately $40. You can also purchase the game online—its current retail cost is $84.99, plus shipping costs.

OVERVIEW

The Landlord Game represents a critique of the ubiquitous board game Monopoly, so some players may be familiar with the concepts of buying and selling properties. The first few pages of the *Rules of Play* should help players to realize the differences between the two games. Because the Landlord Game is designed to help players learn about capitalism and better understand the systemic nature of poverty, it's best if there is at least one player assigned to each of the four socioeconomic classes (Owner, Manager, Employee, and Unemployed). When adding a fifth or sixth player, assign the additional players Unemployed or Employee roles, as this best reflects the current economic reality and will produce the greatest empathy among players.

In a public library setting, the game might be placed on a two-hour reserved time limit or perhaps left out in a designated gaming area. In an academic setting, the game might be played by a single group of players outside of class time (flipped classroom). Alternatively, a librarian may wish to facilitate a seminar-sized session of three to four game tables. Players learn the concepts by playing the game, so little guidance is necessary beyond helping players set up the game, adjudicating the occasional rule, and answering the occasional question. Ultimately, one librarian could easily facilitate game play among a small number of gaming tables and lead the discussion afterward.

The optimum play time for this game seems to be at least one hour, with diminishing returns after about two to three hours, by which time players will likely have exhausted most of the options for social mobility.

NECESSARY EQUIPMENT AND MATERIALS

- one copy of the board game for every four to six players

STEP-BY-STEP INSTRUCTIONS

Preparation

- Visit http://thelandlordgame.com to preview the game materials and instructions and watch the tutorial video to learn more about the learning objectives of the game.
- Obtain a copy of the game. You will need one copy of the game for every four to six players. There are two ways to obtain the game:
  - *Do it yourself*: You may download and print all the game materials from the game website. You may also freely modify or adapt the game materials, which have been released under a Creative Commons BY-NC-SA 4.0 International license.
  - *Purchase a copy*: You may buy a copy of the game online by visiting the manufacturer's website. Follow the link there to purchase through an approved vendor.

Program Instructions

Setting Up the Game

- Give one copy of the Landlord Game to each group of four to six players. Ask them to open the box and remove the game contents.

- Place the board on a flat surface in the center of the patrons. Shuffle the Change Cards and place them on their allotted space on the board.
- With four players, place one Owner token (blue), one Manager token (purple), one Employee token (green), and one Unemployed token (red) in a container. When adding a fifth player, add one additional Unemployed token to the container. When adding a sixth player, add one additional Employee token to the container. Have players draw their tokens randomly from the container.
- Assign each player the Role Card with the symbol (e.g., castle, spatula, keyboard) matching the symbol on the movement token he or she drew.
- Assign the Owner player the Enron Electric and Flint Water utilities.
- Ask a player to volunteer to act as the Bank (alternatively, assign the Bank to the Owner). Have the Bank pay each player the starting salary listed on their Role Card.
- Advise players to read the first few pages of the rule booklet thoroughly and consult the appendices during play as needed.
- Begin play by placing all the player tokens on the Payday square. The Unemployed player moves first. Play then rotates clockwise around the board.

Facilitating Game Play

- Assuming you are moderating the game, clearly establish the length of game play.
- Observe game play, taking notes on specific events, actions, and questions. You may use these notes to lead the discussion by prodding/teasing out students' memories from the game play.

Discussing the Game

- Reserve time for discussion at the end of the game play. Post-play discussion—during which students discuss what they experienced and learned in the game that can transfer over to other domains of knowledge in the real world—is invaluable.
- You may also find the following questions useful as conversation starters:
  - *For game events*: How many of you died? Went to jail? Went bankrupt? Went to college? Joined the military? Had a child? Traded roles with another player?
  - *For social mobility issues*: How many of you weren't able to purchase or keep property?

– *For politics*: How did the power to create new rules impact your game? Who ran for president? Were you elected? What did you promise to change? What did you actually change?
– *Social justice*: How does one get *ahead* in the game? How does this differ from real life? Who *won*? What did winning mean at your table?

RECOMMENDED NEXT PROJECTS

If you chose to download and print the materials for this game—especially if you decide to modify the game to suit your particular patrons—you may develop some insight into all that goes into producing a game along the way. Next, you may want to explore chapter 12, which focuses on creating board games, "Not So Trivial Pursuit: Board Game Creation in Your Library" by Kristen Cinar.

Once you have more experience in creating board games, consider leading a board game creation workshop at your library. I also recommend that you explore chapter 16 on RPG creation by Christopher Bussman and Shea'la Finch, "RPG Writing Workshop: Lead Patrons in Writing Their Own Games."

Hero's Handbook
Steps for Creating a Pathfinder RPG Beginner's Program

DELANEY BULLINGER
Instruction Librarian, Auburn University

ALLISON RAND
Instruction and Outreach Librarian, Park University

ARE YOU READY to *roll for initiative*? Learn how to build a Pathfinder RPG program for beginner players as a beginner Game Master (GM)! The Pathfinder Beginner Box includes all you need to run a successful RPG campaign with little to no further expenses or experience. The Beginner Box, combined with our additional instructions, provides a one-stop shop for easy, engaging library program ideas designed for teens, new adults, and mature adults. In this chapter, you will learn how to plan, implement, and promote RPG sessions, scenarios, and character creation in an academic library setting.

Age Range	Type of Library Best Suited For	Cost Estimate
Young Adults (ages 13–18) Adults	Academic Libraries	$35–$85

OVERVIEW

Pathfinder is an RPG very similar to Dungeons & Dragons involving a set scenario or campaign, a GM who runs the campaign, and participants who act as player characters. The Pathfinder Beginner Box is meant for complete beginners to RPGs and walks both the GM and players through how to run a campaign. When we created the Pathfinder program as graduate assistants at the Undergraduate Library at the University of Illinois at Urbana-Champaign, we were novices to playing RPGs, never mind leading them as GMs. The steps included in this chapter will walk you through how to familiarize yourself with RPGs and how to plan and implement a Pathfinder program in an academic library.

FIGURE 6.1
Pathfinder roleplaying game rulebook

Beginner Box campaigns are standalone sessions that run between one and two hours, not including setup. Campaigns can be run by one staff member with a maximum of four participants, and programs can run more than one campaign simultaneously.

NECESSARY EQUIPMENT AND MATERIALS

- Pathfinder's Beginner Box, which includes the following items:
  - a Hero's Handbook: details character creation, spells, equipment, and general rules for playing the game
  - a Game Master's Guide: offers advice on how to narrate the game and control the challenges faced by the heroes
  - one set of dice
  - 80 pawns
  - four pre-generated character sheets
  - four blank character sheets
  - a double-sided Flip-Mat play surface
- a Pathfinder Core Rulebook (optional, but helpful)
- dice (RPG polyhedral sets and extra six-sided dice)
- pencils and scratch paper
- one to two laptops, tablets, or smartphones (optional, but helpful)

STEP-BY-STEP INSTRUCTIONS

Preparation

- Our first rule (rule zero) is to have fun!
- Before running a program in your library, it's necessary to understand the complexities of running a tabletop RPG. The best way to do this is to play!
- After familiarizing yourself with the content in the Beginner Box, download the Beginner Box Bash Demos from the link provided in the Beginner Box. These will be the four, short, standalone scenarios to begin your program with.
- Gather a group of four to five people (friends, coworkers, student assistants, etc.) to play through all four Beginner Box Bash Demos. Take turns being the GM for each scenario and consider playing as different character types (fighter, rogue, cleric, sorcerer, etc.).
  - Running through these while consulting the Game Master's Guide provided in the Beginner Box will familiarize you with game play as a player and the mechanics of running the back end of an adventure as the GM.
  - Your first few games might be rough, but playing will acclimate you to the unpredictability of RPGs. Be flexible!
- Reach out to gaming-related student groups and promote your events on social media. Emphasize that this is a no-experience-needed program and that beginners are preferred! Make sure interested students RSVP via e-mail or webform. Having an accurate count is crucial to creating balanced groups.
- Annotate or flag any pages in the Game Master's Guide needed for your scenarios. This might include creature stats, spells, items, etc. Anything that you needed as a reference in your playthrough is probably worth flagging.
- Print out your maps for Bash Demos or draw them onto the Flip-Mat.

Program Instructions

- Divide students into groups of three or four. These will be your adventuring parties! You will be their GM.
  - *Note:* This is a firm number, as fewer than three will make the game difficult for players and more than four will result in repeated characters.

- Provide an overview of the game in your own words. Include information about the pre-generated characters provided, the basic mechanics of the game, and how roleplaying works.
- Give students the pre-generated character sheets provided in the Beginner Box. If necessary, print off extra copies for students to write on and provide scratch paper. Allow students to choose which character they want to play.
- Have students thoroughly read through their selected character and discuss the major parts of the character sheet, including ability modifiers, initiative, skills, and weapons/spells. Answer any questions, referring to the Game Master's Guide as needed. Keeping a copy of the Core Rulebook handy to refer to will also help you answer these questions.
- Run the scenario! The Beginner Box Bash Demos provide detailed instructions on how to run each scenario. Refer to the Game Master's Guide as needed.
- Throughout the scenario, be sure to keep the game balanced. If some players are more involved or experienced, make their game more challenging. This allows all players to have equal opportunities for success and fun.
    - *Tip*: Most of the rules of Pathfinder are loose, and the personalities of your players will influence the game play.
- Players should win the game by defeating the creatures in each scenario. The goal is to challenge and interest players, but not for the GM (a.k.a. the library) to win the game.
    - *Tip*: If the game seems difficult because of the chosen characters, number of players, or length of game play, feel free to change the encounters to make them easier (fewer monsters, lower HP, etc.).
- Debrief with players after the game. If they found it too difficult, find out why. If it seemed too easy, invite them to another session with a more challenging scenario.

RECOMMENDED NEXT PROJECTS

- If your Beginner Box Bash Demo scenarios go well, consider running the Black Fang's Dungeon scenario included in the Beginner Box. It is a slightly longer, more in-depth adventure, but still a standalone.

- Host other one-shot Pathfinder scenarios, such as We Be Goblins (available for free online).
- Host a full campaign, starting with Tier 1 adventures where players can use the characters they created.
  - Tier 1 adventures are for characters with low-level experience. As players become more adept, their characters will level up to Tiers 2, 3, 4, etc., thereby increasing the challenge of the scenarios. Scenarios can be found and purchased on the Pathfinder website.
- Run a character creation event! Allow players to roll up their own characters to transition them to the full Pathfinder Core Rulebook rules and out of the Beginner Box. Be sure to practice rolling up characters yourself before you run an event, as this often requires answering a lot of questions and referring to the Hero's Handbook.
- Provide GM training for students interested in running their own groups or write your own adventure sessions.
- Encourage players to continue playing on their own in a space provided to them in the library.

Dewey and Dragons
Dungeons & Dragons at the Library

JAMEY RORIE
Teen Specialist

Beatties Ford Road Regional Library, Charlotte Mecklenburg Library

DUNGEONS & DRAGONS (D&D) is a popular fantasy roleplaying game (RPG) created in the 1970s. It has recently resurged in popularity thanks to it breaking into pop culture in shows such as *Community* and *Stranger Things*, in which the game is featured heavily. Dungeons & Dragons focuses on cooperative play, group story-building, imagination, and the use of simple math. D&D consists of a Dungeon Master (DM), who runs the game and describes the situations for the players, and Adventurers (players who are the heroes of the story attempting to overcome the situations set by the story and the DM). In this program, you, as DM, will be running the game and creating the world for your Adventurers. One special adventure, The Pale Codex, was created at the Charlotte Mecklenburg Library as a starter adventure, but other D&D adventures are certainly welcome at this branch. All those who participate in the game work together to overcome a problem and to create a story that is compelling and fun. Players are encouraged to roleplay their characters and use their problem-solving skills to come up with solutions to the adventure. With a heavy focus on imagination, Dungeons & Dragons can be played with very little investment, relying only on the basic rules provided by Wizards of the Coast—the current publishers of D&D.

FIGURE 7.1
Dewey and Dragons at Beatties Ford Road Regional Library

Age Range	Type of Library Best Suited For	Cost Estimate
Tweens (ages 8–12) Young Adults (ages 13–18) Adults	Public Libraries Academic Libraries School Libraries	$10–$200+

Cost Considerations

Dungeons & Dragons can be played with as little as dice, graph paper, and a pen and pencil. The only essential materials that cost money are the dice specifically used to play D&D. Keeping the basic rules in mind, dice are used by the players and the DM to see whether an action (an attack, looking for tracks, recognizing symbols) succeeds or fails. It is best practice to have a set of dice for each player. You can find multiple sets of dice on Amazon for very reasonable prices, ranging from $10–$30.

You can find the basic rules for Dungeons & Dragons online at https://dnd.wizards.com/articles/features/basicrules, but this just covers the basics of the game. You can also purchase the core set of rule books (*Player's Handbook, Dungeon Masters' Guide, Monster Manual*) along with official adventure and supplement books, miniatures, cards, and other accessories.

Here is a compiled Amazon idea list that includes many accessories you can purchase: http://a.co/7s3jisA.

OVERVIEW

For Dewey and Dragons, I created a short and simple one- to two-hour session that focuses on an adventure set in an ancient library using the fifth edition of Dungeons & Dragons and premade characters found on the Wizards of the Coast website. In the session, three to five Adventurers are tasked with recovering a mysterious and dangerous book from an ancient and forgotten library. In the session, the Adventurers must overcome traps, solve riddles, work together, and fight monsters in order to recover the treasure and win the day. The adventure can be played entirely without using grid paper or a battle mat. You need only use dice and pen and paper. However, you can also play with minis or tokens in order to draw out the adventure.

NECESSARY EQUIPMENT AND MATERIALS

- basic D&D rules (https://dnd.wizards.com/articles/features/basicrules)
- premade character sheets (https://media.wizards.com/downloads/dnd/StarterSet_Charactersv2.pdf)
    - If your players would like to make custom characters later using the basic rules, blank character sheets can be found here: (http://media.wizards.com/2014/downloads/dnd/5E_CHARACTERSHEETSV3.ZIP)
- dice
    - polyhedral dice, one seven-piece set
- D&D cheat sheets (http://bit.ly/DnDCheatSheets)
    - These sheets are notes on how to play for players and new DMs (action reminders, dice type, etc.)
- grid paper
- paper
- pencils and pens
- Your own Dungeons & Dragons adventure—or you can use an adventure created for Dewey and Dragons-The Pale Codex (http://bit.ly/ThePaleCodex).

STEP-BY-STEP INSTRUCTIONS

Preparation

Before Starting the Program
- Read over the basic rules to familiarize yourself with how to run a game as a DM. You don't have to know everything, but you should have a general understanding of what makes up the core game play.
- Read over and become familiar with your D&D adventure.
- Adjust the adventure to fit the number of players. (Suggestions for ways to adjust adventures are located in the DM Tips in The Pale Codex.)

On the Day of the Program
- Set up the game for three to five players. Chairs should be arranged around the table. Gather the appropriate amount of dice, paper, pens, and pencils.
- Set up the DM screen (if you have one) at the head of the table, along with the DM's set of dice, the adventure criteria, the rules, and whatever other reference materials you require.

Optional Setup
- Have your grid paper/battle mat set in the middle of table.
- Have tokens/minis ready for monsters and for player characters.
- Have snacks ready for your Adventurers (i.e., chips, soft drinks, pizza, etc.).

Program Instructions

- Librarians should greet players and begin the program by giving them an overview of Dungeons & Dragons and how it is played.
  - Emphasize that they will be the heroes of the story and will work together to fight monsters while they embark on an adventure of might and magic.
  - Give a quick overview of the rules and the purpose of the dice and how to use them. Explain the cheat sheets and how they will come into use.
  - Ask if they have played or heard of Dungeons & Dragons before to get a sense of your players' knowledge base.
  - Inquire if they have watched *Stranger Things*, *Community*, *Lord of the Rings*, or *The Hobbit*, or if they have seen D&D played online on popular YouTube channels such as Critical Role, Rooster Teeth, TeamFourStar, etc.

- Play Dungeons & Dragons using the provided adventure, The Pale Codex.
  - Tips for running the adventure follow below:
    » Dungeons & Dragons is all about imagination; so, you can ad-lib the story if you are comfortable. As DM, you are in control of the story, its flow, and where it goes.
    » Encourage the players to make a backstory for their character even if they are premade. How did the players' characters meet each other? What are their goals? What is important to them?
    » You and the players can learn how to play together (you won't have all the answers, even if you are already versed in the game). Have the rules handy—along with a laptop with internet access—to do quick reference on the fly.
    » Encourage out-of-the-box thinking and play. If a player wants to try something out of the ordinary (i.e., arm wrestle a disembodied hand), let them attempt it using an ability check. If their actions don't completely destroy the adventure, let them use their imagination and try things out.
    » If players are stuck at a point in the adventure, drop hints as to how to advance in the story.
  - If you do not finish the adventure in the allotted time but still wish to continue, end the session on a cliffhanger to encourage players to come to the next session to see how the adventure will end.
  - At the conclusion of the session, suggest some of the resources included in the recommended section. If your library has any Dungeon & Dragons materials, offer them to your players for checkout and further reading.
    » You can find a list of D&D related materials here: http://bit.ly/DeweyandDragonsList.

ADDITIONAL RESOURCES

The resources below should be useful to those who are new to Dungeons & Dragons and want to run a game.
- Matthew Colville's YouTube series, Running the Game (http://bit.ly/2ZyDsgs)
  - Running the Game offers a fantastic introduction to playing Dungeons & Dragons as a DM. This resource takes you step-by-step through the

process of running the game while engaging players and is highly recommended for anyone who wants to run a game of D&D.
- Critical Role-Handbook Helper (http://bit.ly/2Pc1hGX)
  - This site offers excellent videos regarding the ins and outs of the *Player's Handbook*, from the use of dice to proficiencies to ability checks.
- The Adventure Zone podcast (https://spoti.fi/2LoI9rv)
  - This is an actual play podcast that depicts on-the-fly group storytelling and can give viewers a good feel for how a game of D&D is run. *Warning*: This podcast includes adult language.
- Return of the Lazy DM (https://amzn.to/2LbjfnT)
  - If you plan on making your own D&D sessions or campaigns in the future, consider this excellent source, which streamlines the process for creating an adventure.

RECOMMENDED NEXT PROJECTS

You may also wish to check out other tabletop RPG program chapters in this book such as: chapter 1: "Beyond Dungeons & Dragons: Building a Roleplaying Program" by Robert Taylor and Danielle Costello; chapter 6: "Hero's Handbook: Steps for Creating a Pathfinder RPG Beginner's Program" by Delaney Bullinger and Allison Rand; chapter 10: "Call of Cthulhu: Hosting Roleplaying Events in the World of H. P. Lovecraft" by Michael Furlong; and chapter 16: "RPG Writing Workshop: Lead Patrons in Writing Their Own Games" by Christopher Bussman and Shea'la Finch.

How to Build a Circulating Board Game Collection for a Commuter Campus

TIFFANIE FORD-BAXTER
Science Librarian

DANIEL PALODICHUK
Library Reserves Coordinator

JENNIFER SELGA
Circulation Services Coordinator

University Library at California State University, Los Angeles

COMMUTER STUDENTS ARE typically busy balancing classes, work, and family, which limits the amount of time they can spend on campus. Developing a collection and program(s) tailored toward commuter students can increase their sense of community and cultivate social and strategic-thinking skills. This program outlines how to purchase games, create circulation policies, develop advertising, and plan programs geared toward commuter college students.

Age Range	Type of Library Best Suited For	Cost Estimate
Young Adults (ages 13–18) Adults	Academic Libraries	$160–$1,690

OVERVIEW

In this project, librarians can develop a board game collection and related policies that are mindful of the needs of commuter college students. You will begin by identifying the first five to ten games that you would like to purchase, paying special attention to the number of players required, the complexity level of the game, and play times. The website Boardgamegeek.com includes this information, along with reviews. Games that have shorter play times and smaller containers will typically appeal more to commuter students, who may have limited time on campus to play the game or will be traveling with the games on public transit.

After purchasing the games, you will want to discuss item processing with technical services. They can provide you with a processing timeline, which might be longer than usual if the items require custom cataloging. While meeting with technical services, you should collaborate with them to choose a subject heading to identify the new collection within the library catalog. In addition, if you are circulating the games in plastic containers, inform technical services staff that the original boxes do not need due date slips and call number labels.

Begin developing your circulation policy while you wait for the board games to arrive and be cataloged. If your students are commonly only on campus a few days a week, you should consider setting a seven-day to two-week loan period. Your policy should also include how to handle missing and damaged pieces and games. The total time for purchasing, cataloging, and making the board games available can range from one to two months, depending on the workload and availability of staff at various steps. I recommend that you start building the collection during a break period or intersession. Your budget should include a replacement pieces fund, as you may need to purchase replacement parts for games after heavy use.

NECESSARY EQUIPMENT AND MATERIALS

- an assortment of games, including party and travel-sized games and those with varying complexity levels and time commitments (e.g., UNO, One Night Ultimate Werewolf, Sushi Go, Simon's Cat, Ticket to Ride, Munchkin Legends, Dominion, Yahtzee, Cytosis, Plague Inc.)
- travel cases or plastic containers to replace the original boxes and circulate the games in

Optional Materials

- plastic cases and bags for games (approximately $50)
- shelving for games (approximately $1,400)

STEP-BY-STEP INSTRUCTIONS

Preparation

- Purchase board games for your library. They can be bought online or through gaming stores in your community.
- Meet with technical services to discuss how you want to catalog the games. You will want to tell them what location codes and subject headings you need, along with the level of item processing (e.g., due date slips or call number labels).
- Identify a visible location where patrons can browse the board games in person. Consider purchasing new shelving units to house the games.
- Brainstorm how your commuter students will be able to browse the collection away from campus. You can create a research guide or specific page on your library website about the collection or use a specific subject heading that patrons can search in the library catalog.
- Develop a circulation policy that accommodates commuter students. A seven-day circulation policy allows flexibility for students who may only be on campus two days a week. Decide if you will allow renewals and what fines students will incur for late or lost items.
- Create a Google Form to simplify the check-in procedure. Google Forms allow you to include pictures of each piece in the checklist.
- Decide whether you want to circulate the games in their original boxes or in plastic containers. If your students will frequently be taking games off campus, a plastic container can help preserve the original box and increase the lifespan of the game. You will also want to scan and keep copies of the instructions in case they get lost.
- Establish the check-in and check-out procedures that staff should follow when circulating the games. This includes determining the storage location for the games, how they are organized and sorted, and who will check the pieces when the item is returned.
- Develop advertising and signage for your collection. This can include labels that display information such as the number of players and length or complexity of the game.

Program Instructions

- Prepare your board games to be circulated by placing them in containers. Create lists of components, scan copies of the instructions, and ensure each item has barcodes.
- Start advertising! Share your new collection on social media, with student groups, or even in the student newspaper. You can use these posts as an opportunity to ask students what games they would like to see and play.
- Place your board games in a visible, high-traffic area. Don't forget to include your signage!
- Reflect and evaluate your collection. As your collection begins circulating, you may notice certain games are more popular than others. Use that information to inform future purchases.

RECOMMENDED NEXT PROJECTS

- Once you have your collection, you can begin planning programs. Look at the class schedule to see when most students are on campus. Talk with local student groups to see if they are interested in partnering for an event.
- Review your local courses to identify topic areas that you could support through your board game collection. For example, if you have a history program, consider purchasing the card game Timeline.

Developing Science Literacy through Science-Themed Board Games

BRYCE VAN ROSS
Special Collections and Archives Student Assistant

TIFFANIE FORD-BAXTER
Science Librarian

University Library at California State University, Los Angeles

THIS PROGRAM OFFERS an innovative approach to learning through science-themed board games. Engaging non-STEM majors with science concepts can often be challenging but is achievable with a mindfully developed board game collection. This science-themed collection promotes science literacy and attracts all students, including those who traditionally do not consider themselves scientists or science-literate. This chapter outlines how to select science-themed games relevant to your campus and advertise the collection of games through tutorial and review videos featuring students. Once readily accessible, these videos will help students learn the game rules and lower the threshold barrier for non-STEM students to play science-themed board games. Ultimately, your board game collection and videos will bolster a science community and encourage students to utilize library resources.

Age Range	Type of Library Best Suited For	Cost Estimate
Young Adults (ages 13–18) Adults	Academic Libraries	$60–$1,050

OVERVIEW

A science-themed board game collection encourages students to learn science through means of play. The term *board games* in this chapter includes tabletop games such as card games and roleplaying games (RPGs). By adding science-themed board games to your library's collection, you can demonstrate the interdisciplinary nature of your library and encourage STEM students to engage with science concepts outside of their coursework.

Identifying appropriate games to purchase can take several hours or days, depending on if you review course topics and/or faculty research areas before purchasing the games. These board games offer students the opportunity to learn about science as a piece of culture and can appeal to several personality types that are not necessarily distinct (e.g., gamer, academic, or scientist). Selected games should ideally include varying play times and difficulty levels in order to appeal to the widest audience. You will want to begin with four to six games, which will enable you to create a variety of video content to appeal to a diverse student body.

Videos should be five to ten minutes long and include a short and direct plug-in that highlights the science theme or topic of the game. These videos can be accessed online through your library's homepage, on YouTube, or via a QR code sticker next to the physical game. Typically, you will need one librarian, a library staff member, or a student assistant to film the videos and a group of two to four students to play the game. Game play and video recording time may range from five minutes to an hour, depending on the length of the game. When students view your videos, they have the opportunity to feel empowered and get a sense of belonging with other student learners who are similarly enthused.

NECESSARY EQUIPMENT AND MATERIALS

- video camera
- four to six science-themed board or card games, such as
  - Photosynthesis
  - Chemistry Fluxx
  - Cytosis
  - Evolution
  - Terraforming Mars

Optional Materials

- a camera to record video/audio ($100–$300)
- students hired to appear in videos ($500)

STEP-BY-STEP INSTRUCTIONS

Preparation

- Review your science department's faculty research areas, which you can use to help identify what games to purchase. For example, if your campus has an ornithologist, consider purchasing Wingspan. If you have a microbiology or biology department, consider acquiring Viral, etc.
- Purchase your board games and any video camera equipment you need to record your videos. Board games can be purchased online or through gaming stores in your community.
- Identify student employees who are interested in playing the games and appearing in the videos. Consider reaching out to any student gaming or science clubs to see if any members might like to be involved. You will probably need to have students sign release waivers before they appear in the videos.
- Select a space to record that has good lighting and minimal background noise. If possible, try to identify spaces that reflect a lively or exciting ambiance.
- Determine the type of videos you want to create. Videos can range from short advertisements to full-length playthrough videos. If you are creating a review video, ask the students to type up their reviews beforehand. This will ensure they have topics to discuss.
- If you are unfamiliar with video editing, identify someone who can help with this process. Editing times will vary depending on the type of video you produce.
- Choose where you are going to store your videos (e.g., YouTube or your library website).

Program Instructions

Set Up
- Select the game that you want to feature in your first video. Consider asking your students to read through the instructions a few days before filming starts.
- Gather your students in the room you will be recording in. Remind them to work together to answer any questions that arise once filming begins.
- Place your video camera in a location where you can leave it for the entire shoot. This will provide steadier video footage.

Record
- Start recording. Depending on the type of video you are creating, students should begin either playing the game or discussing their review of the game.
- Double-check to ensure the camera is recording properly and is capturing all the desired audio.

Edit
- Once you have your footage, watch it and note the timestamps for anything that you want to include in your final videos.
- Edit your video to the appropriate length:
    - advertisement for a game: thirty seconds to two minutes
    - game review video: five minutes to ten minutes
    - playthrough video: ten minutes to two hours
- If time permits, have someone unfamiliar with the game watch your video and provide feedback.

Share
- Post your video on your library's social media accounts (e.g., Instagram, Twitter, Twitch, Facebook, YouTube).

Assess
- Reflect on how the videos are received. If you find a certain type of video is more popular than others, you might want to create more of those. You can also use surveys or social media posts to ask students what other science games they want.
- Review circulation statistics to see how game usage was impacted by the release of those videos.

RECOMMENDED NEXT PROJECTS

Begin building your next themed collection. There are a variety of games in subject areas such as history, education, or even business.

Consider expanding your collection to incorporate video games such as virtual reality (VR) and augmented reality (AR) games. Both VR and AR games involve math and computer science concepts, which can be used for further learning opportunities.

Start a monthly board game night in your library. These game nights could include department socials, themed events, or gaming tournaments with prizes (e.g., bookstore gift cards).

Call of Cthulhu
Hosting Roleplaying Events in the World of H. P. Lovecraft

MICHAEL FURLONG
Associate Librarian

University of Central Florida

CALL OF CTHULHU can be a great literary addition to your library games programs. Call of Cthulhu is a tabletop horror roleplaying game (RPG) set in the world of H. P. Lovecraft that involves critical thinking, cooperation, and the fun that comes with solving fantastic mysteries. In Call of Cthulhu, typically five to six players take on the role of investigators, often researching supernatural occurrences. If you want to host a game that rewards teamwork and problem-solving featuring roleplay and mystery, Call of Cthulhu is the game for you.

Age Range	Type of Library Best Suited For	Cost Estimate
Young Adults (ages 13–18) Adults	Public Libraries Academic Libraries	$38–$125

Cost Considerations

The cost is roughly $125 for the Call of Cthulhu books and supplies listed in the Necessary Equipment and Materials section, or optionally, $38 for only the starter set, dice, and photocopies to first gauge interest. Additional costs could include props, music, and setting effects if you would like to enhance the gaming atmosphere. If you decide to use miniatures to keep track of where players' characters are at any given time on a map—especially during combat—those are often $20 and up, but miniatures are optional. Other items can be used to represent characters' physical location on a map, including dice in a pinch.

FIGURE 10.1
Call of Cthulhu Keeper Rulebook

OVERVIEW

Commonly, most RPGs run in four-hour time blocks, particularly one-shot rounds at gaming and game store conventions. However, you could host a pre-game introductory session during which you introduce players to Call of Cthulhu, assign pre-generated characters (or allow players to choose their own characters), answer any rule-related or meeting questions, and then possibly run an introductory Call of Cthulhu scenario. In many cases, three to four hours for a game session of this nature is ideal.

Most roleplaying scenarios are designed for four to seven players, and the Keeper, who runs the game, serves as the referee and storyteller, equivalent to how a DM (Dungeon Master) in Dungeons & Dragons guides the players. A Call of Cthulhu game can have as few as two to four players but can be played optimally with up to six. Seven players or more limits the interaction possible between players and the Keeper. One remedy for larger groups is to designate an assistant Keeper to help with larger investigative parties.

If you decide to use a preexisting story from one of the modules, the Keeper can read and use this storyline for the players. This method requires less prep time than writing the storyline yourself.

There are typically two different types of strategies for hosting roleplaying events: a one-shot adventure that lasts four hours with a single adventure, or ongoing campaigns that also last three to four hours per session but that recur on a regular basis, such as weekly, monthly, and so on, to continue the campaign when unfinished, often using the same characters and players.

Not all players can attend some games regularly; it can be assumed that some players might leave and later reenter an ongoing campaign. General wisdom dictates advertising a series of one-shot campaigns at your library; then, if these prove to be popular enough and players want to meet regularly, you can create a campaign when it seems feasible, if most of the same players would like to continue playing.

NECESSARY EQUIPMENT AND MATERIALS

- *Call of Cthulhu RPG Keeper Rulebook: Horror Roleplaying in the Worlds of H. P. Lovecraft*: $50
- *Call of Cthulhu Investigator's Handbook*: $35
- photocopies of character sheets: $5–$10
- RPG dice: $10 (This should be a regular set of dice as well as an additional D10 so that D100 results can be rolled.) Players can be encouraged to bring their own dice; otherwise, the $10 expense would be per player at the table.
- Modules can be purchased or scenarios written by the Keeper running the game. Most purchased modules range from $20 and up, although some could be purchased for less.
- Optionally, if you want to try the game out before purchasing both rulebooks, you can also purchase the Call of Cthulhu Starter Set to sample the game for $18.
- Of course, all of these issues can be solved and your expenses reduced if you have a librarian who plays Call of Cthulhu or an interested patron with experience and access to the books.

STEP-BY-STEP INSTRUCTIONS

The Keeper is responsible for running the adventure, keeping the events moving, and explaining the world and the story to players as the narrator. The Keeper also makes the final decision about rules, arbitrates what the players can do, and takes on the role of all non-player characters (NPCs) encountered in the game. Being a Keeper requires the biggest time investment because the preparation needed to run the game can take several hours. In contrast, players can play and enjoy the game without advance preparation.

Although H. P. Lovecraft's world is darkly themed, RPGs are social activities. Often a great deal of humor and social activity that has little to do with horror can take place at the gaming table, and players can find amusement in unexpected situations. So, although there may be dark moments in Call of Cthulhu, there are also lighthearted ones, and exploring both gives balance to the game and provides fun.

In Call of Cthulhu, the characters have a Sanity, or SAN, score, and as unsettling events occur and mythos creatures are encountered, players will be required to pass SAN checks or they will eventually develop phobias or potentially experience a serious shock and go insane. So, if a character encounters a shocking event in the game, they may have to roll at or below their SAN score to minimize loss.

A certain maturity level is expected in Call of Cthulhu, and if players have only played heroic fantasy RPGs, they may find this horror-genre game surprisingly different. Often, the forces players contend with are powerful and cannot be fought directly. Call of Cthulhu rewards research, careful planning, and caution, rather than directly confronting monsters and engaging them in combat. In this way, not everything in Call of Cthulhu needs to be encountered, and sometimes the players will lose or experience setbacks during play. Call of Cthulhu is not an ideal game for power gamers or players who prefer hack-and-slash-type campaigns because, after confronting the supernatural in the Lovecraft mythos, their adventures will likely be short-lived.

Preparation

- Attempt to reserve a private room for play. Call of Cthulhu is about building mood, and this is easier to do for the Keeper if there are no outside distractions or competing noise. Effective roleplaying/acting is one way of heightening the mood.
- Although all libraries are different, music can be used to enhance the scenes during Call of Cthulhu, and props and costumes can be used to enhance the overall setting.
- Have pre-generated character sheets prepared for your players. Premade characters are often pre-generated in the game books or can be generated by the Keeper in advance.
- Have dice, pencils, and note sheets available for your players. Experienced players typically bring these materials, but you may have players who are newer to RPGs.

CHAPTER 10 | **Call of Cthulhu**

- Before the start of the game, the Keeper should read the module they are planning to run for the players and have some ideas regarding the direction the story may take while anticipating that the players may choose some unexpected plot angle to pursue. If players are likely to encounter that part of the module, the Keeper should be prepared.
- If the Keeper is new to gaming and storytelling, observing another Keeper as he or she runs RPGs at a gaming convention can be a good way to learn techniques. Additionally, improvisational theater class can help in preparation because the Keeper will be responsible for playing all of the NPCs in the game and so must play individuals with a range of personalities.
- Social media can be an effective tool in helping you keep track of who is expected to attend your program. Players may RSVP via social media for specific events, which will key you in to how many players to expect and thus the number of characters to make available in advance of the event.

Program Instructions

- The Keeper prepares a story or adventure for the players. This scenario can be taken from one of the modules listed above, or an experienced Keeper can write their own adventure. Characters can be provided by the Keeper in advance (which is ideal); these are often pre-generated in some of the books listed above. Or, characters can be rolled up by the players, although this can take away a good deal of game time.
- Creating a vivid story and adventure in Call of Cthulhu is key for engaging your players. In many cases, the characters will be sleuths—perhaps even amateur sleuths trying to solve a mystery. Make sure to present clues your players need to unravel at least some of the mystery they are working on. Players may not always solve the puzzle, but they should have a chance to do so if they are industrious. Also, rules in your world should seem consistent so that people interact realistically as fully developed characters.
- Typically, during game play the Keeper describes a scene and events. Then, players, often going in turn order (but not necessarily), get to state their declared actions. Sometimes the actions happen automatically if they are simple enough, but if the Keeper is uncertain whether an action will succeed, the player must make dice rolls to determine if they succeed, and if so, the level of their success.

- Once actions resolve, or if they do not, the Keeper can introduce new story information as they see fit as things change. Players again can attempt to respond to events in character and make their dice rolls as necessary.
- Most often, this new information will be pointed out as a new character or creature is introduced and/or if the characters explore a new location, usually to investigate the larger mystery.
- Some mechanics in Call of Cthulhu are similar to other RPGs, including hit points. Each character has a certain number of hit points, which determines the health of a character. Losing hit points during the game indicates the character has been wounded in some manner.
- *Library research* is a player skill in Call of Cthulhu games. This is a skill percentage that describes a character's ability to perform library research. For libraries that would like to develop information literacy as a skill with interested players, you could have hands-on activities with books, during which players can actually research and learn about topics in real time and apply information learned to the game. This method is optional but allows players actual research practice in a library and could be fun for those wanting to increase their personal research skills in game time.
- Most skills in Call of Cthulhu are percent-based. For example, a character may have a Dexterity (DEX) percent of 60. If the player tries to dodge an object thrown at them (and avoid losing hit points), the player would be required to roll at 60 percent or below on d100 to be successful. Succeeding allows the player to dodge, but rolling 61 percent or higher would mean that the character is struck by the object and will likely take hit point damage.
- Call of Cthulhu can be set in a variety of time periods, from the Roman Empire to the Jazz Age of the 1920s to modern day, or really any time period you feel comfortable planning. Because of this, you can also include a wealth of historical information in Call of Cthulhu and explore different historical periods. Over time, you may find players prefer playing in different timelines. You can even run a time-travel campaign with players or an adventure set in H. P. Lovecraft's Dreamlands, which is a high-fantasy, otherworldly setting within Call of Cthulhu.
- Chaosium has a comprehensive website featuring additional information on Call of Cthulhu: www.chaosium.com.

RECOMMENDED NEXT PROJECTS

- Some of the most important outcomes you can expect from this program are the development of player friendships, the rich experience of improvised live theater in a tabletop environment, and the enjoyment of exploring a fictional world with your character.
- Creative thinking, storytelling, improvisational acting, leadership, and teamwork are potential learning devices used in Call of Cthulhu.
- After players have finished playing Call of Cthulhu, they should be primed to play most other RPGs as well.
- Also, over time, players often develop into Keepers and can then help run games for other players if there is interest or if players want to branch off in other directions and play in related but different Call of Cthulhu campaigns.

How to Host a Large-Scale Board Games Event for New Student Orientation

ANNETTE M. VADNAIS
Undergraduate Outreach Librarian, Student Success & Engagement
W. E. B. Du Bois Library, University of Massachusetts, Amherst

IN THIS PROGRAM students have the opportunity to meet other students as they play tabletop games as part of their fall orientation at campus. This tabletop gaming program can accommodate a large audience, with over five hundred students in attendance. It is also scalable based on your budget. This event encourages students new to campus to physically enter the library building and its spaces. For many first-year students, this will be their first visit to the library, and the program offers a welcoming and fun first impression. The library then becomes more approachable, making students less wary to visit when they need research help.

Age Range	Type of Library Best Suited For	Cost Estimate
Adults	Academic Libraries	$500–$2,000

OVERVIEW

This event is designed to attract students to visit and get oriented to the library and some of its spaces. It should not feel like a *timeshare pitch*; rather,

FIGURE 11.1
First-year students enjoying Get Your Game On

students should leave the library with a positive first experience. The event is usually 2.5 hours in length, and I have found that this is a good amount of time that encourages most students to stay for the entire event. The event requires at least eight to ten volunteers to help with setup and takedown, answer questions, supervise, and be a welcoming friendly presence. In an attempt to keep students present throughout the event, we typically raffle off a brand new copy of each game and four Kindle Fires (approximately $200). When we announce the winners at the end, students must be present to claim their prize. During the event, we tend to take a hands-off approach and let the students choose their game and the people they want to play with. We do not have a staff member at each table; rather, we let patrons play among themselves.

NECESSARY EQUIPMENT AND MATERIALS

- board games to play (for example, Monopoly, The Game of Life, Settlers of Catan)

Recommended but Optional Materials

- posters, which you can use to advertise the event
- games to raffle off (a new version of each game that is played)
- raffle tickets
- raffle cubes
- candy
- popcorn
- larger prizes
- pizza, salads, and drinks for volunteers
- T-shirts for volunteers
- speakers and microphones for amplification, if participation is high

STEP-BY-STEP INSTRUCTIONS

Necessary Volunteer Positions for the Night of the Event

- facilitator (coordinates volunteers)
- emcee (announces the event and winners at the end)
- photographer
- welcome desk (explains the evening and hands out drink coupons and raffle tickets)
- popcorn maker (if you need one)

Preparation

Three Months before the Event

- Create a planning committee and divide up the labor/costs. (Members of the planning committee can also volunteer the night of the event, but it is not mandatory.)
- Contact other campus entities to see if they are interested in collaborating.
- Contact campus student groups. We reach out to and help advertise for the Game Hobbyist League, a student group on our campus.
- Design the poster for the event.
- Distribute the poster to campus entities that you are working with or that will be advertising for you.
- Advertise your event on your social media accounts.

PART I | **Tabletop Game Programs**

- Put a call out for volunteers to help on the night of the event; let them know about the necessary volunteer positions they can sign up for.
- Design the T-shirt for your volunteers (we use Custom Ink because you can buy T-shirts with no minimum order).
- Order the games you will be raffling off.
- Order candy and popcorn.
- Order raffle cubes (*tip*: Google "ballot," "raffle," or "coin box").
- Order food for your volunteers.

A Week before the Event
- Send a reminder e-mail to volunteers that includes a schedule for that evening.
- Organize carts to make that night easier. Include the following items:
    - welcome desk cart, poster, raffle tickets, drink coupons
    - games to play
    - games for your raffle (cover and leave until a few minutes before the announcement)
    - raffle cubes
    - microphone/speakers

Program Instructions

Event Night Schedule
- 6:30 p.m.: Volunteers arrive, grab their volunteer T-shirt, and eat.
- 7:00 p.m.: Start to set up your welcome desk, tables, chairs, games, and raffle cubes.
    - The welcome desk should be set up first. If you have a poster, you can put it up next to the desk. At our desk, we have volunteers explain the evening and hand out five raffle tickets to each student. We then tell the students to keep one ticket and put the other in whatever raffle cube they want. They can put all of them in one cube to increase their chances or put each one in five different cubes—it's up to them.
    - Next, set up each table to have a game and the raffle cube for that game. We keep multiples of the more popular games on a cart where students can select them, if all the games out on the tables are being used.
    - If using a popcorn machine, turn it on and start making popcorn.

- 7:30 p.m.: The event starts. Students can start to check in at the welcome desk, get their raffle tickets, and start gaming.
- 7:45 p.m.: The emcee gives his/her opening remarks, then mentions the event sponsors and any co-sponsors who would like to speak. This is a great opportunity to advertise the sponsors and welcome them to the campus and libraries.
- During the event: Volunteers walk around and make sure the popcorn and candy supplies are being suitably replenished. They remain on hand to answer any questions students may have.
- 9:55 p.m.: Volunteers should gather all the raffle cubes and bring them to the front area where the emcee is located.
- 10:00 p.m.: Announce the winners (this also encourages them to stay for the whole event, as they cannot win if they are not present when prizes are announced). So, we just open each cube, mention what is being raffled off, and then call the numbers on the ticket. Sometimes, you will have to read more than one ticket until you get a winner, as some students will likely leave before the drawing. At the end, mention the co-sponsors and any student group that wants to promote their club. This can also be a great time to take pictures of each winner to possibly use later in promotion materials.
- 10:02 p.m.: Clean up!

Post-Event
- Hold a committee debrief (e-mail, survey, or meeting). Determine what worked and didn't.
- Make any changes you feel fit for next year's program.

RECOMMENDED NEXT PROJECT

Now that you have a catalog of games, if you find that the event proved successful, you could hold a smaller monthly event during which students come to the library to play games.

Not So Trivial Pursuit
Board Game Creation in Your Library

KRISTEN CINAR
Instructor, Library Services

Suffolk County Community College

THIS PROJECT IS designed to introduce students to library-related information by presenting it in the form of the board games they all know and love. Players can brush up on their library trivia with a clever spin on the classic game Trivial Pursuit by replacing the traditional subjects with library departments (access services, special collections, reference, branches, online services, and wildcard, just to give examples). Similarly, physical library spaces and all they have to offer can be explored by players via a game inspired by a known location-based game such as Clue. Players can also experience the same triumphs and setbacks experienced by characters in their favorite book with a literary-themed twist on Chutes and Ladders.

Age Range	Type of Library Best Suited For	Cost Estimate
Tweens (ages 8–12) Young Adults (ages 13–18) Adults	Public Libraries Academic Libraries School Libraries	$0–$50

Cost Considerations

Cost is dependent on the authenticity you wish to achieve with your game and the resources your library has at its disposal. Players will inherently compare the feeling of your game to commercial versions, perhaps more so as the age level increases.

Repurposing Expenses ($0–$25)

For low-cost options, you can repurpose an old game and give it new life. Utilize a board from a game you own or are willing to purchase cheaply and reface the surface. If you're going for Clue, take some pictures of library locations and paste them over the preexisting rooms on the board. Or, design a new board layout using a custom page size in Microsoft Publisher. Print it out at any office supply store for approximately $25 or for free if your library owns a poster printer! Game pieces can be scavenged as well. If your game requires cards, consider designing them yourself and printing them on some sturdy cardstock. You'll want to keep all your pieces together, so glue a more appropriate face onto your game's old box to complete the look while keeping everything organized.

FIGURE 12.1
Not So Trivial Pursuit, an in-house library creation

In-House Expenses ($0)

Some colleges and universities with a Preservation Department may also be able to save cash by making use of supplies that might ordinarily be used for box creation and book repair. Binder's Board, covered with a nice book cloth, can mimic a standard commercial board. Affix a printout of the game using in-house glue. This will keep the pages secure until they are pulled off at the time of game play. The only additional expense, beyond office supplies for this method, would be any game pieces you require that you did not wish to take from a different game.

Purchased Supplies ($25–$50)

For those who wish to purchase pieces, everything you need is readily available through online retailers such as Amazon. Kits that supply game creators with dry-erase game boards and markers, dice, pawns, other space markers, and a timer can be purchased for the very reasonable price of $25. Blank boards can be had for under $10, as can dice, a large set of pawns, and cards. For those who wish to design a nice game and affix it to a professional-looking board using some spray glue, this option would definitely suit you and would likely come in under $50, when all is said and done.

OVERVIEW

In this project students will learn important library information as they enjoy the competitive and somewhat nostalgic joy unique to board games. Using time-tested commercial models as templates, the games you present to them will be familiar yet exciting due to new content challenges. The boards will resemble classic games in design and rule expectations but will be populated with library and research information to ensure that time is spent achieving educational outcomes, not learning how to play.

Apart from learning library-related information, board game participants will take part in essential face-to-face peer interactions that will also have the added benefit of building on valuable skills such as problem-solving, logic and strategy, effective communication, creative thinking, and good sportsmanship.

Trivial Pursuit

For an academic library version of Trivial Pursuit, players will move about the board, landing on colored squares that correspond with a specific area within the library. Upon landing on an Access Services square, a card relating to this area would be read by an opponent. The student might be challenged to respond to questions such as the following bit of departmental knowledge: How might you request a book be mailed to you from one of our other library branches?

    A. Via Interlibrary Loan
    B. Through Document Delivery
    C. Through virtual chat
    D. The library does not offer this service

Answering this question not only tests the knowledge of those who are familiar with the service but also markets information to those who may have been previously unaware of it. Collecting all the colored books on their bookshelf would be the ultimate goal.

To make this game, repurpose an existing Trivial Pursuit board and add a new set of cards designated to the areas of knowledge that you select. Print cards on cardstock with the questions on the front and corresponding answers on the back. You may also create a board from scratch to better customize the name and appearance, as shown in figure 12.1.

Clue

Libraries with multiple branches or areas of interest might choose a location-based game such as Clue. As opposed to the traditional objective—solving a murder—you might want to pick a more suitable goal, such as discovering where the school's mascot was last seen studying which subject or using which resource. For instance, the Confidential envelope might hold the cards: Main Stacks, History, or Online Databases. The first player to guess correctly wins the game. An incorrect guess results in elimination.

To customize this game, take pictures of the spaces you wish to focus on within your library. Affix printouts of these images to your board and print new cards with a location and a subject and resource type on one side and a design or the game's title on the other. For those librarians wishing to make a custom board, use a program such as MS Publisher to create a layout with your location images and the tile spaces that connect them. You can either create squares in the program that are filled with a color or texture or find a royalty-free game board template online to paste in the background. You can affix this to a board made of Binder's Board and book cloth or use a blank board purchased from an online retailer.

Chutes and Ladders

If you're looking for appropriate games that consist of content based on a title from your on-hand collection of classics, Chutes and Ladders is a great option. Choose a popular title that contains plenty of challenges and setbacks that allow characters to either advance or face push-back in the plot and then incorporate the mechanics of a Chutes and Ladders game. For example, the *Harry Potter* film series provides plenty of inspiration that you can draw on.

Your players can travel forward by broomstick, aboard the Hogwarts Express, and even in Mr. Weasley's flying car. Landing on one of these squares in your game would allow players to advance to an appropriate location on the board, such as the Whomping Willow. Similarly, forgetting the Fat Lady's password may result in the loss of a turn, a dementor's kiss might send them backward (even back to Start!), and a space containing polyjuice might allow them to switch places with another player on the board. You are only limited by your imagination!

When creating this game, it is more appropriate to create your board layout from scratch. Find royalty-free images that capture the general action of that square, such as a car image for the Weasleys' car or a magic wand for spell use. Look for PNG images that have a transparent background to prevent a white box from taking away from the look of your game. Attach your game layout to a board you've created or purchased.

NECESSARY EQUIPMENT AND MATERIALS

- board
- dice
- space markers
- cards
- wooden books for scorekeeping (for Trivial Pursuit)
- printed score sheets (for Clue)
- box
- instructions

STEP-BY-STEP INSTRUCTIONS

Preparation

- Decide on learning objectives to determine what commercial board game fits the type of information covered.
- Assess available supplies to see if you should repurpose an old game, create one in-house, or purchase all new supplies.
- Design a game layout that suits your needs using a program such as MS Publisher, which allows you to create shapes and text to guide players on the board. (Also consider royalty-free websites for colorful graphics!)

- Print out your board design on a poster printer or at a local office supply store and affix it to a board or hard surface.
- Even if your version is based on a popular board game, be sure to include a list of detailed playing instructions!
- Have staff or volunteers test the game and offer feedback.
- If no changes are required, catalog your game and market it through the library's homepage and social media.

Program Instructions

- Players should show proper identification to borrow the game.
- Boxes should be inspected at the points of checkout and return to ensure that all pieces are intact.
- Staff should be knowledgeable of the game in case there are questions.
- Feedback cards should be included that solicit advice for improving the game or suggesting new content for a future project.

RECOMMENDED NEXT PROJECTS

Create a staff-advised volunteer gaming club to guide students and other users as they make a game of their own! Consider an original library game with your own layout, objectives, and rules!

How to Organize a Tabletop Gaming Convention

....

TIFFANY POLFER
Teen Programming Librarian

JAMES TYNER
Adult Services Librarian

Fresno County Public Library

THIS PROGRAM CONSISTS of a large-scale tabletop gaming convention held in the library and holds the potential for local partnerships with businesses and community gaming groups. Tabletop conventions can offer well-known roleplaying games (RPGs), such as Dungeons & Dragons (D&D) and Pathfinder; indie games; newly released game demos; live action roleplaying (LARP) sessions; and board games. It can become a multiday event that can attract people beyond your system; for example, Fresno County Library's Bookwyrm Tabletop Gaming Convention, a two-day event, draws people from all over California, not just from the Central Valley. Finally, a tabletop convention allows gamers and attendees to learn more about library services and library staff to make connections in the local gaming community, which can be helpful for future programs. Through the blueprint included in this chapter, readers will learn the necessary steps to organize a convention-style event, including how to collaborate with local businesses and community groups, build connections, and customize your convention according to community needs and branch size.

Age Range	Type of Library Best Suited For	Cost Estimate
Young Adults (ages 13–18) Adults	Public Libraries	$0–$500

FIGURE 13.1
Bookwyrm Con 2019 at the Woodward Park Library in Fresno, California

Cost Considerations

Tabletop conventions can be cost-free. The expenses for such an event largely depend on any partnerships and collaborations you can obtain with outside organizations. Costs for this program mostly stem from game supplies, which most gamers already have or can be gathered through donation drives (such as a dice drive) or donations from local game stores. If you are offering snacks for purchase or to hand out, the cost will increase. However, a snack bar or game material donation drives can be organized by your local game store or gaming groups. This can be an excellent way to grow your partnership with the gaming community and help promote your program.

OVERVIEW

Library tabletop gaming conventions simulate for-profit gaming conventions, such as BlizzCon or San Diego Comic-Con (SDCC), while being free to the public. The length of the program depends on space and staff availability. It can be held in one afternoon or a whole day, or span multiple days. Games typically run for one to four hours, so consider splitting your program into different time slots. Having separate times allow gamers to choose what they want to play and makes things easier in terms of scheduling staff and recruiting volunteers to serve as Game Masters (GMs) or Dungeon Masters

(DMs). Assigning extra library staff to assist with the program will help it run smoothly. These programs can be presented with minimal staffing levels (two to five people), but the extra hands make it infinitely easier to deal with increased branch traffic. If you do not have extra staff, volunteers can help with the program and free up branch staff to run the usual library services.

In terms of participants, the maximum size of RPGs is four to six players; a higher number of players can make it difficult for the GM to run a smooth game. Keep this size limitation in mind when planning the program's schedule. In our experience, we generally schedule a set number of tables for each type of RPG, depending on its popularity. As D&D's popularity has risen, we have begun to schedule more tables for those games. Your needs will vary depending on branch size, so schedule however many tables your library space can fit. If easier, split the program into two separate time slots and repeat the schedule for both sessions. At FCPL, we use online preregistration to help judge how many tables we will need for our program. A good resource is Warhorn.net, a free online registration software that lets the public sign up for whichever game session and table they desire. There are other options you can explore, but preregistration is a good way to gauge exactly what you are getting into.

Even though we offer preregistration, we still have unexpected people walk in on the day of the program, looking for games to play. To combat this, we offer a board game library for people to check out and play while they wait for a table to open. The main draws tend to be the RPGs and indie games, but more traditional board games provide opportunities for more people to be involved in the program, offer something fun to do while they are waiting, and add to the overall fun atmosphere of the convention. Other solutions for those who are not able to get into a game include game demonstrations or one-shots, which are quick introductions to games.

NECESSARY EQUIPMENT AND MATERIALS

- your imagination and creativity
- a way to separate games, whether by room dividers or separate rooms, because games can get loud
- tables: for sign-in/check-in and games
- chairs: four to six for players, one for GMs/DMs, and a maximum of two for the check-in table

- volunteer GMs/DMs
- game materials: campaign information, pre-generated character sheets for those without premade characters, die, paper, pencils, and a schedule/map of the campaign (can all be found online)

Recommended but Optional Materials

- a board game library for people to check out
- maps of all the game tables and a schedule of the game sessions (very helpful if running an all-day convention)
- a snack bar or list of nearby food locations (with an attached map for attendees from outside the region)
- name badges for attendees to help signify who is participating and who is just observing and can help with stats at the end of the program
- a posted code of conduct

STEP-BY-STEP INSTRUCTIONS

Preparation

- Determine if you are going to hold a half-day program, a full-day program, or a multiday program. After that is decided, pick a date that fits your branch's availability. Make sure the date does not coincide with other large-scale events in the area such as other local conventions, game store events, or even other library programs.
- Once the date is set, reach out to the local gaming community to find volunteers. Volunteers are incredibly helpful in both the planning stages and throughout the day of the program. Free tabletop and RPG programs are hard to find in the community, so use that to appeal to potential volunteers. Reach out to your local game store. These partnerships can be incredibly beneficial to your organization and to the store as well. The library can directly reach the audience they are trying to attract, and the game store can reach people who might never walk through their doors otherwise.
- Figure out exactly what you want to see at your convention. If you are offering multiple games during one session, look into preregistration to control the number of sign-ups. Make sure your location has enough

room and plan accordingly. If you are a small location, keep the number of tables offered low. If you are lucky enough to have a large area, increase the number of tables. Keep in mind that you will need to have DMs/GMs to run the games for you. Use volunteers and contacts within the gaming community to find people to perform these roles.
- Use the planning stages to solidify your connection with local game stores and other community partners (comic shops, games stores, gaming groups). These partnerships can help keep overall costs down, help you find people to assist with running the program, and help with issues during the convention.
- Divvy up tasks if you are working with a committee and have planning meetings to keep everyone communicating. Have someone manage volunteers and enlist another individual to manage game sign-ups and preregistration, if you go this route.
- Work with maintenance. You are going to see an increase in foot traffic through the branch and that usually means an increase in bathroom use.
- Have someone in charge of creating marketing and promotional materials. Make sure your marketing campaign is appealing to the established gaming community but still clear enough for non-gamers to understand (including parents of gamers—you can bring in teens through their parents!).
- Have someone in charge of drawing up a map or a schedule. Everything can be done by a single person, if that is your situation, but it is infinitely easier to tackle all the tasks involved if you have help.
- Market your event! Visit local game stores, local game community meet-ups, comic book shops—anywhere you think your audience will visit before your program.
- Contact local media: newspapers, television stations, radio stations, and blogs. Try to get in contact with nationwide tabletop societies like Wizards of the Coast. Use word of mouth with in-library advertising. If you can find a convention in your area, look into getting a table there to pass out flyers. Use social media to draw more people to your event. It might be a bit difficult at the start to form these connections, but the longer you offer this program, the better chance you have at making the connections that count. Websites such as Paizo.com (the creators of Pathfinder) allow you to register your event on their site for free and offer yet another avenue for people to learn about your event.

Program Instructions

Setup

- Make sure you have enough space to fit all your game tables. Also, if you have the room, think about having an all-beginner table with an experienced DM/GM, an all-female table, and an LGBTQ+-inclusive table, all of which lends to a welcoming environment for attendees.
- If you are using maps, make sure to place them where everyone can see them and include maps that people can take with them at the sign-in table. For the event, make signs pointing people to the game tables. Make sure your tables are clearly labeled with table numbers or your game names.
- Make sure your DMs/GMs have their necessary game materials. Again, a lot of the items needed to run a successful campaign can be found online or in D&D or Pathfinder manuals from the library.
- If you are partnering with vendors (local game stores, comic shops, artists, and so forth), think about carving out a vendor's alley for your convention. This may only be feasible in the larger conventions and is not necessary for a successful program, but if you include it, it is good to have all your vendors in one location.
- Make sure your volunteers know what they will be doing during the program. Hand out name tags so attendees know that they can approach them with questions and pass out timesheets to keep track of their work. This can help when tallying up how much time is spent on this program. Have your volunteers take photos during the program—this can come in handy for reports or presentations.
- Put out signs in front of the convention so people passing through will know what the library is doing. This can attract more people to your program and can also warn regular library users of the potential impact on library services.

Check-In Process

The best place to have your check-in table is at the front of the program space. There, you can pass out schedules, maps, and name tags before attendees even enter the program. Make sure to have a friendly face at the table because this is the first thing attendees will see. This creates a positive experience from the start of the program and makes it more likely for people to return for future events.

Flow of Traffic

Think about how you want to direct traffic. Group your similar games together. For example, have all your D&D tables together, all your Pathfinder tables together, and a specific place for indie RPGs. There may be a delay in checking people in at the front, so plan accordingly. If you have space, make sure there is enough room around your sign-in table to prevent potential traffic jams. Also, create signs directing people to the restrooms and water fountains. If you have time, walk through your location before the program to see where there might be potential snags and plan accordingly to limit or even eliminate these obstacles.

Impact on Branch Services

There will be an increase in the number of people in the library (using the front door, using the restrooms, taking up table space, etc.). To minimize complaints, put out signs in the weeks before the program to alert customers about the event and have extra staff (or even dedicate a staff member already working) handy to handle customer questions and comments. This is where volunteers are helpful because their presence can free you up to handle library customers.

After the Program

Before your program ends, distribute surveys to get feedback on the program. You can also ask attendees to review the library online through Facebook, Yelp, or comments submitted on the library webpage. These reviews can help build your case for a standing program and help you determine which direction to go in the future (planning for a longer program, for example). Plus, they are nice to review to see where you succeeded and which areas you need to revisit in the future.

After-Action Report

If you are working with a committee of any size, it is always a good idea to have a meeting after the program that includes your community partners. There are usually a lot of different opinions and feelings as to how the program went, and this meeting is a good place to discuss how everyone felt about the convention. This also poses a great opportunity to discuss what to change in the future and what to keep. It is usually best to hold these meetings as close to the end of the program as possible, so the events are fresh in everyone's mind. Make sure to include some time to discuss the positives in the program. A lot of work is involved in making an event like this happen, and it is too easy to get bogged down in the details and focus on the negatives. Use this meeting to strengthen the bonds and partnerships formed during the planning stages. Make it a productive meeting but also a celebration—you pulled off the program! If you are answering to a library board, you can also use these meetings to start compiling a physical report to present. Use the photos you took during the event and include the suggestions discussed in the after-action meeting. All of these can be useful in bringing on more administrative support for this program.

Thank Volunteers

This is incredibly important. A lot of work must be done on programs of this scale, and volunteers are vital to making sure the program is a success. Celebrating your volunteers can range from a card or e-mail thanking them for their work to a luncheon commending their efforts. You can also start a mailing list to keep them involved for the next year or next program. Plus, showing volunteer appreciation is an excellent way to wrap up your program and get everyone excited for the next big event on the horizon.

RECOMMENDED NEXT PROJECTS

Based on what your attendees noted in reviews and surveys, you might think about holding other types of gaming programs such as weekly gaming sessions or how-to sessions on how to play tabletop games or RPGs. Also, the convention-style setup of this program lends itself to other pop-culture events. You can use what you've learned and experienced with this tabletop convention to host all-day Harry Potter, Star Wars, and/or Disney conventions. Once you've scheduled and organized a large-scale program, you can expand to other fun programs. Tabletop conventions are just the beginning!

Play Your Cards Right
An Information Literacy Card Game for Undergrads

MARTHA ATTRIDGE BUFTON
Interdisciplinary Studies Librarian

COLIN HARKNESS
Gifts Coordinator

RYAN TUCCI
Subject Specialist

Carleton University Library

SOURCES IS A card game for four players that introduces undergraduate students to the importance of choosing the appropriate academic sources for their assignments. Andrew Walsh and Tanya Williamson (British academic librarians) created the original game and made it available via a Creative Commons license. We have adapted the game to improve the playability, in part by modifying the game mechanics.

Professors frequently ask academic librarians to teach undergraduates how to choose appropriate sources for individual assignments. Faculty find that students can lack a clear understanding of the value of different types of sources (e.g., the differences between academic and popular sources) and thus do not use the appropriate sources for assignments. Inappropriate choices are continually made, despite the fact that professors and teaching assistants define academic sources both in writing (e.g., in a syllabus) and orally in class, often multiple times before an assignment is due.

Sources is an alternative approach to teaching students about sources that leverages the immersive, interactive, and dynamic nature of game-based learning. The game is easy to make, adapt, learn, and play in under thirty minutes in a class or via a tutorial of twenty to twenty-six students (five or six groups). Librarians can integrate the game into information literacy lessons informed by the ACRL *Framework for Information Literacy in Higher Education*.

Note: High school teachers can also use the game with senior students who are preparing for entry into a university or college.

Age Range	Type of Library Best Suited For	Cost Estimate
Young Adults (ages 13–18) Adults	Academic Libraries School Libraries	$40–$55 (for four decks of cards)

OVERVIEW

- To make the decks of cards, allow enough time to download the game materials, print the labels, and attach them to the cards.
- Purchase extra cards and labels in case of printing errors or if label adjustments are needed.
- Ideally, a team of at least two people will be available to teach the game, although one instructor per table is optimum so that players can easily ask questions about the game, including definitions of assignments and sources.
- Instructions include a brief introduction, followed by a short instructional video, which covers the game rules and mechanics.
- Four players per table is optimal but up to six players can play.

NECESSARY EQUIPMENT AND MATERIALS

- decks of playing cards in two colors (the number depends on the number of students in a class or tutorial)
    - For each table, you need one red deck of thirteen assignment cards and one blue deck of fifty-five Sources cards.
    - For four tables, you will need to buy one red deck and five blue decks.
- access to a computer and printer
- adhesive labels (68 labels per the Sources deck), which stick well to paper cards

- Alternatively, you can purchase card protectors, print the card labels on regular paper, and then insert these labels and the individual cards into sleeves.
  - *Note*: Print the labels for the cards in color.
- scissors or a paper cutter
- plastic tokens for bonus points

STEP-BY-STEP INSTRUCTIONS

Preparation

- Access the Sources materials at http://sources.interdisciplinarylib.ca or Dropbox. This site gives you access to:
  - 8x card set in Word Documents (.doc)
  - 8x card set in Word Documents (.pdf)
  - One Rule and Sources Information Word Document (.doc)
  - One Rule and Sources Information Word Document (.pdf)
  - a template: Avery Shipping Labels-Template 8923
  - one instructional video
  - references
- Print the card set onto adhesive labels and attach them to regular playing cards. Each Sources deck includes sixty-eight cards.

Program Instructions

Information Literacy Lecture and Tutorial
- You can integrate the game into a larger information literacy session that includes an in-class lecture on finding the right sources, followed by a tutorial during which the game is played. If you go this route, the lesson should be broken down into two classes: the lecture and then the tutorial.
- If you are teaching a small seminar class, you can deliver the lecture and the game in the same session, providing you have approximately two hours of teaching time to work with. The game works better in the context of a larger discussion involving the value of information and the importance of searching as a strategic inquiry.

Playing the Game

Once you have assembled the decks (have one deck for each group of four students; for example, five decks for a class of twenty students) and printed out the handouts (one for each student):

- introduce students to the game with a brief oral description,
- play the instructional video that reviews the rules of the game,
- distribute the cards, bonus tokens, and handout that outlines the game rules and explains the icons on the cards, and
- have students play a round of the game.
    - Groups of players can play at their own pace, and some groups may finish before others.
    - You can allow groups to play a second round in order to ensure that each group completes at least one round.

RECOMMENDED NEXT PROJECTS

Games can be used in a variety of ways for teaching information literacy. As a follow-up, librarians could:

- play a second round with students using the trading and collaboration rules
- consider adding additional assignments such as group projects or new sources

Advanced D&G (Donations and Grants)
Building Your Game Library without Breaking Your Budget

MATTHEW MORRISON
Public Services Librarian

Tarrant County College

SAY THAT YOU'RE a librarian with a passion for games, but your library has no budget set aside for developing a respectable gaming collection. This project will enable librarians in a wide variety of settings to utilize donations and grants to acquire resources they could not normally access through standard collection development techniques. This project will instruct librarians on how to best approach small businesses, large businesses, and game publishers for assistance in building a game library.

Age Range	Type of Library Best Suited For	Cost Estimate
Kids (ages 3–7) Tweens (ages 8–12) Young Adults (ages 13–18) Adults	Public Libraries Academic Libraries School Libraries	$0 (Ideally, this program will increase the resources of your library without costing a thing.)

OVERVIEW

Developing a library game collection is like developing any other library collection. It requires professional knowledge, research, and a certain degree of investment. Fortunately, it is possible for a library to develop a world-class gaming collection without spending a lot of money. Indeed, through the careful application of specialized grants and donations from gaming-related businesses, big-box stores, and publishers, it is possible for a library to build such a collection without spending a dime!

NECESSARY EQUIPMENT AND MATERIALS

- internet access
- a professional e-mail address
- an electronic device capable of accessing e-mail
- a phone
- up-to-date proof of your nonprofit or tax-exempt status
- thick skin
- time
- patience

STEP-BY-STEP INSTRUCTIONS

Preparation

- Determine the needs of your library and what you want to request ahead of time. This is vital, even if you do not have to write a formal grant application.
- Research the businesses and publishers before you approach them. Find out if they have existing programs or special contacts for helping public organizations such as libraries.
- If the business or publisher is locally based, make an appointment to speak with the management or owners in person rather than making contact by phone or e-mail.

Program Instructions

Approach Small Businesses

- Independently owned local game shops and bookstores that carry gaming paraphernalia can be a wonderful community partner for any library seeking to develop a gaming collection.

- Small business owners tend to be sympathetic to libraries (if not active library users themselves) due to similar problems with limited resources and the shared need for steady community engagement to thrive.
- Small businesses may not be able to offer much in the way of direct financial support compared to larger companies and publishers but can often be persuaded to offer libraries a discount on certain items, even if they cannot donate products to you on a regular basis.
- Some small businesses may be willing to help with running library programs by providing volunteers who can demonstrate various games—if a librarian does not feel comfortable managing such things personally.
- Because they are based in the same communities as your branch, small businesses can also be invaluable as a source of advertising for library programs.

Contact Large Businesses
- Many big-box stores are required by their corporate offices to make regular donations to civic organizations in order to showcase their commitment to helping their communities. While there is rarely a lack of organizations requesting assistance, a savvy librarian can take advantage of this corporate policy to secure resources for their library.
- Given the sheer number of requests a big-box store may receive from community partners, they are more likely to grant simpler, smaller requests for specific board games they carry in stock than requests for financial assistance.
- Big-box stores also often offer a variety of grant programs that allow nonprofit organizations to request financial assistance with special projects.
- Many of these grants are specifically aimed at areas within the library's scope of interest (i.e., afterschool programs for teens, childhood development, STEM programs), and a librarian may be inspired to think of new program ideas built around the requirements of a grant.

Apply for Grants
Grants to Consider
- David L. Hoyt Education Foundation, https://www.davidlhoytfoundation.org/small-grants.html
- Walmart Local Community Grants, https://walmart.org/how-we-give/local-community-grants

- Target community impact grants, https://corporate.target.com/corporate-responsibility/community-impact
- Best Buy Community Grants, https://corporate.bestbuy.com/community-grants/
- H-E-B Community Investment Program, https://www.heb.com/static-page/Apply-for-Community-Investment

Reach Out to Game Publishers
- Many game publishers have specific resources set aside for libraries on their websites, from whole game books available for free to digital resources that can assist with program planning and promotion. This is particularly true of roleplaying game (RPG) publishers.
- Many game publishers are also willing to give free products to tax-exempt organizations such as libraries and have whole departments devoted to managing donations. These departments can be easily contacted through e-mail and often require only a copy of the library's tax-exempt or nonprofit status sent from an e-mail address connected to that library.
- Even publishers that cannot donate materials to a library are usually willing to offer considerable discounts on materials purchased directly from the company.

Game Publishers That Donate Games to Libraries
- Brotherwise Games, www.brotherwisegames.com/contact
- Cheapass Games, https://cheapass.com/contact-us
- CMON Games, https://support.cmon.com/hc/en-us
- Exploding Kittens, https://explodingkittens.com/contact
- Good Games, www.goodgames.com.au/au/join-the-team/faqs.html
- IELLO Games, https://help.iellousa.com/knowledge/kb-tickets/new
- Japanime Games, https://japanimegames.com/pages/contact-us
- Oink Games, https://oinkgms.zendesk.com/hc/en-us/requests/new
- Paizo Publishing, https://paizo.com/paizo/contact
- Red Raven Games, https://redravengames.squarespace.com/contact-1
- SlugFest Games, http://slugfestgames.com/about
- ThinkFun Games, www.thinkfun.com/contact
- Wizards of the Coast, https://company.wizards.com/content/contact-us

Downloadable Free RPG Resources
- Basic Rules for Dungeons & Dragons 5th Edition, https://dnd.wizards.com/articles/features/basicrules
- Pathfinder 1st Edition Reference Document, http://legacy.aonprd.com
- Pathfinder 2nd Edition System Resources Document, https://pf2.d20pfsrd.com
- Call of Cthulhu 7th Edition Quick Start, www.chaosium.com/cthulhu-quickstart
- FATE Core System, https://www.evilhat.com/home/fate-core-downloads
- Vampire: The Masquerade, 5th Edition Quick Start, www.modiphius.net/collections/vampire-the-masquerade/products/vampire-the-masquerade-5th-edition-quickstart

RECOMMENDED NEXT PROJECTS

Organize a game-day event to show off the new gaming collection, perhaps coinciding with International Games Week or a similar annual event. This is a particularly good idea if you receive the assistance of a small local business, as you can partner with them to use the program to cross-promote what you both have to offer your community.

Develop regular game-day events for targeted groups utilizing your new resources (Family Game Night, Teen Game Day, etc.).

RPG Writing Workshop
Lead Patrons in Writing Their Own Games

CHRISTOPHER BUSSMANN
Circulation Manager

SHEA'LA FINCH
West Side Librarian

School of Visual Arts

LEAD ASPIRING GAME writers in creating their own compelling and unique roleplaying games (RPGs)! RPGs, a unique method of gaming that relies on collective imagination, collaborative decision-making, and shared story-building for success, is only as captivating as the creative input of its participants. This workshop will focus on leading participants in developing their ability to imagine interesting characters, worlds, and scenarios through a series of writing exercises. Organized as a collection of writing prompts, examples, and share-backs, this workshop can be coordinated to suit a variety of age groups. The prompts themselves can be used as one-off exercises or can build into a game for participants to test play. RPGs can last for a couple hours (a one-shot) or many years (a campaign), during which participants meet periodically to continue their adventure. RPGs are an excellent way to step outside of ourselves and see the world from a different perspective. They increase our ability to collaborate with others, articulate ourselves, and actively participate in the act of shared imagining that is at the foundation of all communication.

Age Range	Type of Library Best Suited For	Cost Estimate
Young Adults (ages 13–18) Adults	Public Libraries Academic Libraries School Libraries	$0–$50

OVERVIEW

The following workshop focuses on creating worlds, characters, and scenarios using writing prompts. A writing prompt is a common method used in creative writing instruction to expand a writer's boundaries, increase perspective, and deepen empathy. Such prompts are used only as a guide—it is not a rule. Allow your participants to decide how they employ them; some participants may use them like touchstones as they speed through their writing, while others may treat them as instruction guides as they build their pieces block-by-block. Your role is to give them a place to focus on their writing, the prompts to start them off, and the encouragement to keep them going.

Workshop leaders should allot a minimum of two and a half hours to run the workshop. The timing should be flexible and be based on the size of your group. One person per six participants allows for a good balance of attention and time. Providing refreshments is not necessary but is always encouraged to keep the energy up and the mood convivial. There is very little in the way of preparation for this program, aside from taking the time to understand the materials—and, ideally, to become inspired to put your own spin on them. If you have the time beforehand, try these writing prompts yourself! You may soon be surprised to find yourself organizing an RPG of your own.

In addition to the workshop exercises, this outline also includes an overview of what RPGs are, as well as an overview of game systems for follow-up play.

NECESSARY EQUIPMENT AND MATERIALS

- notebooks and writing implements
- colored pencils and/or other drawing materials
- RPG dice—the kind depends on the system; see the game systems section on the following page.

STEP-BY-STEP INSTRUCTIONS

Preparation

- Familiarize yourself with RPGs:
    - What is an RPG? RPGs normally consist of a Game Master (GM) and players. The GM, sometimes also known as the Dungeon Master, creates a story hook and then leads players through an adventure. The

GM is responsible for all non-player characters (NPCs) and adversaries that the player-characters encounter. These are usually generated in advance. Players begin by creating their respective characters and then respond to the GM's story within the boundaries of their character, essentially playing the *role* of their characters and acting accordingly. How they respond to the story, its drama, and its conflicts inevitably changes its path and outcome. In this way, an RPG becomes a flexible, communally developed game. When action is called for, the turns are played out in conversation, and *dice tests* are used to settle moments of chance. For example, a player decides to sneak up on a sleeping monster and then rolls the dice to find out if they succeed in defeating it. This is called a dice test, which is explained in more detail in the game systems section below. Most RPGs take place in the *theater of the mind*, but sometimes props are helpful to create verisimilitude and immersion for players. Such props usually include, but are not limited to, maps, handouts, photos or drawings, miniatures, etc. These props, if used, are usually provided by the GM, and their use is written into the scenario at play.

- Familiarize yourself with the writing prompts for each section, namely world-building, character-design, and scenario-development. Allow yourself to be inspired! These prompts are only a beginning. Include your own ideas as they come to mind. Then, decide how you will deliver the prompts. You can read them aloud with the assistance of a printed list or write them on a board or project them.

- Familiarize yourself with game systems.
    - What are game systems? An RPG system features an established set of dice-rolling mechanics used to simulate action and determine outcomes for the GM and the players. Dice tests accompany narrative story prompts to create an immersive, improvisational gaming experience. Most RPG publishers have a house system that they apply across a spectrum of games. Some systems are proprietary and cannot be replicated outside of their publisher. Other systems are open-license and free for other game designers to use or modify for their own games.
    - What are the most common game systems? The two most popular systems are both open-license: Dungeons & Dragons, 5th Edition (D&D) and basic roleplaying (BRP), the house system for Call of Cthulhu.

The latter is a percentile dice system based around a core set of seven character characteristics. D&D operates on a set of ability scores that can be modified based on character skills and equipment. D&D uses an escalating number of polyhedral dice to resolve dice tests (D4, D6, D8, D10, D12, D20). Percentile dice are either a set of two d10 or one d100.
- Can you create your own game systems? Creating your own system, rather than using an existing system, is always possible. New game designers should study existing systems, particularly those with open licenses, to see the variety of possibilities for dice-rolling mechanics. Randomization via dice-rolling can also be recreated with other materials such as cards, tokens, coins, etc.
- Which game systems do we recommend for participants of this workshop? Most RPG players are familiar with the two most common systems: D&D and BRP, with D&D currently experiencing a renaissance in popularity and BRP being one of the easiest systems to learn and utilize. Participants in this workshop should use a system familiar to them to start and then eventually work toward potentially modifying that system, creating their own, or sticking with their original system.

Program Instructions

World-Building Writing Prompts
Lead participants through the world-building writing prompts (thirty minutes).

About World-Building
RPGs take place in elaborate worlds that serve as settings for one-off adventures or years-long campaigns. The RPG writers create the world their game will take place in. When we use the term *world*, we are referring to the place or environment in which the game takes place, which can indeed be an entire world—but it could also be a single fog-encased ship floating on an unknown body of water. Most worlds arise out of a single scenario setting—for example, a dungeon or a village—that then expands as the game progresses into a fully written world. While it is a good idea to have a general concept of what your greater setting will look like and how your world will operate, focusing on a single, playable, expandable locale is preferable for new RPG writers.

If creating a world seems outside of the age range or timeframe of your event, you can ask participants to choose a familiar pre-existing world from popular culture. For example, participants could choose Middle-earth from J. R. R. Tolkien's *The Lord of the Rings* and modify it. There are many popular, pre-existing worlds to choose from, and most pop-culture, sci-fi, and fantasy properties have their own licensed RPGs.

World-Building Prompts
- Ask participants to consider these prompts while imagining their world. Emphasize that while many of these questions might be helpful, they don't need to answer all of them.
    - What is the climate of the world? Is it varied or consistent?
    - What is the flora of the world? Is it a lush jungle habitat or maybe an icy tundra?
    - What kinds of animals exist in the world? Are they animals we are familiar with or new creatures?
    - Now, consider the impact the climate, flora, and animals of the world have on the inhabitants' way of life. How does this affect what they eat or what kind of clothing they wear?
    - Who are the inhabitants of this land? How did they end up here? Are they diverse or homogeneous?
    - What level of civilization have the inhabitants reached? Are they primitive, advanced, or somewhere in between?
    - If your world were a person, what adjectives would you use to describe it?
    - Do the people have a shared system of belief? They might worship nocturnal creatures and believe the sun is toxic, hence only venturing out at night.
    - What are the core values of the society? Perhaps they value kinship above all else, and therefore believe all people are siblings to one another and live in their community as one gigantic family.
    - Do the people have a government? Perhaps they live under a monarchy—or maybe they rule collaboratively.
- *World-building example 1*: Basalt is a primitive, Iron Age settlement that exists in relative isolation from the nation-state of Agnon. Basalt was founded by thieves fleeing the tyranny of Agnon's law-and-order-based culture and runs on a strict thieves' code of live-and-let-live anarchy.

Basalt attracts outcasts from all over Agnon, allowing players to create unique and diverse characters. The climate is arid and inhospitable to both plants and animals for half of the year. (A year in Basalt is equivalent to three of our years.) The other half of the year is monsoon season, during which endless rains create gigantic lakes where inhabitants can collect and preserve fish, edible seaweed, and other means of sustenance. It is rumored that an eel the color of silver and the size of twenty full-grown people lives in the center of the largest lake and protects people who worship it. Although the Basalt thieves claim to believe nothing, if you look closely enough, throughout the settlement you will find small drawings of eels scratched into surfaces, sand, and stones.
- *Break for share-back*: Invite participants to read aloud and discuss their worlds (fifteen minutes).

Character-Design Writing Prompts

Lead participants through the character-design writing prompts (thirty minutes).

About Characters

RPG characters are created by players to represent themselves in the game-world setting. All RPG game systems have a character creation function, wherein players roll for foundational abilities such as attributes, skills, and equipment. Some RPGs offer archetypes that players can then modify and personalize (for example, a detective or wizard); other systems allow players to create their characters from the ground up, choosing occupations and skills as part of a free-flowing narrative.

There are two sets of characters: one character for each player, and many supporting characters that are played by the GM. While players create their characters via the character creation method mentioned above, the GM is responsible for creating and performing all NPCs, protagonists, and antagonists. The GM's characters can be less developed, as they are often used temporarily to move the game forward or are mysterious in nature so as not to reveal too much of the game and risk spoiling it. If the GM is feeling overwhelmed by the number of characters they need to create, he or she can always employ pre-generated characters, if using an existing game system such as D&D or BRP.

When guiding your participants in creating their characters, make it clear that they do not necessarily need to know everything about that character. Like world-building, it's best to start with a strong foundation and then let the characters further reveal themselves through game play.

Character-Design Prompts
- Ask your participants to consider these prompts while imagining their character's background.
  - What does your character want more than anything else in the world and why?
  - Of Chaucer's seven deadly sins, which sin is your character guilty of and why? How does this impede them from obtaining that which they desire most in the world?
  - What is your character's favorite memory from childhood?
  - Describe your character's community. Do they have parents? Siblings? A best friend? A mentor? A beloved pet? Write about how the people closest to your character influences them.
  - What does your character look like? (Use colored pencils and other drawing supplies to sketch your character.)
  - What values drive your character and why?
  - What is your character's biggest fear? How does this affect their life?
  - Describe one aspect of your character that annoys everyone else but that they have no control over—or maybe don't even know about.
  - Is the way your character feels inside the same as what they reveal to others during their interactions?

- Mix it up! Sometimes we create characters like ourselves or our ideals. Why not get out of your comfort zone and play as someone entirely different? Try writing one paragraph about yourself (desires, flaws, personality, temperament, relationships, interests) and then write a paragraph with completely opposite details.
- *Character-design example 1 (player)*: Kaliko was raised on an island in the sea. In the center of the island is a piping active volcano that streams molten lava down its north side and has done so for as long as recorded time. Maybe as a result of living so close to an active volcano, the people of the island are quite tranquil. Kaliko, however, is not. She is well-known for her inexhaustible energy and simmering temper, which has earned

her the nickname "little volcano." Impetuous and sometimes reckless, Kaliko can normally be found in the coves spearfishing with the others for the village's food stores. Otherwise, she likes to spend time by the edge of the lava flow at the point where it hits the sea. Here, Kaliko and her best friend Lijla dare each other to fish hot, newly made stones out of the water. Lijla is the daughter of the village leader, and though she is as tranquil as the rest of her community, she is as brave as Kaliko, and the two spend most of their time finding small adventures to have around the island that they know as well as the back of their hands. Kaliko has lived in Lijla's house as long as she can remember, although no one will tell her how she came to be there. She has never known her mother or father but considers the whole of the village to be her family. Because of this she is compelled to provide assistance whenever need arises—whether or not she is capable of helping. This can end in success or disaster, but however it ends, Kaliko continues on like a steady river of lava, never hesitating. The thing Kaliko wants more than anything in the world is to find out who her family is.
- *Character-design example 2 (GM)*: Dalin is an ancient dwarf brewer who works at the inn where the player-characters convene. Taking a shine to the group when he sees how much they appreciate his most complex and sophisticated brews, Dalin offers them a tip about a lost dwarven artifact. If the group members agree to undertake recovery of the item, Dalin will give them two casks of his custom, secret-recipe dark ale. Dalin's motivations for recovering this item are not made clear to the group, and the GM can decide whether his intentions are honest or if he is deliberately manipulating the players for his own gain. The GM should also decide what the artifact is, how it works, and what its game-stat attributes are.
- *Break for share-back*: Invite participants to read aloud and discuss their characters (fifteen minutes).
- Take a writing break to lead a short instruction session on game systems (optional, twenty minutes).

Scenario-Development Writing Prompts

Lead participants through the scenario-development writing prompts (thirty minutes).

What Is a Scenario?

Once a setting is established, RPG writers need to construct a scenario—in other words, a story conflict that will motivate the player-characters to undertake an adventure. A scenario consists of a series of story hooks and inflection points that allow player-characters agency while also driving them toward the story goals generated by the GM. RPG scenarios are not fully written stories but a series of story hooks, conflicts, and abilities tests that allow for improvisation and adventure. The design of the scenario should be flexible enough to handle different outcomes, including the potential death of the player-characters.

For the GM's part, a compelling scenario customarily includes some level of risk and mystery. That is the *hook* that lures the characters into undertaking an adventure that could put them at personal risk.

From the players' perspectives, there should be some reason for their attraction to the proposed adventure that draws them in and keeps them committed throughout the journey. Are they dominated by greed and therefore lured into pursuing treasure? Are they compassionate and driven to protect anyone in need? Are they reckless and attracted to adventure for its own sake? The values you set up in the character-design will help you establish their motivations.

When writing an intriguing scenario, try to include the unexpected—but nothing too outlandish. For example, meeting a strange barkeeper in a tavern and being offered a map to seek some treasure is a good start but perhaps a bit predictable. What if your characters met each other in a tavern but the barkeeper isn't mysterious at all—in fact, he is quite friendly!—and after a few hours of conversation, he confesses to you that he found something unusual in the forest earlier that day, and it's made him nervous ever since, only he can't quite put his finger on what it is about this unexpected item that puts him ill at ease. How would your characters pry more information out of the barkeeper? What would the item be, and how could it lead into a longer quest?

Be careful. If you include something too outlandish, you may lose your player's *willing suspension of disbelief*, which is a person's willingness to go along with an imaginary scenario. Trying to push the boundaries of what is believable without crossing them is part of the fun of writing a scenario!

The following prompts are the foundation of common scenarios. Take them and twist them around—while adding in the unexpected—to see how compelling you can make each one.

Scenario-Development Prompts

- *Example 1A (GM perspective)*: An abandoned space station suddenly starts broadcasting an emergency signal. An official search party is needed to investigate the station and search for survivors. Players are offered the contract and first dibs on any salvageable material. What the players don't know is that the emergency signal is a ruse designed to lure them into a trap.
- *Example 1B (player perspective)*: You are given a contract to search a recently abandoned space station that is now broadcasting an emergency signal. The money is excellent, but the mission is personal. Your grandfather was a scientist in the genetics lab, and you wish to find out what happened to him. The other player-characters are concerned that your character won't act in the team's best interests.
- *Example 2A (GM perspective)*: An ancient relic is stolen from the restricted stacks of a local university library by a group of daring thieves. This relic has an illicit provenance, and the university decides to hire a group of private investigators (PIs) to recover the item rather than report it stolen to traditional law enforcement agencies. The players are requested to discreetly reacquire the object, no expense spared. What the players don't know is that this relic was originally stolen by looters before being donated to the library, and its original owners were the ones who reclaimed it.
- *Example 2B (player perspective)*: When the local university library calls and asks you to discreetly reacquire a stolen object from their antiquities collection, you take the case, though you are more used to working on your own than with a team of other PIs. What seems like a routine case takes an interesting turn when the provenance of the missing item is uncovered.
- *Example 3A (GM perspective)*: A bizarre series of grisly ritual murders has 1930's Brooklyn on edge. The police have made no headway in the case, nor have they realized that the murders are connected to a series of burglaries. A private lawyer hires a disgraced journalist to investigate the thefts, thinking they are connected. What the player doesn't know is that the lawyer is the murderer and that the burglaries are red herrings.
- *Example 3B (player perspective)*: You wake up in a jail cell, head splitting and bandaged. You are unsure how you got there. A guard approaches and unlocks the door. "You've made bail," he says and motions you to follow him to a desk, where a rumpled-looking clerk asks you to sign a

form. He then hands you an embossed business card you don't recognize. Printed on the card in stamped gold foil is the name "Harold Ladislaw, Esq.," with an address and phone number printed beneath it. Underneath that are four words written in hasty, scratchy pencil mark: "call or come by." The sleepy clerk nods at the card and confirms that this Ladislaw fellow posted your bail an hour earlier via courier. He hands you a receipt for the certified check. "Nice to know people in high places," the clerk sighs before turning away. There is a pay phone nearby. Do you . . . ? (Players' decisions follow).

- *Break for share-back*: Invite participants to read aloud and discuss their scenarios (fifteen minutes).
- *Testing the game*: Once your writing workshop has concluded, you can gauge your participants' interest in reconvening to play a game. If that is their intention, you will need to:
  – schedule a three-hour block of time for game play.
  – ask participants to review the scenarios developed in your workshop and decide which they would like to play. (Or perhaps there was a particularly compelling world that everyone would like to play in. If so, invite someone to write a scenario for that one.)
  – Choose your GM. Before reconvening, this person will be responsible for reflecting on the world and scenario, dreaming up storylines and action, and sketching out the necessary supporting characters for the game.
  – Meanwhile, the other players will need to reflect on their character. Maybe they want to revise it to better suit the upcoming scenario, or perhaps they would like to develop an entirely new one. They also need to roll their stats (see the section on game systems) or pull pre-generated stats off the internet for their chosen game system.

RECOMMENDED NEXT PROJECTS

You may also wish to check out other tabletop RPG program chapters in this book such as: chapter 1: "Beyond Dungeons & Dragons: Building a Roleplaying Program" by Robert Taylor and Danielle Costello; chapter 6: "Hero's Handbook: Steps for Creating a Pathfinder RPG Beginner's Program" by Delaney Bullinger and Allison Rand; chapter 7: "Dewey and Dragons: Dungeons & Dragons at the Library" by Jamey Rorie; and chapter 10: "Call of Cthulhu: Hosting Roleplaying Events in the World of H. P. Lovecraft" by Michael Furlong.

How to Highlight Locally Designed Board Games in Your Library

MAGGIE BLOCK
Teen Services Librarian

King County Library System, Skyway Library

THIS IS NOT your average game day! Instead of pulling out your dusty old board game collection, organize game days that will give your patrons the chance to try brand-new, rarely before played games—all being taught to them by the game designers themselves! Designers are eager to bring their finished games to showcase, but more importantly, they can get direct feedback about the games they have in development by *playtesting* them. This program can be easily tailored to meet different library and community needs, such as those posed at an all-day event in which dozens of local designers bring their games for patrons to play; or, you could create a regular series in which a handful of game designers bring their games for patrons to play. This program can also work in a large library system, rotating from branch to branch and featuring different regions' game designers.

Age Range	Type of Library Best Suited For	Cost Estimate
Kids (ages 3–7) Tweens (ages 8–12) Young Adults (ages 13–18) Adults	Public Libraries Academic Libraries School Libraries	$0

PART I | **Tabletop Game Programs**

FIGURE 17.1
Library game day

OVERVIEW

This program is designed to foster fun and engaging intergenerational community events. Tabletop games offer people who otherwise wouldn't have an organic way to spend time together a framework to collaborate, imagine, laugh, and compete against each other. Giving patrons the chance to not only play games with their neighbors but learn the game their neighbor designed, and even help their neighbor tighten up aspects of the game, strengthens the bonds of those in attendance further than an average board game day. Giving designers a space where they can showcase and playtest their games is a real benefit that libraries can offer. Game designers often have to pay for such an audience.

The first and most important task to this type of program is to make partnerships with local game designers (more details below). After assessing the tabletop designers and local games available to you, you can then start to design the event to fit your library's needs. You could offer an all-day program or one as short as three hours. You could offer an all-ages program, a family program, an adult program, or a teen program. Depending on how many game designers you are hosting, you may need only one staff member present. Bear in mind, because the designers are there, staff will not be necessary to pass along game instructions to players. Working with the designers, you, as the host, can figure out how large to make your player groups. If it's a fifteen-minute or one-hour game, drop-ins should work well; if it's for a two-hour or longer game event, preregistration probably makes more sense.

NECESSARY EQUIPMENT AND MATERIALS

- tables
- chairs
- We recommend that you also have alternative tabletop games available—ideally, games that fill a gap based on what's offered (if all the designers have games for ages thirteen and over, have some age-six-and-over games for families, etc.).

STEP-BY-STEP INSTRUCTIONS

Preparation

- Find local tabletop game designers. Here are some recommended avenues to help you locate designers in your area:
    - Go to local comic conventions. Visit gaming areas and introduce yourself to those running different tables. You can also walk by the vendors' tables and talk to the folks selling games.
    - Stop by your local game or comics shop. Ask if they know of any local designers or design groups.
    - Conduct an online search. Beyond Google, Facebook and Meetup are all good resources. Some recommended search terms are: "playtesting," "indie games," "indie game creators," "indie game designers," and "tabletop games." Be sure to include your area in these searches.
    - Once you find a designer, ask them for recommendations as to who else and where else to recruit.

Program Instructions

- Decide what kind of an event you want to offer. You can do this ahead of time based on library and community needs and then acquire games that fit those needs. Alternatively, you can see what kinds of games your local designers have made and design the event around those.
- Set the date and publicize. Try to conduct outreach to local gaming groups, comics and gaming shops, and area schools.
- Make sure you give your game designers plenty of reminders.
- Make sure you know your gaming needs before you set up the library area for them. Be sure the table you had in mind will fit the game in question. Know how many players the game will need and have an extra chair or two ready for the designer and a potential observer.
- Make sure you have back-ups in place (such as some alternative games for different age groups). Most independent game designers create games as an unpaid hobby and can be flaky as a result.
- If you are doing a drop-in event, be ready to work as a greeter throughout the event time. Invite newcomers into the room and facilitate them in finding a good game to play, based on their interest or which game will be available next.
- Get contact information from your attendees for future events.

RECOMMENDED NEXT PROJECTS

- If you're featuring games that are being playtested, bring the designers back to show any changes and improvements they've incorporated since the last event. Allow patrons to watch the games grow and evolve with their feedback.
- Host a program where patrons design their own games! This is also a great alternative if you cannot find local game designers.
- Have patrons who regularly come out to tabletop game programs bring in their favorite game and teach their neighbors how to play.
- Have teen volunteers learn how to play a game and then teach it in a program.

PART II
Video Game Programs

Exam Cram
Providing Video Games for Final Exam Study Breaks

KYLE NEILL
Instruction and Digital Archivist

BRAD CASSELBERRY
University Archivist

University of Wisconsin-Stevens Point Archives and Area Research Center

THIS PROGRAM WILL provide college or high school students who are studying for final exams with valuable and mentally beneficial study breaks within what is otherwise a stressful time. Students will have the opportunity to experience modern and classic video game systems using a wide assortment of games while having fun and relieving some of the stress that preparing for final exams inevitably causes. This program is also a great opportunity for librarians to attract students who may not make regular use of their libraries.

Age Range	Type of Library Best Suited For	Cost Estimate
Young Adults (ages 13–18) Adults	Academic Libraries School Libraries	$0–$1,500

Cost Considerations

Costs can vary greatly depending on the quantity of gaming systems and TVs used, as well as whether your materials are bought, donated, borrowed, or brought in.

FIGURE 18.1
Students enjoy unwinding with video games during UW–Stevens Point Library's exam cram event.

OVERVIEW

This program is intended to provide students with a fun and relaxing escape from the stresses of final-exam preparation. Video games have become increasingly prevalent in recent years, and many students already rely on them as a type of break or stress relief. This program invites that established culture into the study arena. Your role is to provide students with a fun and inviting atmosphere in which to enjoy video games ranging from classic to modern.

This program should be held for four to six hours and twice a year, or however often final exams are administered at your institution. This period will allow for students to spend adequate time experiencing games they enjoy, as well as give some students the opportunity to take study breaks and play games, go and study again, and then return. There should be a minimum of one staff member available to supervise the use of your systems, though it would be beneficial to have more people present to watch items and engage with students.

While any type or number of games would suffice for this program, we suggest that you offer a variety of game genres, as well as both classic and modern systems. This will give students the widest range of experiences and allow them to juxtapose older gaming technology with newer systems. A selection of genres, including party, racing, sports, and dancing games, are great for multiplayer stations, while roleplaying, story, adventure, and puzzle games are more appropriate for single-player stations. Systems can range from the older Atari 2600 to the Nintendo 64, the PlayStation 2, the newer Xbox One, the Nintendo Switch, or any console generation in between.

The most challenging aspects of coordinating this program will be preparation and planning. If your library has an available budget for this program, you may be able to purchase systems and games. But if—like so many other libraries—you do not have available funding, you will have to either borrow systems and games from willing lenders or bring in your own personal items and request that your colleagues contribute. After collecting your necessary equipment, it is simply a matter of setting up the event and engaging students as they arrive.

NECESSARY EQUIPMENT AND MATERIALS

- video game consoles with games (include controllers or accessories as required by chosen games or as optional additions)
- TVs, one per system—ensure appropriate inputs are available for your chosen system(s). Also, make sure your TVs are not too large. That way, you will be able to fit multiple units in your program area.
- tables and chairs
- designated room/space

Recommended Equipment and Materials

- power cords or extension cables
- fans
- signage

STEP-BY-STEP INSTRUCTIONS

Preparation

- Decide what gaming systems, how many systems, and what generations of systems (older, newer, or a mix) you want to provide.
- Decide what games to pair with your chosen systems. If you will be setting up several systems, be sure to make available a diverse assortment of genres of games to provide a variety of options and experiences to students.
- Consider the number of students who may participate and allow a mixture of both single and multiplayer games.
- Consider holding high-score contests or miniature tournaments for games, if applicable.
- Designate a program space where noise will not cause disruption for or distraction to other patrons.
- Ensure adequate availability of a power source for your gaming systems. You do not want many systems drawing power from a single outlet.
- Draw a floor map of the room you will use and map out your system setup to make the most efficient use of your space.
- Set up tables in your program area as appropriate, with enough chairs at each station to accommodate single or multiplayer games.
- Set up TVs and gaming systems at each station and test to make sure they are operable.
- Consider placing a fan in a corner of your room, as temperatures may rise with multiple systems and bodies in the room.
- Consider rules surrounding the use of your systems (no food or drink, time limits, etc.) and place signage where appropriate.

Program Instructions

- Ensure that at least one staff member is present in the program area at all times to supervise the use of your systems and enforce posted rules.
- Welcome students warmly and invite them to sit and play a system.
- Encourage students to rotate systems and play more than one game.
- Keep in mind students can feel uncomfortable playing video games in an academic setting, so be inviting. This will help you break down student-perceived barriers regarding what activities are appropriate in the library for study breaks and stress relief.

- If you notice timid students who don't feel comfortable sitting alone at a system, begin your own multiplayer game and invite them to join you.
- Equip yourself with fun-fact gaming knowledge to share with students who seem interested in a specific game or system. Students will be particularly appreciative of information about older games and systems that they may never have experienced.

RECOMMENDED NEXT PROJECTS

- If the overall reception is positive for this program, consider creating a collection development policy around your video games and designate a smaller permanent space for game-related study breaks. Consider whether you would like to allow circulation of your new collection.
- A similar video game program may be implemented as part of a welcome week activity for new students to get acquainted with the library and meet other students with similar interests.
- Develop a program for genre-specific or topical gaming (e.g., racing games, puzzle games, or a 1990s-themed gaming event).
- Perform outreach to faculty members regarding the possible incorporation of video games into their curriculum.
- Reach out to related clubs or student organizations for collaboration opportunities on this or other gaming programs.

How to Start a Kerbal Space Program Club

JACQUELINE LOCKWOOD
Teen Services Librarian

King County Library System

GET KIDS AND teens excited about space travel, engineering, and teaching each other with a Kerbal Space Program (KSP) Club! KSP is a video game that simulates building and using rockets, spacecraft, and airplanes. Its fiery explosions and cute characters make challenging concepts such as getting into orbit fun to learn. Plus, with its LEGO-like building capabilities, there are a lot of ways for patrons to get creative and play again. At a KSP Club, patrons have fun learning about rocket science, design, the importance of learning from failures, and how to be a mentor. They also feel immense pride when they accomplish something difficult in the game and have other people there to share in the experience! KSP is currently available for play on computers, the PlayStation 4 (PS4), and Xbox One consoles.

Age Range	Type of Library Best Suited For	Cost Estimate
Tweens (ages 8–12) Young Adults (ages 13–18) Adults	Public Libraries Academic Libraries School Libraries	$40 per seat, plus hardware costs

FIGURE 19.1
Teens celebrate winning a moon landing race at the KCLS Newcastle Library's Kerbal Space Program Club.

Cost Considerations

The version of KSP sold on the Steam platform sometimes goes on sale during holidays and special events and can be purchased at as much as 50 to 75 percent off.

Computers, peripherals, and PS4 or Xbox One gaming consoles with televisions will add to the expense if you don't have a video gaming platform already established in your library.

OVERVIEW

A KSP Club meeting is a dedicated time for creating, experimenting, failing, and learning to laugh and try again. All of this happens on computers or consoles; so, there are no fizzing Alka-Seltzer rocket engines to clean up afterward.

Two hours once per month is a good amount of time for the program. If you don't have time or space available for a two-hour program, plan to provide more instruction or structure to your club so that members can still accomplish something productive during play time.

The program can be run entirely with library equipment, or you can allow patrons to bring their own computers if they already play the game at home.

One staff person can run the program comfortably up to an attendance of about twelve players. If you have more participants, it's helpful to have a second staff person who knows the basics of the game, assistance from someone from a partner organization, or mentors on hand who already play the game and are willing to teach younger participants. Offer small incentives to reluctant mentors to encourage them to attend and help those who need it.

NECESSARY EQUIPMENT AND MATERIALS

- Computers with KSP installed. If you have laptops, adding an external mouse will make game play easier. Or, you can use Xbox One or PS4 gaming consoles instead.
- A projector (optional) is a bonus! Encourage patrons to demonstrate their skills and the spacecraft they have built and teach others so that the whole group can see.

STEP-BY-STEP INSTRUCTIONS

Preparation

- Learn how to play KSP. While you don't need to be an expert, knowing the basics, such as how to build a simple rocket, perform a launch, or even get a rocket into orbit, will go a long way toward helping patrons engage with the game. The best way to start is to dive in, fail, and learn. You can also watch the excellent KSP tutorials on YouTube by gamer and real-life rocket scientist Scott Manley.
- Reach out to people, groups, or organizations that may have an interest in helping you start a KSP Club. Museums, schools, or businesses in the space industry are some examples. You may find someone who already plays the game and is willing to help.
- Prepare a sign-in sheet and other optional supplies such as whiteboard markers, candy, and other incentives.
- If you create any written instructions for your patrons, such as the steps to getting a rocket into orbit, print a sufficient number of copies before your program starts to ensure you don't run out.
    - Steps for getting a rocket into orbit:
        » Use a preloaded game rocket, such as the Kerbal X, or design your own orbit-capable rocket.

- » Set the throttle to max for launch (Z key).
- » Turn on Stability Assist (T key).
- » Launch (spacebar)!
- » At a speed of 100 m/s (meters per second), start turning to the east (D key). Don't turn too far too fast! Look at the nav ball and try to keep your nose inside the prograde indicator (yellow circle) to keep from flipping as you gradually turn to the east.
- » Once you reach an altitude of approximately 15,000 meters (m), point your craft forty-five degrees from the horizon on the nav ball. The horizon is the line between the blue and brown hemispheres.
- » Press M to go to map mode and see your path. Right click on the apoapsis marker to keep it visible. When your apoapsis (highest point) rises above 70,000 m, turn off your engines (X key). Then, look at the nav ball and point your nose indicator dot onto the horizon (where blue and brown meet). Time to coast!
- » Once your apoapsis is about thirty seconds away, burn prograde (Z key) to raise your periapsis (lowest point). Your periapsis isn't visible at first because it's inside the planet! When it appears, right click it to keep it visible.
- » Once both your apoapsis and your periapsis are above 70,000 m, you're in orbit! Press the X key to turn off your engines.

Program Instructions

- After your meeting space and equipment have been set up, your KSP Club meeting can begin. If you are using laptops, save time by asking your patrons to select one and set it up themselves as they arrive. Offer patrons a sign-in sheet and ask for their name, grade, and e-mail address so you can send out club meeting reminders. Welcome them to the club and ask if they have played KSP before. Depending on their answer, try to seat beginning players near experienced players to encourage knowledge-sharing. Patrons can work in pairs at computers, if necessary. Help facilitate taking turns and working together so that no patrons are left out.

- When your patrons have settled in, officially kick off the meeting with a short welcome. Introduce yourself and briefly explain the purpose of the club and any rules you have. This is also a good time to share exciting library or space industry news. If you have a specific plan in mind for the club that day, explain it to your patrons. For the first club meeting, focus on introducing the game, explaining basics, and discovering any experienced players who may be present. If you locate a community partner who can help you teach KSP, your first club meeting is a great time to kick everything off with a special event and invite your partner to be a special guest teacher.
- During the club meeting, rove around and admire the work of your patrons. Answer questions if you can or connect patrons to other patrons who know the answers.
- Toward the end of the meeting, give patrons a warning that they have only fifteen minutes or so left. Ask your patrons if there is anything specific that they would like to do at the next club meeting.
- At future club meetings, expand on the basics. Offer to help teach patrons how to get a rocket into orbit. A great pre-built rocket for this that is already loaded into the game is the Kerbal X. If you have a projector and a screen, use it to aid your instructions. Spend time getting to know your patrons and find out what they like to do in the game. Some may enjoy building space planes or piloting a mission to a moon or planet. Others, especially younger patrons, might simply enjoy creating huge, unwieldy rockets that explode on launch.

RECOMMENDED NEXT PROJECTS

- Continue to add new content to your club meetings to keep things interesting. For example, show and discuss videos of SpaceX and Blue Origin rocket launches and landings. Introduce a competitive element by issuing challenges such as being the first team to land on a moon and plant a flag. Asking them to plant a flag ensures that their Kerbal must survive the landing!
- Incorporate crafting and building into your program. Printing their screenshots and using a button maker to create custom buttons is just one idea you can draw on.

- There are a variety of mods available for the computer version of this game. Explore possibilities, such as using the Kerbal Operating System (kOS), to introduce a coding element to your program.
- Expansions for the basic game are available. Making History adds a mission builder, a history pack that allows players to recreate historic human achievements in space exploration, and dozens of new parts. Breaking Ground adds more equipment for science experiments, improved surface landscapes, robotic parts, and a new futuristic space suit.
- The release of the sequel, Kerbal Space Program 2, has been announced for spring 2020! Some of the features advertised include improved tutorials, new parts and technology, the ability to build colonies, interstellar travel, and a multiplayer option!

Game and Learn
How to Create a Library Augmented Reality Tour

YINGQI TANG
Associate Professor, Distance Education/Electronic Resources Manager

CHARLCIE VANN
Associate Professor; Psychology, Philosophy, and Religion Librarian

Houston Cole Library, Jacksonville State University

THIS IS A self-paced library-orientation tour project developed with augmented reality (AR) technology. Students follow directions on their mobile electronic devices to visit designated public service stations in the library and learn what kinds of services are offered, at which time they are asked to solve clues in order to continue the tour. The purpose of the project is to reduce library anxiety among first-year college students. The AR program helps students become familiar with your academic library's spaces, services, and resources, as well as establish a connection with the librarians who work there.

Age Range	Type of Library Best Suited For	Cost Estimate
Young Adults (ages 13–18) Adults	Academic Libraries	$0

Cost Considerations

There is no fee to use the application. However, some promotional products are recommended for encouraging participation.

OVERVIEW

The goal of this program is to introduce the spaces, services, and resources in your library. After the library AR tour, students should know the locations and functions of your library's public service stations and recognize subject librarians who can provide in-depth reference service to them.

The project follows a treasure hunt theme. The scenario of the story involves a group of construction workers, who, while repairing the roof of the library building damaged by a tornado, discover a locked chest in the attic. A secret code is needed to unlock the chest. Students are asked to finish two tasks and six quests (one clue is digital and the other five clues are on paper) to find *six letter* keys. Then, the player must put the keys in the correct order to unlock the chest.

- *Task 1*: Select a subject area of interest, visit the floor, and find out who the correct subject librarian is.
- *Task 2*: Visit five service stations (Reference Desk, Children's Corner, Computer Lab, Multimedia Lab, and Group Study Room), and then find and solve the clue at each station.

After students successfully unlock the chest, a "Congratulations" note will pop up, and students can redeem a prize for participation. At the end of the tour, students are asked to rate their experience, and the results will be displayed on a wall.

NECESSARY EQUIPMENT AND MATERIALS

- a computer, smartphone, electronic device, and printer
- the Metaverse application

STEP-BY-STEP INSTRUCTIONS

Preparation

- Familiarize yourself with the Metaverse application and experiment with all the features. Understand how to use Scenes (Character, Text Input, Request Item, Give Item, Webview, Camera, YouTube, Photo Portal, Video, Wall, Poll, 360 Video, and 360 Photo) and Blocks (Walls, Text, Polls, Probability, Leaderboard, etc.) to create an experience.

- Come up with a story theme. Then, create a tour map that shows the places you want students to visit.
- Build a collection of customized materials, such as characters, images, audio, and videos, for each activity.
- Generate a break code. The length of the code should equal the number of quests. It is best to have a code that has a meaning. For instance, we used "askus!" because we have six quests, and we welcome patrons' questions throughout these adventures.
- Create an alphabet game for each quest. Figure 20.1 is a sample of one such alphabet game.

FIGURE 20.1
Alphabet game sample

Program Instructions

- Take a photo of the area where you want to post the librarian's information. We selected a location near the office of a public service librarian.
- Take a photo and write a brief description for each public service station you want students to visit.
- Register for an account at Metaverse (https://studio.gometa.io/landing).
- Create a new experience. Use Scenes and Blocks to create a game based on the tour map. Upload photos to the Character Scene or Text Input Scene. Use Check Text Response Block to check answers. The experience will not be continued unless a participant provides a correct answer.
- Use Poll Scene and Record Vote Block to record and post your students' ratings of the experience.
- Use Background style to switch a scene from AR mode to background mode as needed.
- Use Response style to select the shape and color of a response button.
- Use Transition control to move from one scene to another.

PART II | **Video Game Programs**

- Create a flyer for a participant to scan. The content on the flyer should include the QR code for the experience involved, along with basic information such as where, when, and how to start the experience (see figure 20.2).

Clues
- For Task 1, we used our librarians' LibGuide profile pages. The pages can contain your institution's librarians' contact information, duties and responsibilities, and biographies. Students are asked to find the initials of the appropriate librarian's first and last name.

FIGURE 20.2
Libr-AR-y Treasure Hunt flyer

- For Task 2, we printed alphabet games and placed them on the areas where the photos were taken. We kept our game challenges simple so students wouldn't take up too much of their time solving them. Our alphabet games include Letter Illusion, Hidden Letter, Find Letter Pattern, etc.

RECOMMENDED NEXT PROJECTS

There are many features in the Metaverse application that can be applied for future projects. We plan to create another project that targets potential incoming students. Jacksonville State University hosts Preview Days each year for high school seniors to encourage them to visit their campus. Houston Cole Library, the tallest academic building in Alabama, attracts many visitors during this period. The purpose of the project is to make the library tour more fun and memorable. To that end, the AR experience for this project includes the following steps:
- Use Character Scene and Check Text Response Block to create choice questions about facts regarding your library.
- Use Camera Scene, Text Input Scene, and Media Wall to post students' selfies and comments regarding their library visiting experience.

Level Up!
Library Orientation with a Phone-Based Exploration Game

BETH JANE TOREN
Interdisciplinary, Cultural, and Film Studies Librarian

West Virginia University Libraries

THIS SELF-PACED, REASONABLY priced, and imaginatively blended activity provides an effective, customizable, and scalable alternative to in-person tours. The Green Door Labs Edventure Builder is specifically targeted to libraries and museums and has an interface with game mechanics built into its menus, allowing users with no programming experience to independently create games. Students learn about their library in an engaging way, and instructors can obtain game scores, which they can use to offer students credit for the activity.

Individuals or teams new to the library can play an exploration game on their mobile phone while exploring your library's physical and/or virtual locations, services, and resources. Players experience easy wins through a variety of methods: congratulations,

FIGURE 21.1
At the end of this game, students were invited, optionally, to share a photo of their favorite spot in the library with social media.

badges, points, or a level-up in a game, all of which create a successful, fun, and positive introduction to the library, building confidence and reducing anxiety. Blending game content and graphics on printed posters and then placing them in the game, along with adding in photos of areas within your library, can add depth and familiarity for players.

Age Range	Type of Library Best Suited For	Cost Estimate
Young Adults (ages 13–18) Adults	Public Libraries Academic Libraries	$250–$500

Cost Considerations

- charges per month of live play, negotiable based on time commitment
- includes ongoing hosting, development space, and analytics
- Separate server space is required to host game graphics, but the game, statistics, and uploads by players are hosted by Green Door Labs.
- options include professional or in-house graphics and photos

OVERVIEW

Following the initial investment of time for planning, developing, and testing, which can all be accomplished by a small number of people working in collaboration, this program can become an effective and efficient replacement of in-person tours. Students actively participate in their exploration, moving forward in the tour by answering questions and completing tasks. The game allows a higher level of individual engagement, with both the physical environment and intellectual content utilized at the player's own pace, essentially allowing each student a private tour. In addition, the program saves time previously spent giving less-efficient group tours.

A significant amount of planning time is required to make this game effective. Creative and logistical tasks must be performed. One person could potentially manage the game with consultations from others; or, up to three people or more people with clear roles can manage it (one being a tiebreaker may be most effective).

Via the game, players go on a self-paced library tour, completing tasks, taking and uploading photos, and answering questions at various steps. Playtime may take thirty to fifty minutes, or ten minutes per floor, depending on the layout of the library and number of steps involved. Players should be encouraged to play independently at random times. A large group playing at the same time—during class time, for example—can potentially cause bottlenecks and work against the theme of independent exploration. However, players should still be allowed to partner up or play in small groups, particularly to enable folks without a smartphone to play. If you anticipate a high number of participants playing simultaneously, randomizing game paths and questions may decrease bottlenecks. The tradeoff is an uneven flow of game play for players—random paths potentially create unpleasant backtracking.

Players begin with a fully charged smartphone and must have internet access to upload photos. Players without a phone are given the option to play with a partner or small team. They are free to choose without penalty or reward whether to take selfies while there and grant the library permission to use those photos.

NECESSARY EQUIPMENT AND MATERIALS

Developers Need

- computers with reliable internet access
- server space to host graphics
- cameras
- smartphones
- software for graphic editing
- a spreadsheet to align all game components (narrative, media, tasks, responses, etc.)

Players Need

- fully charged smartphones (or the option to play with a partner or team if they don't have a smartphone)
- a QR code scanner (optional, based on your questions)
- dependable wireless internet access

STEP-BY-STEP INSTRUCTIONS

Preparation

- Review design cycles and plan for iterative versions.
- Make a list of your available resources.
  - Focus on high-quality content and being creative with what you have at hand rather than depending on high-production value.
- Use your audience as a source of inspiration.
  - Reach out to people in your target audience and get them talking to you about why they enjoy playing their favorite games.
- If you aren't a gamer, study up on what makes games engaging. For example, constant feedback is critical. Continuously displaying your level and how much life you have is a video game standard. Narrative-driven games in which the player has at least the illusion of choice and open-worlds are popular and can be mimicked with simple tools. Videos and links to other web content can be embedded in the game as well.
- Build the mission and the team.
- Establish a buy-in from your administration and other stakeholders.
- Gather a team of three or more interested people, making sure everyone's role is clear.
  - Visit the Edventure Builder site at Green Door Labs. Watch their tutorials and examples with your students.
- Establish who your point of contact is. This person should communicate with the company representative and relay everything back to the team.
- Determine your audience and goal, along with your learning outcomes. For example, you could state, "New undergraduate students who play and complete the library game will visit significant physical locations and engage with virtual services and resources to support their academic success." A clear goal statement will help answer questions that arise and avoid scope creep.
- Tasks to be performed separately:
  - Explore library tours online for inspiration.
  - Brainstorm—especially based on any variety of games you enjoy.
- Meet with the team to
  - demonstrate inspiring tours and/or tour features
  - share and compile brainstorming results

- Game design and development:
  - Design options include incorporating your physical location(s) and facilities into the virtual world of the game using an imaginative scenario (such as a zombie apocalypse or roleplaying) and taking selfies or shelfies (taking a photo of books on the shelf).
  - Development is built-in, making this a great platform for first-time game creators or builders. The defaults are useful, and some are customizable, making development easier and ensuring consistency. Each step you add has menus and a WYSIWYG interface to add text and graphics. Options appear in drop-down menus and check boxes. This simple tool provides plenty of options for variety and creativity. Seasoned game developers might become frustrated with the simplicity, but the ease of selecting from a menu of predetermined mechanics allows less-experienced users to devote the bulk of their energy to creativity and customizing content for their unique library environment and target audience.
  - Options for question formats, called *step types*, include fixed-answer, open-answer, validation-code, multiple-choice, and photo-response. You can include hint text, determine the maximum number of attempts allowed, or add success text and failure text. You assign the number of points (or no points), and the type of step logic you'd like to use to determine what happens to the player next. They may then go to the next step, go to a random step, jump to a step, or make a selection.

Planning

- Plan to get a simple working game delivered and continually ask two questions about your ideas:
  - Does this support the outcome we seek for our target audience?
  - Is this necessary and doable? If the answer is no, move the idea to a *futures* folder.
- Gather library tour suggestions from as many people as possible and consult existing tour materials to identify significant locations, services, and resources. Identify fifteen or fewer reasonable ones, but no more than twenty. These become the steps.
- Develop tasks or questions to align with the steps.
- Plan a path through the library that begins and ends at the entrance or lobby.

TASK	1	2
Question	Select the next button to begin exploring.	Take a photo of the statue in the lobby and upload it. Optionally, take a selfie with it in the same pose.	Scan the QR code on the poster beside the water fountain.
Image	smiling avatar	smiling avatar	Benito's face, smiling
Narrative	Welcome to the library. My name is . . . This game will . . . You will . . . (*Several screens are needed to explain game play and options as well as gather user information if students are playing for course credit.*)	The bronze statue of a boy reading was donated by a local family to welcome people of all ages to the library. He is named Benito.	Comfortable furniture in the circular area at the back of the main floor is my favorite place to wait for someone or read. Restrooms and a water fountain are in the same area.
Category	Story mechanics	Experience	Awareness
Question Type	N/A - Next button navigates to next step	image/selfie upload [*upload button*]	QR code
Response	N/A	Great shot! There are ten more steps in our exploration. [*next button*]	Excellent! You completed two tasks; only thirteen to go. And now you know where to go if you need a break or a drink! Beverages with a lid are allowed in all areas of the library. Food is limited to the snack room. Let's go there next! [*next button*]

FIGURE 21.2
Simplified example of a spreadsheet to plan and align your narrative

- Create basic characters and a storyline.
- Draft a narrative.
- Plan to build in assessment in the form of no more than two before and after questions based on your desired outcomes. A multiple-choice Likert scale will do.
- Create a spreadsheet to plan and align your narrative, steps, media, and outcomes. See figure 21.2 for a sample spreadsheet.

Build

- Build the game in the development area.
- Completely develop a couple of steps with all the options included and test them before expanding to additional steps or batching development tasks.

Playtest

- Playtest thoroughly, getting all the questions right and then getting them all wrong.
- Playtest each iteration.
- Make each response assure the player they are doing fine and remind them where they are in the game.
    - *Example of reassuring fail text*: "I'm sorry, that wasn't the response I was looking for. Rest assured if you have further questions about the location of printers or anything else, we will be happy to assist you in person or chat with you online. Only three (3) more steps. You can do it!"
    - *Example of success text*: "Fantastic! If you find a book you'd like to read, take it to the service desk with your library card. Only three (3) more steps. You got this!"
- You can play through the game on any device or desktop while not on site, uploading any photo or getting questions wrong as needed to proceed.
- After the development team members have played through the game—a physical walk-through of the library included—and have identified and fixed any issues, invite the widest possible audience to playtest.
- Playtest with individuals and groups if you can, gathering their feedback in writing if possible.

- The best people to playtest a library orientation game are completely new to the library.
  - Try to get them to play and provide feedback with as little interaction beforehand with you as possible.
- Conduct focus groups with local gaming and game development groups.

Program Instructions

Game Play
Players can do the following:
- begin at the library entrance and use a QR code or webpage to launch the game
- earn points, and game developers can share final scores and outcomes with instructors
- allow or deny permission for the library to use the photos they upload for marketing and publications
- be given an option to indicate they are playing for fun and can skip recording identifying information required when tracking instruction records
- be prompted to share their comments and suggestions about the game in an open text box
- be invited to upload selfies with reassurance that this is optional, and their choice will not impact their score

Soft Launch
- Do a soft launch with instructors and others in your network who have brought groups of students to the library for traditional tours.

Launch
- When you have a viable product, promote and market your game.
- Wide marketing strategies may capture additional audiences.

RECOMMENDED NEXT PROJECTS

- Once players have gone through orientation, keep up the fun by inviting them to library events and programs and encourage them to attend higher-level library instruction sessions.

- Once you have a working game and have analyzed your data for ideas, turn to your assessment data and *futures* list. Potential more advanced developments include:
    - choosing your own adventure between different paths based on player interests
    - adding mini-games within the game
    - adding contests and utilizing social media
    - inviting student groups and courses to assist with future game development
- If graphics were initially kept simple, there is potential for library location photos to be Photoshopped to incorporate characters or other content from game graphics using simple tools to mimic augmented reality.

Smash Your Programming Goals with a Super Smash Bros. Ultimate Tournament

SARAH PROSSER
Teen Librarian

Rye Free Reading Room

GREAT FOR DRAWING in tweens and teens, this program always gathers a crowd as players of all experience levels battle to see who the best is! Kids can compete against each other, learn good sportsmanship characteristics, and work on social skills. This program is a lot of fun but does require some setup. This chapter will offer best practices for setting up the game, and learning how to host a Smash Bros. Tournament will help lay the foundation for running other tournament-style events at your library!

Age Range	Type of Library Best Suited For	Cost Estimate
Tweens (ages 8–12) Young Adults (ages 13–18)	Public Libraries	$0–$680

Cost Considerations

This cost estimate factors in the range between a library that has no components and a library with some or all the necessary components.

OVERVIEW

This is a program that engages teens and tweens to compete against each other in a safe environment. It is best run on a seasonal basis, two to four times a year. Librarians running this program can expect about thirty minutes of setup beforehand, and the event itself usually takes about two and a half to three hours to run *if* your library has only one Switch and doesn't allow a free-play period beforehand. One staff person can run this, but two is ideal in case any problems arise.

This program runs best if you incorporate a power of 2 in terms of participants (i.e., 4, 8, 16, 32, etc.). Sixteen is the ideal number of players, but more or less than that can still work. The Program Instructions section in this chapter explains how to place participants into brackets, as well as what to do when you have a different player total than a power of 2.

Some players may be brand new to the game, while others may be veterans. The goal for this program is to make sure everyone has a fun time and that the event runs as smoothly and painlessly as possible.

This program will be loud; therefore, hosting it in a room or space where high noise levels are acceptable is important. Using a room in which the lights can be dimmed or turned off can make the program even more special.

NECESSARY EQUIPMENT AND MATERIALS

- Nintendo Switch (two Joy-Cons and one HDMI cable included)
- Nintendo Super Smash Bros. Ultimate game
- TV or screen/projector
- a pen and paper for sign-up and establishing the brackets
- snacks and drinks
- seating for participants

Optional Equipment and Materials

- $20 GameStop gift card as a prize
- extension cords
- two to four Pro Controllers
- secondary Switch
- secondary Super Smash Bros. Ultimate game
- secondary TV or screen/projector and HDMI cable

STEP-BY-STEP INSTRUCTIONS

Preparation

- Two to six weeks out, host character unlocking events if your library is purchasing a brand-new Super Smash Bros. Ultimate game; these can be informal or formally planned. If you do not offer an opportunity to unlock characters before the game, it is likely that during the tournament a character will randomly appear as a challenger after each match until they are defeated and then added to the roster of choices.
- One to three days out, charge your Pro Controllers and Joy-Cons and purchase a gift card.

Program Instructions

- Thirty minutes before the program begins, set up the Switch, the game, and any controllers.
    - Set up for the game to ensure that:
        » players have only three stocks (lives)
        » matches last for no more than five minutes
        » no items will appear during the match
- Start the sign-in fifteen minutes before your program is set to start, and if your library allows last-minute drop-ins, register them to play. Fill in the brackets as people sign in/register. A sample bracket is below.
    - *How to do byes*: If you have more or less than sixteen players, bring your total up to the nearest power of 2 (4, 8, 16, 32, etc.) and offer your

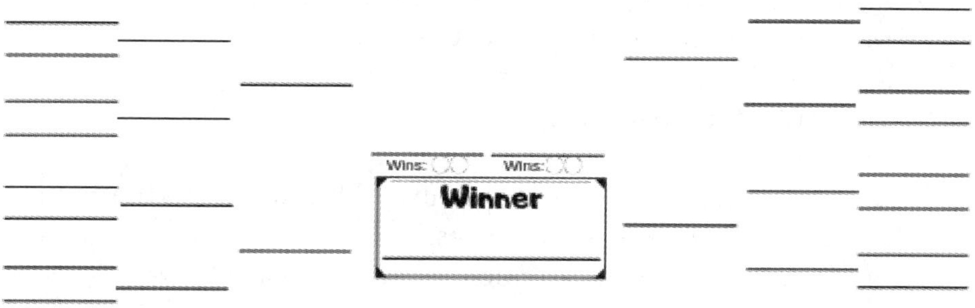

FIGURE 22.1
A sample of an unfilled bracket containing sixteen slots for players

players *byes*. Byes are a free pass going into the next round and are awarded during the first round of play. The number of byes needed is determined by subtracting the number of players from the total amount of slots. Awarding byes is best done by numbering slips of paper equal to the amount needed for your bracket. You can have players pull the slips from a hat; those players who pick numbers one through however many byes you need will win the bye.
    – For example, if you have nineteen players signed up, your bracket will be thirty-two slots, and you will need to award thirteen byes. If you have seven players signed up, your bracket will have eight slots and you will need to award one bye.
- While you are making the brackets, allow players to free play against each other.
- When you are ready to begin, go over the rules with the players. Please note the rules below, which often work best for libraries.
    – General Rules
        » Rounds will consist of one match. (If you have a low number of participants, all rounds can be best two out of three.)
        » Participants will play in one-on-one, player-versus-player rounds.
        » Participants will have three stocks (lives) per match.
        » Matches have a five-minute time limit.
        » No items will be allowed.
        » There are no kill stages. (A list of *legal* stages can be found here: https://dotesports.com/fgc/news/what-are-the-legal-competitive-stages-in-super-smash-bros-ultimate.)
        » There are no banned characters (optional), such as Hero—a controversial character in the game.
        » Winners advance to the later rounds.
        » Good sportsmanship is required.
    – Final Rules
        » Whoever gets the best two out of three matches is the winner.
        » Players get three stock (lives).
        » A five-minute time limit is set on each match.
        » There are no items.
        » There are no kill stages.

- » The winner of the match must stay as the same character and gets to pick the next stage; the loser can choose a different character.
- » Announce which two players are first up, and then which two players are on deck to play in the next round. Circle winners (or those who have byes for the first round) and advance them to the next round.
- » Feed players liberally.
- » Continue play until you have a final winner.

RECOMMENDED NEXT PROJECTS

- Recommend after-school gaming programs.
- You can expand your video game collections and apply these tournament rules to other fighting games, such as Naruto Shippuden: Ultimate Ninja Storm Trilogy or Dragon Ball FighterZ.
- Have kids build their own levels with the Stage Builder portion of the game.

Get the Most out of VR

HALEY T. LEE
Mobile and Educational Services Librarian

Warren County Public Library

TO INTRODUCE VIRTUAL reality (VR) to the library and to those who have never experienced it, libraries should begin with Playroom VR, a simple and accessible game for those new to VR. Playroom VR has five mini-games that allow up to five players to play at once with only one VR headset. The user with the VR helmet picks the mini-game, while the rest of the players play off the TV screen with PlayStation DualShock controllers. Players then take turns using the VR helmet and selecting their game. Not only can programs using games such as Playroom VR allow users to have an immersive VR experience, but they can also help players learn cooperation, communication, and team building.

Age Range	Type of Library Best Suited For	Cost Estimate
Tweens (ages 8–12) Young Adults (ages 13–18) Adults	Public Libraries School Libraries	$300–$700

Cost Considerations

There are several VR headsets on the market and, in my opinion, the PlayStation VR (PS4 VR) is the best deal. Though Oculus Rift is considered the best hardware option, it is very expensive; requires a gaming computer, which is far more than the cost of a decent gaming console; and requires significantly more setup. PS4 VR, on the other hand, is affordable and offers a quality experience. Plus, it is far more durable than an Oculus headset.

OVERVIEW

The Playroom VR enables one person to use the VR helmet and allows up to four other players to play with regular controllers off the TV screen. The player with the VR helmet gets to pick the game, and the others play along. The following games for this program are:

- *Cat and Mouse*: The player with the VR helmet plays as a cat, while the other players with PlayStation controllers play as mice collecting cheese while avoiding the cat's sight.
- *Monster Escape*: The VR player is a sea monster destroying the city, and the other players are robots trying to stop it.
- *Ghost House*: The VR player goes into a haunted house to catch ghosts but cannot see them. The other players can see where the ghosts are via the TV screen and need to tell the VR player where to catch them.
- *Wanted*: This game is similar to Ghost House, only the VR player is a sheriff and has to listen to the other players, who tell the VR player who the wanted robot is so it can be arrested.
- *Robot Rescue*: This is a two-player game in which a VR player and one other player work together to rescue robots in a platformer game.
- *Playroom Invasion*: The VR player and the other players work together to shoot down an alien invasion.

These mini-games are great tools for assisting teens and tweens in their communication and team-building skills in a fun way.

If you have already started a VR program or have a different VR headset and just need ideas, skip down to the Recommended Next Projects section for more suggestions on how to get the most out of your VR events or program.

CHAPTER 23 | **Get the Most out of VR**

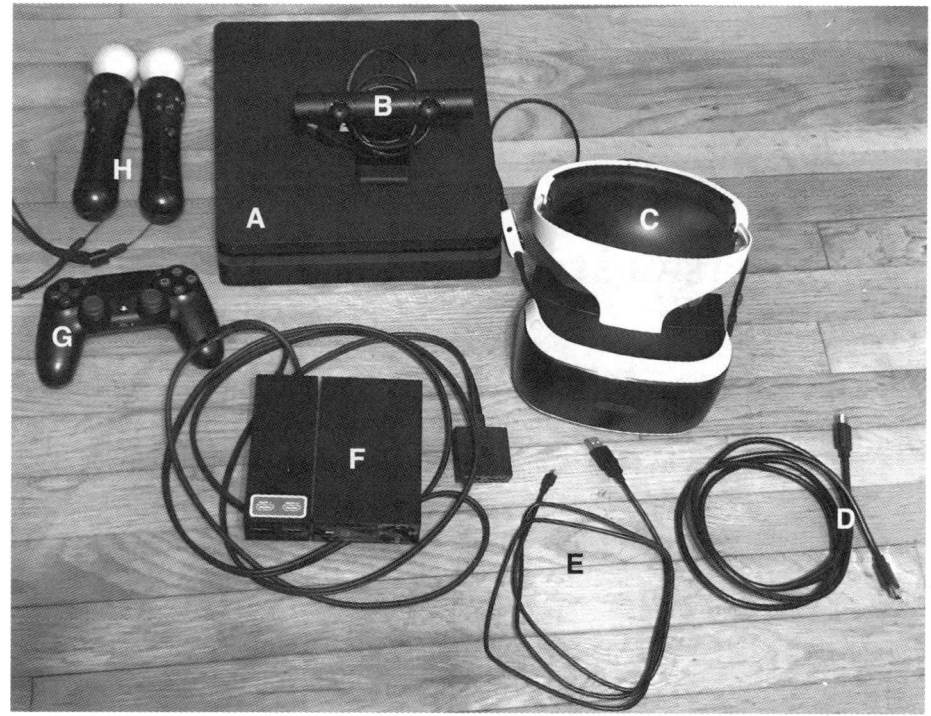

FIGURE 23.1
A: PlayStation 4, B: PlayStation Camera, C: VR Headset, D: 2 HDMI cables, E: USB cable,
F: processor unit with power cord, G: PlayStation 4 controller, H: PlayStation Move controllers

NECESSARY EQUIPMENT AND MATERIALS

- PlayStation 4 with power cord and HDMI cords
- PlayStation VR Headset and Camera (Unlike the Oculus, this headset requires only one camera.)
- projector or TV
- one to four PlayStation DualShock controllers
- the Playroom VR (This is a free game that will automatically download once you set up the VR Headset.)
  - There is also a free demo disc of other VR games that you can try out before buying them.
- A PlayStation Charging Station (optional)—while not necessary, this would be helpful for keeping multiple controllers live for the program. The VR headset will occupy most of the ports.

- PlayStation Move controllers (optional)—these are not needed for this program or even for many VR games. However, for some games, these controllers may be optimal because they would help with the players' immersion. So, be sure to look into the games you'll use before purchasing them.

STEP-BY-STEP INSTRUCTIONS

Preparation

- If you are unboxing the VR headset and/or PlayStation 4, be sure to give yourself some time to set up the system and perform all the updates.
- The day before the program, you might want to check to ensure no new updates are needed. If there is an update, you can often skip it and go directly to the game, especially if you play offline.
- Make sure your PS controllers are charged because you might not be able to charge them during the program.
- While not necessary, you might want to play around so you can unlock harder-difficulty levels for any games in which the VR player must rely on information given by the other players.
- Give yourself plenty of time to set up the equipment. Twenty minutes should be ample time to plug in the equipment and boot up your Playroom VR game.

Program Instructions

- One player starts with the VR headset and gets to pick which game in the Playroom VR they wish to play. Up to four other people can join, depending on the mini-game.
- Players can play one mini-game before they pass the VR headset to someone else. Monitor everyone to make sure all players get a chance to play with the VR headset and controllers, if desired.
- To get players more engaged, you can add more rules to the game.
  - *Example*: With mini-games that have the players feeding information to the VR player to catch something, limit the vocabulary they can use.
- These instructions and guidelines are only meant to serve as a starting point for those new to VR. The next step is what to do after you've familiarized yourself with VR. In the Recommended Next Projects section, I illustrate how to get the most out of your VR system.

CHAPTER 23 | **Get the Most out of VR**

RECOMMENDED NEXT PROJECTS

Here is how you can get more out of the PlayStation VR:

- *Keep Talking and Nobody Explodes*: This is a great game that requires two players; the goal is to work together to defuse a bomb. The VR player will handle the bomb and will be the only one who sees what the bomb looks like. The other player is known as the expert and has the manual to defuse bombs but doesn't get to see the bomb. The two players must communicate based on what they see and work together to solve simple coding to defuse the bomb. This is a great team-building exercise that simulates a stressful situation that requires two people to work together to resolve.
- *Fruit Ninja and/or Beat Saber*: These two games work great with motion controllers, which focus on rhythm and reflex. For larger groups, these games are great for turn-taking—everyone gets to play. The mechanics of the game get them up and active as they compete for a high score.
- *VR Worlds**: This is another great game that allows people to enjoy a solid VR experience. Players can deep-sea dive while dealing with a shark attack, plunge down a road with a board, play Pong with your head, and even be an alien scavenger. Just don't let students play London Heists. It's a shooting game with a lot of swearing!
- *AFFECTED: The Manor*: This horror game lets people explore a creepy haunted mansion—a perfect Halloween program to run in October. This could be a test of courage for some teens and an entertaining romp through a virtual haunted house for others. The game would also work well as a haunted house scavenger hunt as players seek out a list of items in the mansion. A second person could write down and verify that the item has been found by watching the TV screen. You'll likely have a lot of participants who prefer watching the game to playing it.
- *Five Nights at Freddy's: Help Wanted*: Most likely your teen patrons will ask for this game. The player takes on the role of a security guard for a Chuck E. Cheese rip-off, and the animatronics are trying to get you. This would also be a good game for the Halloween season—or any time, really. This game title offers all the Five Nights at Freddy's games; so, players can pick whatever game or night they want to play and take turns that way. This game is known for its jump scares, but it also has the player use resource management skills because they have to conserve their power through the night to protect themselves from Freddy and the other animatronics.

- *Statik**: This is like an escape room game. The player has a device on their hands that has different tools on it. The device must be turned certain ways in order to solve the puzzle to get out of the room. Players will need to use their problem-solving skills to get out within the time limit. An escape room activity, if you'd enjoy hosting one, would be a good addition to this program to attract more participants. The game can also be used as a group activity, with the players not using the VR headset helping by watching the TV screen and reporting on what they see.
- *Tumble*: This is similar to Playroom VR but involves more players. The VR player's goal is to use blocks and other objects and stack them into a tower. However, the other players' goal is to sabotage the tower by dropping things on top of it. The VR player then has to make their tower sturdy enough to keep from falling. This enables players to work on keeping their cool under stress and on being good winners and losers.
- *Apollo/Titanic*: This is a simulation and exploration game that can be bought as a bundle or separately. The player can simulate taking off in a spacecraft in the Apollo game. In the Titanic game, the player can explore the sunken *Titanic*. There are more games such as these that are very educational and could be used as a passive program and tool if the library has a space or sea theme event going on.
- *Job Simulator*: This one-player game lets players work a basic job, such as a store clerk or mechanic, for robots. They are given a scenario involving a customer, and it is up to the player to figure out how to solve it. Though it is only a one-player game, others often enjoy spectating.

*PlayStation game exclusive

How to Create and Sustain a Gamer's Club Even if You Are Not a Gamer

MAYA BERRY
Digital Librarian, R. C. Pugh Library

Northwest Mississippi Community College

LIBRARIANS WHO DO not consider themselves gamers can still create and sustain a successful gamer's club in their library. Although it may sound intimidating to run a club if you have little knowledge of board games, card games, roleplaying games (RPGs), video games, and/or other games, your lack of experience may actually be of benefit, as you can then focus on the games your club is most interested in instead of playing others that you may be biased toward or against. You can find club members to enthusiastically teach you all you need to know about their favorite games, and you may find that these games become your favorites too!

Age Range	Type of Library Best Suited For	Cost Estimate
Tweens (ages 8–12) Young Adults (ages 13–18) Adults	Public Libraries Academic Libraries School Libraries	$0–$500+

Cost Considerations

Costs will vary according to the games that your club members want to play. Purchasing gently used items is one way to cut costs. Visiting local thrift shops or garage sales or asking for game donations are other cost-cutting measures. Watching for sales in big-box stores or online can also reduce your expenses.

You may also have club members willing to bring in their board games, cards, dice, video game consoles, and so on. If your club members share games, they should be aware that they are doing it at their own risk becuase normal wear and tear (bent corners on cards, etc.) may occur during a gaming session.

OVERVIEW

Provide a welcoming space in your library for your club members to use. Depending on the space you have, choose the most appropriate room or location where tables and chairs can be set up for multiple groups of four to eight. Video games require not only games and video game consoles but also televisions or projectors and adequate power outlets. You will need at least two hours for a club meeting or the program so that you can dedicate an hour and a half to actual game play and still have fifteen minutes for setup and fifteen minutes for cleanup.

To sustain your club over time, you will need to be flexible. The group you have this year may want to play entirely different games than the participants you see next year, and new games launch all the time. Make sure to always support the club with game resources that the majority want to explore and try out. Be prepared to purchase expansion decks, update manuals, obtain the newest popular game, acquire donations, and, whenever applicable, ask players for any copies of games they may have that they don't mind sharing with the group. Talk with your club frequently about the games they are playing and observe which ones are most popular during the club meeting.

Staffing will depend on the size of your club. If you have a small club (eight to ten members), only one staff person is needed to facilitate the players and manage game play. If you have a larger club, you may need more staff to assist, especially if you would like to play during a club meeting. That way there will be someone available to answer questions and assist players without players feeling like they are interrupting someone else's game. Recruit experienced volunteers from within the club's ranks to assist in being *in charge* of a game in progress so you will not have to familiarize yourself with all of the rules involved with it.

Do your own research on games that are being played during club meetings to familiarize yourself with the game play. You don't have to be an expert on playing these games—unless of course you want to be. You just need to know what's required to make the gaming session go smoothly. For example, are whiteboards needed to keep score? Should handouts be printed or extra dice brought in? Your club members will respond positively to your interest in their games and keep you updated on changes or things they need if you just ask!

NECESSARY EQUIPMENT AND MATERIALS

- tables
- chairs
- games (board games, card games, video games, etc.)
- TVs, if video games will be played
- projectors, if you want to project a video game or game rules so everyone can see

STEP-BY-STEP INSTRUCTIONS

Preparation

- Determine the age rating of the games you will/will not play based upon your expected audience and community standards. Will you play M-rated video games; allow games that are rated for only seventeen-year-olds and up, such as Cards Against Humanity; set some limits because you may be expecting a range of ages/comfort levels to adult humor; or are you limited by school guidelines? If you don't know anything about a game that has been proposed during a club meeting, research it on game review sites or watch YouTube videos that walk you through it. Most games will have ratings and/or suggested age ranges listed on the packaging.
- List out behavioral guidelines for the club. What happens if someone thinks someone is cheating or not playing according to the rules? What do you do if you have a sore loser after a game? What consequences might you list if someone says the game that someone else is enjoying is stupid?
- Determine your role in the group. Are you going to sit and play with club members or act as a moderator by sitting separately and welcoming new club members and answering questions?

- Advertise the formation of your gaming club.
- Obtain some games that seem popular, according to your research of games currently played in your library; or, you can use games that your library already owns. Do not invest too much money or time on games until you have spoken with club members about what they want to play.
- Have your first club formation meeting and discuss what games club members like to play and what games they recommend for the club or program time. They may wish to play a variety of games or stick to one game that everyone plays in multiple groups. This will change depending on who comes to the meeting and as the years pass. This is a wonderful time to learn more about games! Everyone may want to discuss their favorite game and what they are currently playing, which will help you determine what games they are interested in.

Program Instructions

- Have tables and chairs set up for small groups of four to eight before people arrive.
- Bring the library's copies of the games and put them in a spot where game players can use them during the club meeting.
- Assist anyone who is looking for a group to play with and answer any questions about the group/library.
- You may need to give an announcement that the gaming time will end in fifteen to twenty minutes so that people can start finishing up their game and/or pack it up if they brought their own games.

RECOMMENDED NEXT PROJECTS

- Use input from members to host a gaming tournament.
- Have club members host a learning session for people who are gaming beginners, like you! For example, if you have Dungeons & Dragons players, ask them to give an overview of the game and teach people how to start playing. This is a good advertisement opportunity for the club and gives club members public-speaking experience on a topic they enjoy.

How to Create an Arcade Program in the Library

NICHOLAS DEASE
Digital Learning Librarian

Pratt Institute Libraries

IN THIS PROGRAM librarians will survey and identify appropriate game consoles, peripheral devices, and game software for the purpose of building an arcade-style video game event in the library. Librarians will learn the characteristics of major game consoles, online services, games, and optional devices that are appropriate for multiplayer social events and their audience.

Age Range	Type of Library Best Suited For	Cost Estimate
Kids (ages 3–7)* Tweens (ages 8–12)* Young Adults (ages 13–18) Adults	Academic Libraries School Libraries Public Libraries	$0–$2,000+

Cost Considerations

The cost is dependent on any consoles acquired, peripherals used, or devices already available.

---

*Librarians should consult ESRB ratings on the backsides of game cases in order to determine the appropriate audience.

OVERVIEW

Running an arcade-style video game event in the library is a great way for patrons to de-stress, socialize, and play games together. However, these events are often costly to assemble and require a good degree of familiarity with current video game trends in order to effectively pull off. This chapter aims to provide foundational knowledge for librarians to select what games and consoles are appropriate for their patrons.

To be sure, the landscape of video gaming is large, vibrant, and sometimes mysterious. What is popular or interesting to a library's patron base may not be intuitive or obvious. To help guarantee the success of the event, this chapter goes in-depth with full descriptions of all major consoles, their audience, and a list of critically acclaimed titles across the video game landscape. Special consideration is given to software exclusivity, optional online services, and unique peripherals.

NECESSARY EQUIPMENT AND MATERIALS

- video game consoles: PlayStation 4, Xbox One, Nintendo Switch, or PC
- classic game consoles: SNES Classic and NES Classic, PlayStation Classic, SEGA Genesis Mini
- video game peripherals: two controllers per console/device
- optional video game peripherals: PlayStation VR, fight sticks, unique controllers
- monitors: HDTVs or computer monitors
- video games: digital downloads or discs
- optional online services: PlayStation Plus, Xbox Live, Nintendo Switch Online
- a room with tables, chairs, access to electricity, and potentially Wi-Fi for online play

STEP-BY-STEP INSTRUCTIONS

Preparation

- Determine your budget based on devices already available. Video game consoles and games are expensive. Savvy librarians can save money by reusing materials already owned by the library. Most modern PC monitors allow for HDMI input, and many libraries have a handful of monitors lying around. As it turns out, HDMI is the most common type of video game console display input and can therefore be used in lieu of HDTVs. Further, many arcade-style video games have been released on PC through digital distribution platforms such as Steam. They often do not have demanding system requirements; so, old PCs can be recycled as dedicated game stations. As an added bonus, Xbox One controllers are natively supported on modern Windows operating systems. Using these with PCs can provide a seamless game-playing experience.

Selecting Game Consoles ($300–$400 each)

- *Exclusivity*: Most video games are cross-platform, which means they are released on multiple modern consoles. However, some consoles have first- and third-party exclusive games that can only be found on its originating platform. Because of this, popular exclusive multiplayer games may be a determining factor in deciding which consoles should be purchased for this event. Librarians can search Metacritic.com by console to see the current most popular games offered on that console. Further, many online multiplayer games do not allow for cross-platform play (for example, PS4 players cannot play games with Xbox One players). Each individual game's multiplayer feature specs must be researched before making plans for cross-platform multiplayer setups. Game cases and digital store fronts, such as Steam or PlayStation Store, are good places to find this information.
- *Optional online subscriptions*: All of today's modern first-party consoles require a paid subscription in order to access online multiplayer features. However, many multiplayer games feature split-screen or local multiplayer options. These are excellent options for arcade-style events because patrons can play with each other in real time without the need of setting up accounts that must connect to the internet. That said, there are many games that only have an online multiplayer option, yet some of these are the most popular games available. As an example, Fortnite is a multiplayer shooter game that requires an online connection to play—there are no local or split-screen multiplayer options.
- *PlayStation 4*: This console is Sony's current flagship device. Although not backward-compatible with older generations of PlayStation games, it features a massive game library with an array of first-class exclusive titles. This makes it a solid purchase for libraries that serve a wide audience

range. The basic console bundle comes with only one controller; so, librarians must purchase additional controllers for local multiplayer games. Online play requires a paid subscription to the PlayStation Plus service. As is the case with Xbox One, PlayStation's software catalog is directed at all age ranges, and all genres are well-represented.
- *Xbox One*: Microsoft's Xbox One is a powerful modern console. Unlike Sony's platform, the Xbox is partially compatible with earlier generations of Xbox games, but it is all done through emulation. Microsoft is in the process of adding support for more titles. Many Xbox and Xbox 360 games are currently playable on Xbox One. However, individual games should be researched for support online. The basic console bundle comes with only one controller; so, librarians must purchase additional controllers for local multiplayer games. Online play requires a paid subscription to the Xbox Live service. As is the case with PlayStation, Xbox One's software catalog is directed at every age range, with all gaming genres well-represented.
- *Nintendo Switch*: Nintendo's most recent console is unique and features an excellent selection of first-party exclusive titles. Combining the portability of Nintendo's earlier handheld consoles with a dock station for traditional console play, the Switch has less graphical power than Sony or Microsoft, but it makes up for it with high-quality games. Much of its software lineup is aimed at younger audiences, but game players of all ages routinely play and sing the praises of Nintendo's first-party exclusive titles. Unlike Microsoft and Sony, the Nintendo Switch has two controllers in the basic bundle for local multiplayer games. Online play requires a paid subscription to Nintendo Switch Online.
- *Classic consoles*: In recent years, nostalgia for 1990s-era video games has surged. Nintendo, Sega, and Sony have released several so-called *classic consoles* that come pre-loaded with greatest hits software at an affordable price. The SNES Classic, NES classic, PlayStation Classic, and SEGA Genesis Mini feature modern HDMI display input, two controllers in the box, and excellent pre-loaded games. These consoles are a great way to pad out an arcade event with a little extra cash. The games often have a wide audience appeal as well.
- *Peripheral hardware*: If extra funds are available, peripheral devices, such as custom controllers, can take the event to the next level (for example, Rock Band Guitar Controllers, the Dance Revolution Dance Pad, or PlayStation Move controllers). These devices are more welcoming to

casual game players because they lack the complicated controller layouts. Furthermore, they can completely change the game-playing experience or open up new software libraries for the console. For example, PlayStation VR is a virtual reality (VR) headset that works with a number of VR-specific games in the PlayStation 4 library. One particularly good VR rhythm game is Beat Saber, which utilizes the VR headset and PlayStation Move controllers to allow game players to dance to the music and slash incoming notes to the beat. Please note that these devices are expensive but totally optional.

Picking Games and Software ($29–$59 each)
- *About the genres*: The game genres that work best for arcade-style events are arcade games, rhythm games, multiplayer shooters, racing games, and fighting games. Arcade games have wildly different mechanics but are usually action-based affairs with flashy graphics and score systems. They're great for short game-play sessions and usually appeal to a wide audience. Rhythm games force players to respond to music via inputting commands according to a rhythm. They're excellent for all age ranges and generally appeal to users with little or no video game experience. Shooters involve moving through space and shooting enemies in a first-person or third-person perspective. They are often violent and geared toward more mature audiences. Racing games put players in the position of a competitive race-car driver and usually appeal to all age ranges. Fighting games are one-on-one competitive brawling events. While some can be extraordinarily violent, many feature cartoonish violence and are appropriate for a younger audience. The genre appeals to a niche and skilled player base, but casual players can and do pick up fighting games from time to time. That said, the genre can be off-putting for first-timers or casual players.
- *About single-player*: Generally, single-player, story-oriented games are not ideal for larger-scale social events, as they can sometimes take upwards of twenty hours to complete.
- Below are a few examples of good titles in each genre. It is not an exhaustive list, but any of the games below would be a great fit for a video game event. Further resources you can use to research games include IGN.com, GameSpot.com, Metacritic.com, and Co-optimus.com.
    - *arcade games*: Pac-Man, Galaga, Frogger, Bubble Bobble, Donkey Kong, Final Fight

- *rhythm games*: Guitar Hero (any), Dance Revolution (any), Rock Band (any), Amplitude, Just Dance (any), Beatmania, Beat Saber (PS VR or PC only)
- *shooters*: Borderlands, Overwatch, Counter-Strike: Global Offensive, Call of Duty (any), Halo (any), Gears of War (any), Doom (any), Fortnite, Destiny, or Destiny 2
- *racing games*: Mario Kart (any), Crash Team Racing, Forza (any), Need for Speed (any)
- *fighter games*: Street Fighter (any), Super Smash Bros. (any), Mortal Kombat (any), Tekken (any), Marvel vs. Capcom 2, Dragon Ball Fighterz

Assembling Devices and Double-Checking

- Install the game consoles in the gaming space, plug the devices into an electricity source, and connect them to the monitors. It is important to test-run the devices before the event. This ensures they work but also provides an opportunity to address any electricity or compatibility issues.
- Install your games on the console. Today's games are very big and must be installed on the console's hard drive before play. This is true even for disc-based titles. Usually, this process takes only a few minutes, but it should be done prior to the event in order to ensure things go smoothly.
- Many wireless controllers/peripherals must be charged before use. Make sure your devices are charged in anticipation of the event.
- Many games require large updates before online play is possible. Make sure to test the games and update as needed before the event.

Program Instructions

Initiate the Arcade

- After assembling the devices in the game space and testing the equipment, the arcade is ready to go. Be sure to individually launch the games on each console. Let the games sit at the start screen or main screen. This will be the most inviting to patrons and signal that the game is available for play.
- Turn down the volume on the monitors low enough that individual sounds can be heard but not so loud as to make a cacophony when all the consoles are simultaneously being played.

- Depending on the environment, the lights may be dimmed to achieve a classic darkened arcade room atmosphere. This will help make the monitors appear more vivid and draw attention to the games.
- As patrons enter the space, encourage them to take turns trying different games. In the ideal scenario, the librarian should focus primarily on providing a welcoming atmosphere and not structuring what patrons play. However, depending on how the event is progressing, the librarian may need to engage patrons more directly to get game play going.

Engaging the Audience
- Patrons gravitate to certain video games based on personal preference and experience. Sometimes games are ignored because the peripheral devices appear complicated or the game looks difficult. If a game or console is being neglected, the librarian may draw attention to it by directly inviting patrons to give it a try. Having a staff member on hand to publicly initiate game play can sometimes motivate uncertain players to try an unfamiliar or intimidating game.
- Often patrons will come to an event with lots of experience in one game or game genre. As a result, they may spend an inordinate amount of time playing one game, which can sometimes prevent others from trying it. The librarian should monitor the space to ensure everyone gets a chance. Gentle reminders given to patrons to try other games may help motivate them to broaden their horizons.

Troubleshoot Challenges
- Games sometimes crash and must be reset manually. If possible, it is helpful to have an extra staff member on hand during the event to troubleshoot difficulties.
- Users may accidentally navigate back to the console's main menu and not know how to return to the game. The librarian should survey the space to ensure that all monitors and consoles are available and ready for immediate play. If an empty game station has a paused or frozen game, relaunch the game and let it start up naturally.

Wrapping Up

Thirty minutes prior to the end of the event, the librarian should announce how much time is left to all who are in attendance. This will help patrons mentally prepare to wrap up their game play. This is especially important during competitive games, wherein the *one more round* effect can sometimes make it difficult to end things in a timely manner.

RECOMMENDED NEXT PROJECTS

Depending on community preferences, librarians may wish to arrange game-specific tournaments using the hardware/software purchased for the arcade event.

How to Create a Video Game Recreational League

LEAH CANNER
STEM Specialist

Baltimore County Public Library

RECREATIONAL SPORTS LEAGUES offer kids and teens a great opportunity to meet new friends, develop positive practice habits, and experience what it's like to be a part of a team and engage in healthy competition. However, not all kids and teens find sports interesting or accessible—but video games can be a great alternative! By hosting a recreational video game league at your library, you'll create an opportunity for participants to band together and learn, practice, and play as a team. If you play online, you'll have the perfect forum to demonstrate positive digital citizenship.

Age Range	Type of Library Best Suited For	Cost Estimate
Young Adults (ages 13–18)	Public Libraries	$100–$250

OVERVIEW

This program series is intended to be more comprehensive than a standard gaming event. You'll want to construct and host it in a way that encourages participants to keep coming back and to bring their friends. Consider

FIGURE 26.1
Smite developers at Hi-Rez Studios were kind enough to hook our gamers up with all kinds of loot, including T-shirts, comic books, bracelets, lanyards, and even thunderstix!

offering prizes to incentivize attendance. It's tough to build camaraderie in a single afternoon!

There are two core ways you could approach planning the content for a video game recreational league:

1. You could feature a new game each week and create a more casual environment in which participants utilize their gaming strengths and backgrounds to teach each other new things.
2. You could stick with one game for the entirety of the series and focus on learning and growing as a team. This requires significant working knowledge of the featured game; so, you'd want to choose a title your host is well-versed in.

If you don't have staff who are interested in gaming, turn to your next best option: your community. Ask around in your library's teen area or at a teen-based program. Visit local high schools and colleges with a small gaming display to talk up the program. Chances are you'll find a couple of volunteers who would love to act as gaming ambassadors or mentors and participate in more of a facilitating manner.

Program occurrence and length are mostly dependent on technology, staffing, and space availability. If possible, pick a weekly time slot and stick to it for as long as you'd like—consistency in a series increases the likelihood of participant retention and makes it easier to invite friends.

Once you have your dates and games chosen, and you've found your facilitators and ambassadors, it's time to have some fun and grow a little in the process!

NECESSARY EQUIPMENT AND MATERIALS

- laptops—one per participant
- mice—one per laptop
- unfiltered internet access—if you want to play online, you'll want to test your system's Wi-Fi ahead of time. Make sure the game you want to play isn't blocked by anything.
- Mi-Fi or wireless hotspot devices—useful in a pinch or to get around blocked internet access
- extension cables—so you can place power strips beneath groups of tables
- power strips—so you can power multiple laptops at groups of tables
- jerseys—blank T-shirts, heat transfer paper, irons, cardboard to place inside shirts during transfer

Optional Materials

- participation prizes or swag—some game developers are ready and willing to support library programs with resources such as posters, shirts, keychains, in-game items, and more. You never know until you ask!
- snacks

STEP-BY-STEP INSTRUCTIONS

Preparation

- *Create a schedule*. Make arrangements for access to the technology and space you'll need to host your series. Note that you may want to avoid meeting on Tuesdays or Wednesdays if possible—most major games release their patches on Tuesday or Wednesday cycles, which means that you might be faced with an unexpected update on the day of your program.

PART II | **Video Game Programs**

- *Recruit help*. If you're a gamer and plan on running the programs on your own, consider your workload to make sure you'll have time to dedicate to set up and break down, as well as hanging out and engaging with participants. If you're not a gamer, ask your peers and find someone who would be interested in facilitating.
- *Choose your game(s)*. Once you establish a series schedule, choose a game or games on which to focus. If you have a game that you cherish and would like to share with your participants, talk to them ahead of time and ask if they've heard of it. If they aren't into it, ask for suggestions on other games they'd like to play week in and week out. Suggested free-to-play titles, by genre:
    - multiplayer online battle arenas (MOBAs): League of Legends (LoL), Defense of the Ancients 2 (Dota 2), Smite
    - shooters: Counter-Strike: Global Offensive (CS:GO), Fortnite, Apex Legends, Destiny 2
    - trading card games (TCGs): Magic: The Gathering Arena, Hearthstone
    - action/roleplaying: Path of Exile, Dauntless
- *Solicit swag*. After selecting a game or games, research the game developers and publishers. Contact their events and outreach representatives via social media, e-mail, phone, etc., and explain that you're a library looking to feature their game during a program series about making friends and building connections through teamwork. Ask if they'd be willing to donate any merchandise to be used as giveaways for participants, or if they have any suggestions regarding what you could do during the program to make it more engaging for participants such as Skyping with developers, holding a fan art competition, or if there any Twitch streamers with whom they could put you in contact with. If you're lucky enough to score some giveaway swag, great! If not, that's okay. You can still purchase snacks, raffle giveaways, etc., for the event.
- *Make jerseys*. Whether you obtain swag from partners or not, you can acquire simple supplies to make DIY team jerseys to keep participants coming back. You can also build on these jerseys throughout the series.
    - For an easy DIY jersey, visit your local craft store and buy a bunch of blank T-shirts (preferably of the same color—team uniforms promote solidarity). Purchase heat transfer paper and an iron for affixing decals and in-game names to your T-shirts. Check your maker supplies and

FIGURE 26.2
Custom-made jerseys give participants a great way to feel included as part of the team as they proudly show off their in-game names.

check in with your Youth Services Department—you may already have this stuff!
- Check out your chosen games' websites for press kits. They'll most likely have some cool images or logos that you could use or adapt into a graphic for the front of your jerseys. If possible, make the background of the graphic transparent so it doesn't transfer onto the shirt. If you have a peer on staff who is well-versed in graphic design/photoshop/image manipulation, consider asking them for assistance in making any changes.
- For the first one or two programs, ask participants to come up with in-game names to be used to create friends' lists and team up together. Have them write down their names for you (I cannot stress this enough—demand that they write as legibly as humanly possible). Using this list of handles, create a graphic for each name to be ironed onto the back of the jersey. Consider using a font from the press kit or one reminiscent of other video games.
- At the beginning of program two or three, set up a jersey-crafting station on which to gather the blank T-shirts, printed out heat transfers,

scissors, and a big piece of cardboard to put inside the shirt so you don't accidentally burn through to the other side like I did. Have participants carefully cut out their in-game names and a logo and then work with them to transfer the graphics to the T-shirts. Consider enlisting the assistance of another staff member to help with the jerseys while you facilitate the program so there can be gaming and jerseys happening at the same time. That way, nobody gets bored.
  – *Note*: Consider setting a stipulation for jerseys in which participants must attend at least two sessions to get one, lest it become too expensive as newcomers drop in and friends bring friends to see what the series is about.

- *Market your event*. As the date of your premiere event draws close, ramp up your advertising. Post signs or flyers near on-the-floor gaming areas in your branch. Leave handouts in a visible area during teen programs. Ask your system's marketing department to create social media posts about the series. Plan visits to local schools and set up a console/PC during lunch hours in the cafeteria to show off the game and generate hype.

- *Prep your tech*. The day before your first—and every subsequent—program, launch the game on each device on which participants will be playing. Make sure to download any patches or updates beforehand so you aren't stuck waiting for installations during program hours.
  – Create a couple of generic accounts for the game you're playing with names such as "librarygamer2019" or "XXPLgaming1" to be used later. Some interested participants will want to try the game before taking the time to create an account. Others may not have e-mail access and won't be able to create an account. Some won't care at all and will just want to play. Keep track of the accounts you create and consider printing a document with the compiled login information.

Program Instructions

- *Set up the room*. On the day of the event, budget yourself at least an hour of setup time. Arrange tables and chairs into groups of four to six (depending on how many outlets your power strips have). Run an extension cable and a power strip on the floor beneath the center of the group and run laptop power cables down the gaps between the tables to connect to the power strips. If you're using Mi-Fi connections, place one at each group.

Once tables, chairs, and PCs are set up, power them on and connect to the internet. Test the game launcher and make sure there wasn't a sneaky overnight patch.
- Consider setting up a special station with a PC and a projector for any participant to use if they want to be in the spotlight and let others watch their game play, streamer style. If there are multiple participants interested in being the main gamer, create a schedule for them to share over the series so everyone gets a turn and they're more likely to come back multiple times!

- *Connect participants*. As participants arrive, welcome them and help them set up game accounts if they haven't already done so. As they come up with their in-game names, create a list of gamers and their handles so it'll be easier for participants to identify one another and build their in-game friends lists. Ask participants if they have any experience playing the game and then indicate that on the list. A big part of collaborative gaming is forming connections between new players and experienced ones who can act as game ambassadors. Once participants are logged in and playing, circulate the list of names and get everyone added to friends' lists for easy reference as the series meets.

- *Build relationships*. Make it a point to talk to each participant individually and ask them about the game. Who is their favorite character? What is their favorite map or level? What's the best strategy they've used so far? What's the story behind their in-game name? Demonstrate communicative behaviors in a social setting, and others will likely follow.

- *Play and learn*. Encourage teamwork and collaborative play between participants. Suggest that they form groups and play with or against each other, swapping teammates after each game. Act as mediator for participants who may feel shy about asking to team up. Consider creating superlative awards to hand out at the end of the league such as "most improved player," "best teacher," "most positive attitude," etc.

RECOMMENDED NEXT PROJECTS

Looking to elaborate on the concept of a recreational gaming league? Consult with your community teens and utilize your library's teen advisory board for input and ideas into what your next project should look like.

- If you have enough interest, consider planning a gaming ambassador program during which teens pair off with less experienced participants and act as gaming buddies. Let the participant do the bulk of the playing while the teen provides encouragement and assistance when needed.
- Think about converting your recreational league into an outreach program and partner with a local gaming store or community center. Involve their staff in the facilitating process to build familiarity with your library and its patrons.
- Pare down the recreational league experience and host a series of gaming pop-up events at various community locations. Meet up with teen volunteers or work with other staff members to host a small table that is set up with a gaming opportunity and information about services and upcoming programs. Consider bringing library-branded giveaways for participants who complete a gaming challenge of your choosing—placing in the top three in Mario Kart, for example.
- To strengthen the bonds formed during your recreational league, plan a video game program in which participants are invited to, for example, *1v1 a librarian*, and try to best library staff in a variety of games. Print in 3D a variety of tiny trophies or make unique buttons to be rewarded, depending on which game participants choose to play or which staff members they beat.

Culper Spies
Choose Your Own Adventure Online Gamification

KRISTEN CINAR
Instructor, Library Services

Suffolk County Community College

THIS PROGRAM WILL help students navigate a thrilling spy narrative as they use research skills to carefully evade enemy detection in an online game. The virtual choose-your-own-adventure-style activity presents players with the challenge of uncovering secret messages by accessing information found on the library's webpage and through the catalog and databases. Only with the solutions decoded can they pass the information along to their proper contact. A list of two or more options for each clue will allow players the opportunity to alter the course of the game based on their response. Those who solve each clue correctly using answers found in the electronic resources will successfully proceed in the narrative and ensure their message is passed along in the resistance effort. This activity lends itself well to distance learning courses and is a good choice for those looking for assignments that are not time- and location-sensitive.

Age Range	Type of Library Best Suited For	Cost Estimate
Adults	Academic Libraries	$0–$50

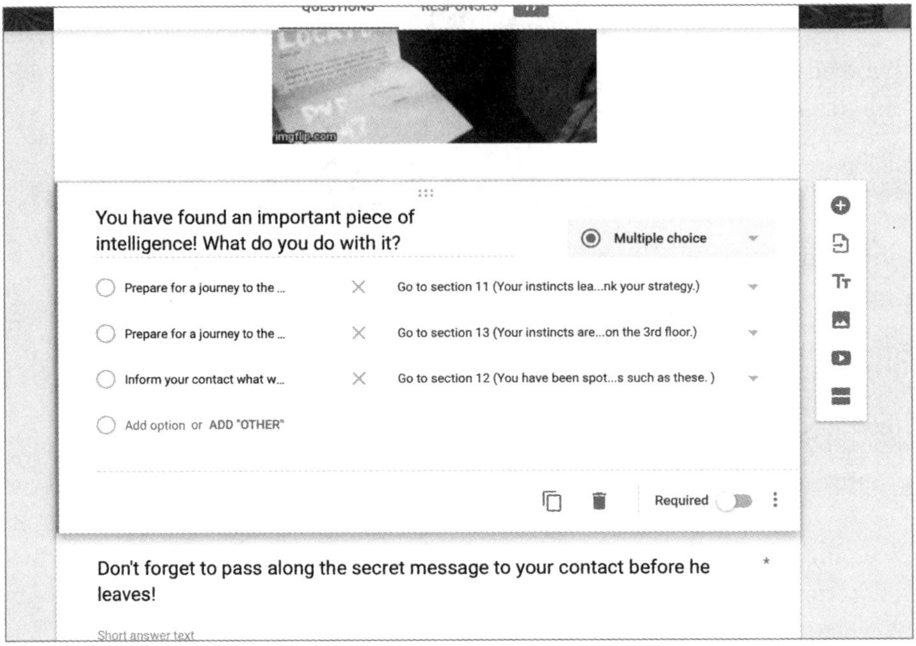

FIGURE 27-1
Customizing Google Forms to optimize game play

Cost Considerations

Google Forms is a free program available to anyone with an active Gmail account. All videos and other media for this project can easily be captured with a smartphone or other device. Costs would only accrue if you were to use small props or professional-quality puzzles for players to solve as they play.

OVERVIEW

For this activity, a narrative can be created based on the historical Culper Spy Ring. The story will be built in Google Forms, a free program that allows pages to be linked by multiple-choice commands. Each page should contain a portion of the narrative and an action prompt in the form of two or more choices. The combination of a player-driven storyline and corresponding media provides all the basics of a functioning game. Requiring students to solve puzzles and clues using library information that is easily found or researched online ensures that they will gain practice putting valuable research skills to use as they play.

Visual media immerses players in the story's world as they're able to see their choices come to life. Puzzles that need to be solved would have media capturing the results of correct and incorrect choice selections. Pictures, self-made GIFs, and videos help players see their actions played out. For a cipher wheel that requires call numbers, citation information, or other content to be placed in proper order as the puzzle is aligned, a video would show the act of aligning it in whichever order players choose. Students who learn that an invisible ink message can only be read using heat might be asked to choose which author from the list of options has published articles on heat-related topics. After some practice searching for authors' works by name, the reward for a correct choice could be a video clip of a letter being moved under a UV light to reveal its hidden message.

Decoded intelligence must be passed on to the proper contact. To motivate students to find and practice using online research guides, the game provides a picture of a librarian (plug the photo into a free online photo sketch converter for an authentic look!) and hints at a guide they may want to consult to determine if the librarian is the person they're looking for. Such a clue may look something like this:

> A traveler approaches you carrying a bundle of parchment rolls that look to be maps. He nods as he passes. Could this be your contact? Consult the research guides to learn who the map librarian is. If his face matches the one you've been given, circle back and pass along the information you've uncovered!

Accessing the research guides is a way of marketing the existence of these helpful tools so players know where they might look for help in other areas in the future! Multiple-choice boxes that indicate that this is or is not the player's contact would need to be inserted to advance the page, while a short-answer box could also be inserted to provide a space for players to type the decoded information if they believe they've identified the proper ally.

NECESSARY EQUIPMENT AND MATERIALS

- a computer for accessing Google Forms
- a smartphone or other device for capturing images and videos

- any props or puzzles you wish to include in the clues (I have assembled some of my personal favorites at https://sites.google.com/view/kristenspuzzles)

STEP-BY-STEP INSTRUCTIONS

Preparation

- Create a new file in Google Forms.
- For each page, insert a visual media object, a small bit of narrative, and a question with corresponding options.
    - For further examples of game narratives, learning outcomes, and puzzle options, visit https://sites.google.com/view/kristensspygames (feel free to borrow content from this page).
- Create a page for each option players might choose.
- Select "Multiple choice" and "Go to page based on my answer" and select the page that each response will be directed to.
- Mark each page as "Required."

Program Instructions

- Market the game before launching, unless it will be used as a classroom assignment.
- To track answers, require students to register so they can be sent a link to the game that requires e-mail authentication.
    - Click the "Responses" tab to view answers for assessment purposes.
- For use that isn't monitored, embed the game or provide a link online.
- Use responses to determine the game's success and inform what changes should be made in the future.

RECOMMENDED NEXT PROJECTS

Experiment with new storylines. This method of gamification can be easily applied to alternative themes and storylines. While spy techniques may have been appropriate for a Culper Spy–themed game, other puzzles can easily be inserted to suit new material, now that your learning objectives and game layout have been created.

Hosting Pokémon GO PVP Tournaments in Your Library

EMILY BURKOT
Teen Librarian II

Chesapeake Public Library

POKÉMON GO MAY have lost some momentum since its initial 2016 release, but the game still enjoys a large fanbase that remains devoted and super-competitive. According to Nielsen Company SuperData, Pokémon GO made $1.3 billion in 2018, making it the fourth most successful free-to-play game on the market (behind Fortnite, Dungeon Fighter Online, and League of Legends).[1] Pokémon is a great theme for all-ages programs, and you will have just as many adults in attendance who grew up on the first-generation games as you will have kids attending who just really like Pikachu. Bring your community together for a Pokémon GO Player versus Player (PVP) tournament and encourage literacy, critical-thinking skills, and fun in the library!

Age Range	Type of Library Best Suited For	Cost Estimate
Tweens (ages 8–12) Young Adults (ages 13–18) Adults	Public Libraries School Libraries	$0–$100

Cost Considerations

This program can be run inexpensively if you play for bragging rights instead of physical prizes. If you choose to provide prizes, you can give them to as many or as few players as you want, depending on your budget. A one-time purchase of Reflector software will allow participants to see the battle on a larger screen but isn't strictly necessary.

OVERVIEW

Pokémon GO has a built-in PVP module that allows players to compete with other players remotely if they have a certain level of friendship in-game, but players can compete with anyone locally. There is even a great equalizing component to the module, called leagues, that limits players to competing with their Pokémon under a certain level. Determine how many players you have, what leagues are most appropriate for them to play in, and then start playing!

Preregistration can help you take care of a lot of that ahead of time, but if most of your customers are drop-ins, try allowing for half an hour of registration at the beginning of the program and choose a lower league that will accommodate most users. Each match takes approximately five minutes, depending on how long it takes players to choose their Pokémon, so double up on matches if you have a lot of attendees. Allot at least two hours for the tournament and plan to have at least one other person in the room with you for scorekeeping or crowd control.

NECESSARY EQUIPMENT AND MATERIALS

- blank brackets for scorekeeping (or use a bracket generator such as Challonge.com)
- tables/chairs (Participants may choose to stand when playing, but spectators will probably want seats.)
- Participants should bring their own devices to play.

Optional Equipment

- prizes
- Reflector software (https://www.airsquirrels.com/reflector)
- laptop and projector

STEP-BY-STEP INSTRUCTIONS

Preparation

- Determine whether you will be purchasing prizes and how many. Digital gift cards for the Apple Store or Google Play Store are good prizes because they can be used in-game for supplies and Pokémon Trainer avatar items. Digital allows you to purchase exactly what you need at the end rather than guessing what kind of phone your winner might have.
- Determine how long you want the tournament to go and then plan your brackets accordingly. Remember, a sixteen-person bracket includes fifteen games, and each game can take about five minutes. Determine a registration limit or plan to have more staff so you can keep up with multiple matches at the same time. Also keep in mind that only brackets in multiples of eight are going to turn out even. This can be done in other multiples, but some unlucky people are going to have to win more games than others.
- If you have patrons at a variety of age levels and with various levels of experience participating, consider creating multiple brackets. A children's bracket or beginner's bracket can keep participants from feeling like they don't stand a chance.
- Determine which league you will be playing. Well-matched, high-level players can play Ultra or Master League, but if you have a variety of experience levels, Great League will help level the field.
- If using Reflector software, test the setup on your network before the day of the event. All devices must be on the same network, and some libraries have a staff network their devices default to.

Program Instructions

Registration
- If you had participants preregister, you will still want people to check in or sign in; that way, you'll know to rethink your brackets if a large number of preregistered gamers don't show up.
- If you didn't have them preregister, take half an hour and register participants so you can put together the brackets.

Tournament
- If you have allotted enough time, play one match at a time using Reflector software to cast the match onto a large screen for spectators. If using Reflector, have players face away from the screen so they cannot see what their opponent is doing.
- If you have a very large bracket, you can play all of round one simultaneously to save time. You will want some way to verify who won, whether via a screen-capture of the win screen or by staff members watching each match to confirm the winner. You may even be able to just let them tell you who won. You know your patrons.
- Players can then go to the Nearby screen in the bottom-right corner of the screen and select Battle. One player can select Challenge a Trainer and scan their opponent's Battle Code. The person who scans the code selects the league. Make sure players know which league to choose.
- Players then pick three Pokémon they will use to compete. Players can rotate between these three during a match but cannot choose from any others. If you are playing Great League, the Pokémon chosen must be under 1500 CP. Ultra League requires that Pokémon be under 2500 CP, but Master League has no limits on your Pokémon level.
- Once both players are ready, the match will begin. The game takes care of itself from there!

Scoring
- Once a player has won, they move on to the next match on the bracket, and play continues.
- If you are using double elimination or some other type of bracket, play according to those rules.

- At the end of the tournament, you will have a winner! Prizes can be awarded to just the champion; to the first-, second-, and third-place winners; or to winners in each level if you chose to break up the brackets by experience.
- In the Pokémon games, you are awarded badges for achievements. In the original games, each gym location had its own badge, which you were awarded if you beat their Trainer. Consider making buttons with your own unique emblem and awarding them to all your participants!

RECOMMENDED NEXT PROJECTS

- If you have any customers who are Harry Potter fans, the company that created Pokémon GO also offers Harry Potter: Wizards Unite. There is no PVP yet, but you can still consider using these games to interact with your customers. Encourage AR photos in the library; or, if you have a good walking path nearby, arrange a meetup for library customers to play together.
- If you really want to take this to the next level, hold a tournament like this at each of your locations, followed by a Grand Championship to determine the best Pokémon Trainer in your community!

NOTE

1. SuperData, "Market Brief – 2018 Digital Games & Interactive Entertainment Industry Year in Review," 2019, www.superdataresearch.com/market-data/market-brief-year-in-review.

Building a Video Game Collection for Programming (And Keeping It Current!)

EMILY BURKOT
Teen Librarian II

Chesapeake Public Library

CURATING A COLLECTION of video games to be used as part of your branch's programming can give your library the ability to provide successful activities on-the-fly in addition to scheduled events. However, developing a collection of video games can be expensive—and confusing—if you are unfamiliar with console gaming. Creating a thorough plan before purchasing any games will help you spend your budget efficiently while developing your collection. A plan will also help you keep the collection current as well as help you determine when it is necessary to buy newer versions of games and how you plan to pay for their upkeep. Here, I will highlight some questions you will want to answer before getting started and things to look out for along the way. Also included are some best practices for building a programming collection of video games that will draw in patrons.

Age Range	Type of Library Best Suited For	Cost Estimate
Kids (ages 3–7) Tweens (ages 8–12) Young Adults (ages 13–18) Adults	Public Libraries School Libraries	$5–$300+

Cost Considerations

Digital independent games can run you as little as $4.99, while brand-new physical copies of mainstream games can run as high as $59.99.

OVERVIEW

It is important to remember that you do not have to develop a collection of video games for your library programs all at once. The initial cost of gaming supplies (consoles, controllers, and games) can be expensive and may limit how much you can buy at once. Do not assume that you cannot create a video game collection because you can only purchase one or two titles each year. Choose wisely, and in a few years, you will have a collection!

NECESSARY EQUIPMENT AND MATERIALS

- gaming consoles and accessories
- television or projector
- games

STEP-BY-STEP INSTRUCTIONS

Preparation

What games are popular in your community? Should you buy digital or physical copies of games? Is it better to purchase several older games or spend that money on one copy of whatever the hottest game is at the moment? Should you replace sports games every year? Can your library trade in old games for store credit? Is it necessary to buy games when they are first released, or can you wait for used prices or other sales? These are all things to think about before you begin building a video game collection.

Make a Plan

- Consider your community. Who do you plan on providing video game programming for? If your library has any rules limiting you to games with specific age ratings during library programs, knowing what audience you plan to reach will help you pick the right games.

- Talk with your community. What kinds of games are they interested in playing? Sports? Party games? Fighting games? Are there specific games they want? Keep a list and refer to it when you are ready to buy more.
- You may be surprised by the game requests you get. Your community may be happy starting out with a used copy of Super Smash Bros. Brawl and a console borrowed from your library staff or even an inexpensive independent game.
- Speak with your library administration about vendors and verify if there are any limitations on where you can purchase your consoles and games.

Program Instructions

Buying Your Games

- Once you have a plan for developing your collection, start browsing potential vendors. If limitations are not an issue, check all your purchasing options for the best prices. You can look for deals via big-box stores, GameStop, Amazon, and even digitally through the console's store.
- Pay close attention to the number of players a game supports. Online multiplayer support means that participants will be playing with teammates or opponents over the console's network (an added subscription purchase), not against other customers attending the program. Try to find local multiplayer games so everyone in the room can have a good time.
- Consider whether deluxe or collector's edition games are worth the extra cost for your library programs. Often, the bonuses are subscriptions to download add-on content, weapons, or avatar skins. If you are only using the games once or twice a month, those bonuses are probably not going to affect your students' game-play experience.
- Digital games downloaded to the hard drive of your console have the bonus of being theft-proof and can be switched without staff intervention. However, if your upkeep plan includes trading games in for store credit later, these are not the best choice for your collection.
- If you are willing to go digital, you can create a wish list in the console's store and check it periodically. Any games on that list that go on sale will display at the lower price for the sale's duration, allowing you to purchase games at a discount.
- If someone on your staff has a GameStop PowerUp Rewards membership, you can get an additional discount on pre-owned games, as well as access to members-only sales, using their membership card.

- If your customers are interested in sports games, NBA, Madden, and FIFA are published by Electronic Arts (EA). They publish new editions annually, but these don't necessarily need replacement every year. (There are some game-play changes from year to year, but mostly the updates consist of the addition of new players.)

Subscription Services
- Consider a subscription service, such as PS Now or Xbox Game Pass, if you want to provide more games than you have the budget to purchase or wish to try a variety of games with your community before you buy. These give access to a selection of digital games that can be played as long as the subscription is active.
- EA also has the EA Access subscription service, which gives you unlimited access to most of the EA games up through the previous year. The newest games can be played in early access trials and purchased at a discount.

Keeping It Current
- Many stores that sell video games have trade-in/buy-back programs that enable customers to get store credit for new games. Keep in mind, however, that older games don't generally have a high trade-in value. Some trade-in programs are only available online; so, check the store's website for details.
- If your library allows it, utilize Black Friday sales for popular game purchases at lower prices.
- Make use of your community's feedback. Keep a running list of ideas based on suggestions from your community to assist you in purchasing new games they will be excited about.
- Gaming magazines and websites are good sources of video game knowledge. The streaming site Twitch can also provide valuable input. Look at which games are currently being streamed by the most players, as well as which games have the most viewers. Those games might be popular in your programs too. (In addition, watching game play on Twitch will give you a good idea of the game's content before you purchase.)

RECOMMENDED NEXT PROJECTS

- Many multiplayer games can be used for gaming tournaments. Players can compete for prizes or bragging rights, depending on your budget.
- The same customers who attend your gaming programs may also be interested in workshops on coding and video game design. You can utilize games such as Code Combat (https://codecombat.com) to make the class engaging for fans of video games.

It's Locked
Combining Video Games with Real-Life STEM Challenges

SELENIA PAZ
Senior Children's Services Specialist

Harris County Public Library

THIS PROGRAM WILL begin with participants starting a Nancy Drew PC mystery game called Warnings at Waverly Academy. Players accompany Nancy as she attempts to solve a mystery at Waverly Academy. As participants attempt to solve this mystery, they will complete STEM tasks similar to those completed in the game, utilize their critical-thinking skills and knowledge of science, and become more familiar with searches and library catalogs in the process.

Age Range	Type of Library Best Suited For	Cost Estimate
Young Adults (ages 13–18) Adults	Public Libraries Academic Libraries School Libraries	$20–$120 (depending on supplies used)

OVERVIEW

In this program, participants will start off by entering the computer game world of Nancy Drew as she attempts to solve a mystery at Waverly Academy. In Warnings at Waverly Academy, players learn that someone has been trying to scare valedictorian students in an attempt to reduce the competition. Nancy must solve puzzles and gather clues to find the culprit. Participants will continue the adventure and will pause in order to solve puzzles similar to those Nancy must solve in the game.

The program can run one and a half to two hours but can also be broken up into more than one session if participants are interested in playing the PC game through to the end after they have completed their own tasks and puzzles. There can be one person on staff for the program, but two to three staff members would be ideal and would allow each staff member to participate in at least one of the puzzles participants will solve.

FIGURE 30.1
Examples of activities. Use already-made items or prepare item with materials such as construction paper.

Because the computer game will need to be played by all participants, the group can work together at the beginning when taking on the role of Nancy Drew and suggesting steps or actions the character can take while playing the game. If the group is large (for example, ten or more participants), it can be broken up into smaller ones after the initial game play. These smaller groups (two to four participants) can then each have a turn at the puzzles and activities.

It is recommended that at least one staff member play the game beforehand or have knowledge of the events and who the culprit is in the game. If desired and time permits, or if there is more than one session of this program, the computer game may be played to completion, or staff can provide clues when participants successfully complete puzzles and tasks. These clues can lead the group(s) in solving the Nancy Drew: Warnings at Waverly Academy PC game mystery.

NECESSARY EQUIPMENT AND MATERIALS

- Nancy Drew: Warnings at Waverly Academy PC game
- computer capable of connecting to a projector
- projector and screen
- DNA model kit or craft materials to create a DNA model
- access to Scratch on a computer or a small piano keyboard

- one or more computers with access to your library's catalog
- a large piece of bulletin board paper with a map of fifty states outlined

STEP-BY-STEP INSTRUCTIONS
Preparation

- Acquire the Nancy Drew: Warnings at Waverly Academy PC game. This can be purchased on the official website, herinteractive.com, as both a virtual download and a physical game. Install the game and ensure it is working properly.
- Ensure the computer you will be using is compatible with the PC game and able to connect to your projector.
- Decide whether you will be using an already-made DNA model kit and piano keyboard or if you plan on creating them by hand utilizing a website such as Scratch or the invention tool Makey-Makey. Additional assembly time will be required if you decide to make these items instead of purchasing them premade.
- Decide whether you will have enough time to play the game to its finish in one session or whether you would prefer to break up the program into more than one session. This will allow you to plan your activities accordingly.
- If you will not be playing the game to the end, and participants are eager to solve the mystery, plan to have clues that will be awarded to groups as they complete the activities. These clues together will help participants solve the mystery.

Program Instructions

- Connect your computer to your projector and turn both on. Open up Nancy Drew: Warnings at Waverly Academy.
- If providing clues to participants after they complete activities, choose what those clues will be, write them down on small Post-its or pieces of paper, and fold the paper so the clues cannot be seen.
- Prepare your stations. There should be four activity stations:
  - *DNA Model Kit*: This kit can be a premade DNA model kit, if available, or one that you prepare out of crafting materials such as beads, pipe

cleaners, or construction paper. Your DNA model kit will require adenine, thymine, cytosine, guanine, phosphate, and deoxyribose sugar.
- *Piano Song*: A small piano keyboard can be used for this activity, but one of the best and least expensive methods is to have access to Scratch (scratch.mit.edu). Various piano projects exist on Scratch, and several of these already have the piano keys labeled. Printed music sheets, preferably labeled with notes for beginners, will also be needed. These sheets can be of any song you choose. If you choose to use/have a Makey kit, you can incorporate the kit in this activity.
- *Map of the United States*: Create a large map of the United States on a large sheet of bulletin board paper but do not label the states with their names. Depending on the number of groups, you may need more than one map, or you may choose to split up the number of states, giving a set number to each group to label. You may also choose to trace the map using a projector or to print out an unlabeled map(s).
- *Library Catalog Search*: At least one computer with access to your library catalog is needed. Prepare five to ten reference-search questions that can be solved using your catalog. Depending on the time you have available, you may add more questions. Print out the questions and have them available for the group(s).

Activity: DNA Model Kit
- Have participants put together the DNA model, connecting all the corresponding nucleotides and linking the pairs together with the sugar and phosphate.
- Participants can put together the DNA model from scratch or complete one that has missing parts, such as in a puzzle.
- Check to ensure the DNA model is accurate and complete or provide tips on parts that are not in their correct spot.
- *Optional*: After the group has put together the DNA model, provide a clue as to the identity of the culprit in the game.

Activity: Piano Song
- Access Scratch (scratch.mit.edu) and search for Piano projects; select a Piano with labeled notes.
- Using the printed music sheets, have participants play one of the songs from beginning to end.

- If interested in adding coding to the program, use Scratch and select the Music (Play instruments and drums) extension, which will allow participants to use the notes using the Scratch piano.
- A keyboard piano or a Makey can be utilized with Scratch.
- *Optional*: When the group has played a song completely, provide a clue as to the identity of the culprit in the game.

Activity: Map of the United States
- Place the large bulletin board paper with the outline of the United States on a table or large area of the floor, or you can hand out the printed map(s).
- The group will label the states.
- If there is more than one group, more than one map can be provided, and the map can be separated into sections or a group can be given a certain number of states to label.
- *Optional clue*: When the group has finished labeling, provide a clue as to the identity of the culprit in the game.

Activity: Library Catalog Search
- Participants will answer five to ten questions (or more, depending on the time available) using your library's catalog.
- Searches can also require participants to visit the library stacks to find answers; make questions as complex as you would like for your activity.
- If there is one group, participants can search together. If there is more than one group, each group can have the same questions or different questions.
- *Optional clue*: When the group has finished finding answers to the questions, provide a clue as to the identity of the culprit in the game.

Solving the Mystery
- *Discuss the responses*: Go over the DNA model, all of the piano music or one song, the map of the states, and the answers to the reference questions.
- *Discuss the activities*: How familiar were participants with DNA, music notes, or the library's catalog before participating?
- *Discuss the mystery*: When first beginning the game, did participants accurately guess the solution to the mystery? Did they suspect one suspect more than another? Discuss the solution to the mystery.

RECOMMENDED NEXT PROJECTS

Nancy Drew: Warnings at Waverly Academy is one of many PC games featuring Nancy Drew. All of these PC games include activities and puzzles that encourage critical thinking and are educational. For example, in Nancy Drew: Tomb of the Lost Queen, players are introduced to and play the Ancient Egyptian board game Senet, and in Nancy Drew: Shadow at the Water's Edge, Nancy solves Sudoku and origami puzzles, all of which are great activity ideas that can be replicated in a library program.

How to Explore STEM Programming through VR

ZACHARY STIER ("MR. Z")
Children's Librarian

Ericson Public Library

THIS PROGRAM LAUNCHES learners into immersive gaming experiences using Oculus Go. Oculus Go is a standalone virtual reality (VR) headset. The headset requires an internet connection for setup and to download applications. Once any necessary applications are downloaded, the internet is not needed to play. This is a fun learning experience, during which patrons play VR games and can complete challenges and missions, become a superhero, find monsters, race a car, and more! Each gaming experience supports STEM learning by helping patrons learn skills such as strategizing, critical thinking, and coding. You can enjoy taking patrons to virtual worlds!

Age Range	Type of Library Best Suited For	Cost Estimate
Tweens (ages 8–12) Young Adults (ages 13–18)	Public Libraries School Libraries	$25–$250

Cost Considerations

Expect to pay $199 for a standalone Oculus Go headset, 32GB, or $249 for a 64GB Oculus Go standalone headset. The prices for games vary and can be found in the Oculus Go store. *Please note*: Oculus Go is one of many VR systems on the market. Google Cardboard, which can mount to your smartphone, is a low-cost option and offers games through Google Play.

OVERVIEW

This program provides a variety of choices of what to provide to learners and the time to complete each stage. I recommend that this program be offered as a series to ensure patrons have enough time to complete each stage. You should have two to three staff members or volunteers on hand to assist with this program. For public libraries, a total of twenty-two players per program is suggested, and registration should be required. For school libraries, the total amount of learners is dependent on the class size. You can have patrons play a few games for each program or center your VR program around one specific game.

NECESSARY EQUIPMENT AND MATERIALS

- Oculus Gos (the number of Oculus Gos you need depends on the number of participants)
- charge cords for the Oculus Gos (make sure the Oculus Go controllers are charged, but bring extra AA batteries in case you need them at some point during game play)
- Optional equipment includes a laptop and a VGA or HDMI cord to connect a computer to a projector.

STEP-BY-STEP INSTRUCTIONS

Preparation

- Make sure the Oculus Gos are fully charged, but bring your charging cords in case your headsets must be recharged during the program.
- Depending on your space, you might need to set up tables and chairs.
- Download the Oculus Go app. This is free. You will need an IOS device such as an iPhone (the iPhone app for Oculus Go is available on the iPad, but it can have download issues) or an Android device (the Android app for Oculus GO is available through Google Play).

- Make sure you have a good Wi-Fi connection. After downloading the Oculus Go app, look through the store to locate games you believe patrons will enjoy. See table 31.1 for a list of recommended games.
- Speak with your administration about using the library's credit card for any game purchases.
- Pre-load the games on each Oculus Go prior to the start of the program. Oculus offers many games for free, but some games have costs associated with them. See table 31.1 for more information.

Program Instructions

Equipment Overview

- Attendees will immerse themselves in the world of VR. Each group should have one to two Oculus Gos at their table, depending on how many headsets you have.
- Demonstrate how to put on the headset. The headset has a strap for the back of the head and one for the top of the head. All straps can be adjusted.
- Go over all the gaming tools on the controller, which include a touchpad, back button, the Oculus Go button, and the trigger.
- You can connect Oculus Go to Facebook Live. Connecting your headset to Facebook Live will help guide you through the applications and demonstrate how to use the controller. If possible, connect the computer to a projector/screen for the walk-through. If you do not have a projector/screen, a computer screen will work. The easiest way to connect to Facebook Live is by completing the following steps as describe by the Oculus support website under the heading Oculus Quest or Go (https://support.oculus.com/1775053542763938/).

    1. Open the Oculus app on your phone.
    2. Tap Setting and then tap Linked Accounts.
    3. Tap next to Link to Facebook to link or unlink your account with Oculus.
    4. Once Oculus Go is turned on, the individual will choose Sharing on the bottom of the home screen and then click Go Live.

TABLE 31.1
Top Oculus Go experiences for patrons to explore

Name of the Game	Cost
Bait: Relax by the lake and enjoy a virtual game of fishing.	Free
Dodge This VR: Take control of a cannon to protect yourself from medieval knights, wizards, and more crazy characters trying to get past you.	$2.99
Doritos VR Battle: Wander the Dorito caves to collect as many flavors as you can.	Free
Epic Rollercoaster: No need to go to an amusement park for this joyride. Patrons will enjoy a variety of rollercoaster experiences.	Free
Escape from Bunker 14: You begin the game by not knowing where or who you are. The objective of this adventure-style game is to complete challenges and solve puzzles to find your way out.	$2.99
Evil Robot Traffic Jam: Play as an Evil Robot Defense Force character and access destructive abilities to disrupt robots and create traffic jams.	$3.99
Fancy Beats: Musical rhythm and 3D effects create a unique dancing experience.	Free
Hardlight Blade: Use your controller as a sword to cut through robotic enemies.	Free
Hidden Fortune: This is an enhancing treasure hunt in which patrons use magic wands and orbs to explore the world around them.	Free
Jake and Tess' Finding Monster Adventure: Your task is to try to take photos of the monsters you spot. The objective might seem simple, but the challenges get difficult.	$2.99
Joy Lab: A wonderful laboratory where you can build machines, launch fireworks, and enjoy fun experiments.	$3.99
Justice League VR: This VR experience, provided by Warner Bros., enables patrons to become a superhero, utilizing their powers to defeat obstacles.	$4.99
Lila's Tale: Enter a dungeon and search for Lila's brother. This game offers puzzles, enhancements, and obstacles.	$2.49
Mr. Cat's Adventures: Enjoy the adventure while solving puzzles, dodging monsters, and avoiding traps.	Free
My Principal Is an Alien: Uncover the truth and find out if the new principal is an alien.	Free
Oculus Arcade: Enjoy a collection of classic arcade games.	Free
Overtake: Traffic Racing: Grab your controller and enjoy the thrill of car racing.	$3.99
Race on Mars: Go to Mars in the year 2131 and experience the technology of jetpack racing.	$1.99
Ropes and Dragons: Play the role of a wizard and help a charming dragon find sweets. Complete puzzles and use a magic wand.	Free
SwingStar: Use a giant sticky hand to solve puzzles to save your home.	$2.99
Tiny Magic Carpet: Patrons will go on a trip using a magic carpet. They will collect all the coins but will need to watch out for the coin robber.	Free
Tomb Rader VR: Lar's Escape: Become Lara Croft and go into an ancient tomb.	Free
Wonderglade: A funny theme park experience with classic carnival games.	Free

5. After clicking Go Live, a screen appears that says Livestream to Facebook and will provide information to the Facebook account that they will Live Stream to along with the option to make it public or private.
6. They will then click Start Livestreaming.

Experience
- VR games take time to complete. You need to decide on the amount of games you want patrons to experience during a program.
- Make sure patrons are sitting when they have the Oculus Go on and the volume on it is turned up.
- You can connect Oculus Go to Facebook Live by choosing the Live option on the selection panel. Make sure you connect the headset to your Wi-Fi. By connecting it to Facebook Live, patrons who visit your library Facebook page will be able to see other patrons' gaming experiences.
- The following table includes games from the Oculus Go Store: www.oculus.com/experiences/go. Prices may vary.

RECOMMENDED NEXT PROJECTS

- Following this VR gaming program, create a Scratch coding program during which patrons work on their coding skills to create their own video game. After they create their game, invite the community into the library to try it out.
- Go beyond a standalone headset and test out a new VR system. Oculus has the Rift S, which provides a PC gaming experience, and the Google Cardboard VR headset can be used with an IOS or Android device.
- Search for community and/or state partners to expand your VR gaming programs. Partners can provide expertise on gamification, additional VR headsets and systems to use, and help facilitate programs.

Teach Young Patrons Cybersecurity Using Minecraft

CHRIS MARKMAN
Senior Librarian

Palo Alto City Library

THIS PROGRAM IS based on Minecraft's survival mode of game play but does not require a computer or computer lab to make it happen—it's more about giving patrons a specific design challenge and facilitating discussion. As the program lead, you do not even need to know how to play Minecraft that well (although someone in the room probably should!). Instead, this program uses the core game mechanics of Minecraft to illustrate a thought process or decision tree. This thought process, called *threat modeling* in the information security community, is a fundamental component of a cybersecurity tool set all internet users should have in their arsenal.

Age Range	Type of Library Best Suited For	Cost Estimate
Tweens (ages 8–12) Young Adults (ages 13–18) Adults	Public Libraries Academic Libraries School Libraries	$0–$300

Cost Considerations

Minecraft is available on multiple video game platforms (including most phones, tablet computers, and even some Chromebooks). It typically costs under $30 per patron, but you may find that many of your patrons who are interested in this program already own an account.

The game *does not* require a super-fast computer to play. It was first released in 2009, and most computer labs built in 2019 and beyond are more than capable of running the Java versions of the game. For that reason, costs in this section do not include hardware, but you may want to invest in handheld video game controllers for younger patrons less familiar with a keyboard and mouse setup.

There is also a free version of the game included with most Raspberry Pi computers. The popular 3D printing design website Tinkercad (https://tinkercad.com) also has a *blocks* design mode that can serve as a substitute for the full game, similar to Minecraft's creative mode.

Minecraft also offers a free one hundred-minute time-limited demo version of the game packaged with Windows 10. You only need an e-mail account to register. A demo version for other operating systems is also available to download via Microsoft's website (www.minecraft.net/demo).

OVERVIEW

Working in teams or individually, patrons design a personal *digital fortress* based on what they consider to be the greatest in-game Minecraft threats. The key element that makes this different from other Minecraft design events is that before building anything in-game, patrons must first go through the process of creating a threat model (a mental map, essentially) based on their knowledge of the game and the *probability* and *impact* of an attack occurring.

This program is very flexible in terms of duration and participant skills. It could be repeated several times in one day, building on design ideas, or repeated as a weekly activity. It is important that participants review the designs created by their classmates and compare the final result with each associated threat model.

The goal is to show there is no single perfect design solution in Minecraft (because threat models are subjective) and how these models mirror how real-world cybersecurity practices must adjust to threats.

If you plan to work with a large group, consider the use of a digital projector, multiplayer server, or remote desktop system to make reviewing and presenting individual fort designs easier.

NECESSARY EQUIPMENT AND MATERIALS

- at least one computer capable of running Minecraft (online or offline)
- printed threat model templates
- pencil(s) or pen(s)

STEP-BY-STEP INSTRUCTIONS

Preparation

- It's important to accurately advertise this workshop and its associated game-play style. Minecraft is an open-ended, sandbox-style game in which some players focus on things other than building, such as exploring the world or player-vs.-player combat. If your audience is primarily teens and tweens, marketing material might be more visible to parents, who may need a more in-depth explanation about how you are linking the game with a cybersecurity theme.
- Also consider the number of available computers or game stations at your library. Will this be a *bring your own laptop/mobile device–style* event, or do you need to limit the number of participants so you can walk through the process of threat modeling as a group?
- Review the process of cybersecurity threat modeling yourself. There are several high-quality guides online, most notably Electronic Frontier Foundation's online Security Self-Defense course (https://ssd.eff.org/en).

Program Instructions

- Begin the program by explaining the three workshop steps to your students.
    - *Introduction*: Explain what threat modeling is, how it can be used in the real world, and how that same skill can be practiced in Minecraft.
    - *Building*: Create a threat model and Minecraft fort based on this model as a group or individually.
    - *Critique*: Look at and discuss the different outputs from the second step. What did they miss? How could they be improved?

- It may also be helpful at this point to illustrate how threat modeling can save you from disaster by using an example from the game. You could talk about why you should never place lava near a wall made of wood—it will eventually burn down, and the fire could spread to other parts of your base as well. In this example, the process of threat modeling would allow a person to forecast or predict different security scenarios and create a defense strategy before it's too late.
- Create a threat model. The easiest way to do this is to provide several examples based on different mobs found in the game, allowing students to *fill in the blank* for the remaining monsters they've encountered. Focusing on the probability and impact of each mob attack is critical for the following step.
- Now it's time to start building in Minecraft. Before your group begins, refer to the threat models that were just completed and suggest they focus their design based on monsters or security events that have the highest probability and impact should they occur.
- Some students are going to finish their design faster than others. Others might have lots of questions about the game. It may be helpful to reassign more advanced players to pair up with newer players, so they don't get lost. In this step you need to pay close attention to the clock; time will go by faster than you think!
- Finally, provide time for students to show off their design ideas. As they present their Minecraft fort, you can refer to their threat model or call out unique security features that they employed. The most important part in this step is to show the similarities between cybersecurity and Minecraft. In both cases, security designs are unique because they match a corresponding threat model. Similarly, someone who is new to Minecraft won't be well-versed in the game and might rate the probability or impact of an event higher than an advanced player. This is also true for cybersecurity. For example, knowledge of a software company being involved in previous data breaches might lead a more advanced user to trust their security less or provide fewer account details than a novice user who is unaware of those events. In both cases, knowledge shapes *both* their threat model *and* corresponding security.

RECOMMENDED NEXT PROJECTS

- Export the fort designs from this project for 3D printing or collect screenshots and showcase these designs on your website. Visitors can vote for their favorites!
- Try the same workshop setup but with different design restrictions in place. What is the most secure fort design that can be created using limited resources? Who can create the best base using the *smallest* number of blocks? What is the best base you can build in the shortest amount of time? What if there was a new mob added to the game that could jump over walls or dig tunnels? The possibilities for variations are endless.
- Draw classroom inspiration from historic castle and fort designs from around the globe or even from YouTubers who showcase complex designs in their videos.

PART III
Live Action Game Programs

How to Run a Vampire LARP in the Library

ERROL LOGAN
Teen and Adult Services Librarian
Somerville Public Library, a branch of the Somerset County Library System

LARP STANDS FOR live action roleplay. It's an increasingly popular hobby for teens and adults. Players take on the roles of characters in a fantasy, science fiction, or, in this case, modern horror world. LARP players dress in costume and act out mundane actions and have conversations while in character. When conflict is called for, however, they use the rules of the game to resolve it. Our program's LARP takes place in the popular Vampire: The Masquerade rules set, published by Night Studios and based on White Wolf's World of Darkness games.

Vampire: The Masquerade is a game of modern horror in which the characters take on the roles of assorted vampire clans. As secret masters of the world, they compete with each other politically and socially in an eternal struggle of brinksmanship as they struggle for control over a darker version of our own world while trying to manage their own inner beast—which drives them to commit violent acts and degrade their humanity to the point that they become mindless creatures that must be put down for the good of all.

The program can take place after hours or in a spacious programming room. Ideally, participants are best isolated from patrons, as animated conversations and outlandish costumes are part of the overall experience.

A LARP can be a great way to upsell library services. We always try to include a local history component in our LARPs so that participants can learn about the resources we have available. If you've got a good relationship with a nearby historical site, perhaps you can arrange a visit as part of the overall experience. You can also take advantage of this opportunity to suggest additional readings from your horror or modern fantasy collections. If your library agrees to purchase copies of the rulebook to add to your collection, they can be checked out by people who want to learn more about the game.

Age Range	Type of Library Best Suited For	Cost Estimate
Adults*	Public Libraries Academic Libraries	$0

Cost Considerations

One of the greatest things about a LARP is that it can cost as much or as little as you like. There is usually a small setup fee needed for the purchase of rulebooks, but it's easy to get them donated as well. The experience can be

FIGURE 33.1
Members of the Mind's Eye Society at a vampire LARP

---

*Because of the mature themes involved, most vampire LARP groups are adult-only. It's a harder rule for some patrons than others, but we recommend partnering with a group that excludes minors. This is an ideal chance to court the elusive new adult demographic. If you've garnered a lot of interest from minors, you can consider running a separate age-appropriate program for them.

greatly enhanced via the purchase of props, but this can get pricey. The level of investment you put into setting the stage is entirely up to you, however. In the past we've just told patrons, "The setting is this library. What you see is what you see," and gone with that.

OVERVIEW

First, we recommend that you partner with a local LARP organization. For vampire games the Mind's Eye Society (MES) is recommended. They have groups all over the country and are moderately likely to have one near your library. This society should have all the expertise you need to get started, including a built-in player base, an administrative support system, and rules support. Some local groups have access to props that can really help set the stage and are often grateful to acquire free space and increase their audience. Learn more about them at their website: www.mindseyesociety.org.

Your best role is as a facilitator, assisting with what they already have planned. Conducting outreach and recruiting your patrons, thus expanding their player base, will likely be the most important part of your job. Of secondary importance will likely be finding a way to get the privacy that they and your patrons will need. This kind of program is best held after hours or in a large, relatively isolated program space. Acquiring permission to run an after-hours program can be challenging and requires more buy-in from your library's administration but can reap the rewards of being able to use more of the building and accommodate working patrons' schedules.

It is possible to run an event without that partnership, but it's highly recommended that you have a staff member or volunteer who has LARPed before. If you decide to go it alone, I recommend one staff member per ten participants, if that can be arranged. Also, if you run an after-hours program, we recommend that at least two staff supervise the program.

The ideal program lasts about four hours from start to end—including about an hour to set up and a half hour to break down. The LARP group you partner with will be best able to determine what their maximum number of attendees will be, and as always, the needs of your facility and the capacity of your program room are key to deciding how many participants to allow in your game. On average, a high-quality LARP experience requires a minimum of six people. It can be difficult to justify paying two staff members to supervise an after-hours program if only two or three participants show up. If at least a dozen patrons are not preregistered, it's usually advisable to cancel if the program is to take place after hours.

NECESSARY EQUIPMENT AND MATERIALS

- A copy or two of the Vampire: The Masquerade rulebook by Night Studios can help, though MES members usually own their own. It's available in print or as a PDF from www.drivethrurpg.com.
- Everything else, including props or costuming, is completely optional. Vampire: The Masquerade is a modern horror game, and vampires can look like regular people; so, excessive costuming and set decoration, while fun and immersion-building, isn't required.

STEP-BY-STEP INSTRUCTIONS

Preparation

- Get permission to run an after-hours program or have a program room that is large enough to accommodate upwards of thirty people in relative quiet and privacy.
- Partner with your local LARP club or work with a staff member who is familiar with the rules.
- Purchase any props or costumes that you can afford that you think will enhance the overall experience. Generally, props are better than costumes, as they'll have more uses after the program is over.
- In order to get people started as soon as possible, you should have enough pre-generated characters to accommodate your entire anticipated player base. Nothing pulls people out of the mood to play like having to create characters on game day. Be sure to have a wide selection of character concepts that appeal to players who might want to try a combat scenario or a social character.
- If running the game, familiarize yourself with all the rules. You don't have to master them, but you should have access to a rulebook or a more experienced helper if you're not 100 percent up on how the game should be played. If joining in, learn the rules that you need to know in order to play along.

- After the game, have everyone sit or stand in a circle and talk about their experience. Encourage them to share a good thing that happened to them during game play, any constructive criticism they might have, and to call out another player for exceptional roleplay. It helps community-building and assists people in transitioning back into their mundane, reality-based mindset.

Program Instructions

- Build the program that you want. Patrons like consistency. If you wish to eventually hold a monthly LARP meetup, start your program with that in mind. Don't just *try it once to see what happens*. Patrons will notice your lack of commitment and perhaps decide not to come to a theoretical second event.
- Participants tend to get excited during tense scenes. Remind everyone that they can step back or ask questions *out of character*. Your LARP group partners will usually have tools to help deal with that. If they don't, don't work with them.

RECOMMENDED NEXT PROJECTS

- MES games usually run monthly. Your patrons can attend those if they desire additional gaming experiences.
- You can run another event or make the game a recurring program.
- Encourage participants to make their own characters. Vampires are immortal and can come from historic settings. You can help them with their research to increase verisimilitude.
- Some players enjoy making their own costumes. If you have a makerspace with sewing machines, encourage them to use it. You can also run a separate costume-making program in support of your monthly game.
- Encourage players to try science fiction–style games or games in other genres. The MES supports several genres of games.

How to Run an Instagram Scavenger Hunt for New Student Orientation

SUSAN M. HANSEN
Director of Library Services

Hoffman Family Library, Goodwin College

THIS PROGRAM ALLOWS you to engage patrons in an easy and enjoyable scavenger hunt while demonstrating the library's social media savvy. An Instagram scavenger hunt is simple to create and accessible even to library users who don't consider themselves social media experts. Partner with other groups in town (or on campus) to make the hunt as wide-reaching as you like. Use it to highlight community services, upcoming programs, famous landmarks, local businesses, parks, restaurants, and more! All you need to do is advertise and have a prize to reward at the end.

Age Range	Type of Library Best Suited For	Cost Estimate
Young Adults (ages 13–18) Adults	Public Libraries Academic Libraries School Libraries	$0–$100+

Cost Considerations

- advertising costs (e.g., printed flyers, bookmarks)
- purchase a prize (if donated prizes aren't a possibility)

Clue	Hashtag
The library's mascot is always ready for Halloween and Day of the Dead!	#barebones
Three of these on the library's second floor let you work as a group without disturbing others.	#studyroom
Need to know what's going on inside? These show you without needing X-ray vision.	#Anatomymodels
Help the library make 1,000 of these as a wish for world peace—and make an extra to keep.	#origamicrane
This second floor space invites you to relax and enjoy the vending machines.	#lounging@Goodwin

FIGURE 34.1
Example of clues and related hashtags

OVERVIEW

The primary purpose of an Instagram scavenger hunt is to offer library users an engaging way to learn something new about the library and its surrounding community. However, it can double nicely as a way to increase library Instagram followers. Depending on its scope, your hunt can last anywhere from one day to a week or month. For example, our academic library scavenger hunt—as an orientation exercise for new students—was designed to lead students around campus as they identified locations for student support services and places to relax or have fun (the student lounge, a café, a campus selfie spot). Students were given a week to locate all the clues and post a photograph with the assigned hashtag. A public library scavenger hunt, with the support of community partners, can keep the hunt active for a month, allowing people in town time to locate businesses, arts and entertainment spots, and specific items of interest (for example, a statue on the town green) included in the hunt. A clue can also be created to elicit a variety of individual responses such as, "Where is your favorite spot to study?" or "Where was the last place you bought ice cream?" There is no need to limit the number of participants. One or two library staff members will need to monitor the library's Instagram account for hashtag posts and to track participants' progress.

NECESSARY EQUIPMENT AND MATERIALS

- library Instagram account
- prize (possibilities include gift cards to local restaurants, tickets to movies or athletic events, etc.)

STEP-BY-STEP INSTRUCTIONS

Preparation

- Determine the scope of the project. Will it take place within one building or on one campus, or will it be town-wide?
- Identify partners for the hunt. Any businesses or organizations you want participants to visit should be alerted to the hunt ahead of time and be willing to participate.
- Identify a prize.
- Create a library Instagram account if you don't already have one.
- Create a list of places/items to be photographed.
- Create clues to lead people to those places and create a hashtag for each clue.
- Create rules for participants. (Will people play as individuals or in teams? Will the game be open to members of your library only or to the general public? Will the first person to complete the challenge win, or will the challenge remain open until a specific day and time, at which point the winner's name can be drawn from all who completed the challenge?)
- Advertise!

Program Instructions

- Have people register to participate, either online or in person. Record their name, contact information, and Instagram ID.
- Create a spreadsheet with participant information and columns for each hashtag.
- Create a hashtag with the name of your hunt. Instruct participants to post all pictures with both the hunt hashtag and the clue-specific hashtag; this will make tracking easy.

- Decide how to provide the clues. The clues can be made available at once, or a small number of clues can be posted over time (daily, weekly). Post the clues on social media as well as on a written display in the library.
- Start the hunt!
- Library staff should monitor the Instagram account daily for hashtag posts and verify that the photographs are taken in the correct place. Note progress on the spreadsheet.
- Monitor hashtag posts until the hunt ends.
- Notify the winner and award the prize.

RECOMMENDED NEXT PROJECT

Try a smaller or larger scavenger hunt next year and ask previous participants to help plan it.

How to Create a Life-Sized Game of Life

LINDSEY TOMSU
Teen/YA Librarian

Algonquin Area Public Library District

LIFE-SIZED BOARD GAMES can go beyond large-scale versions of Candy Land and Clue. In this project, you will learn how to turn the classic board game The Game of Life into a real-life interactive experience. The preparation of such programs is also a great way to get teen volunteers involved in library programming, as they can earn volunteer hours for assisting with creative and hands-on tasks rather than just doing busywork.

Age Range	Type of Library Best Suited For	Cost Estimate
Tweens (ages 8–12) Young Adults (ages 13–18)	Public Libraries	$100–$1,000

Cost Considerations

Not everything needs to be bought new! Consider what items the library may already own, what items can be made by volunteers, and what items can be donated/borrowed by patrons before you budget to purchase everything.

For items you must purchase, remember that your local dollar store is your best friend!

For items that must be crafted, laminate anything that must be done on paper. This way you can keep these elements of the program in good condition and re-use them multiple times (instead of just once), which helps justify a higher initial program budget.

OVERVIEW

The idea for doing a life-sized Game of Life event came about when my teens had already made and played life-sized versions of Candy Land and Arkham Horror. Having enjoyed the experience of volunteering to make such a large-scale program a reality, along with the fun of getting to play life-sized versions of games they adored and put hours into making, my teens decided to try their hand at The Game of Life.

The key thing to keep in mind with creating any life-sized game is how detailed you want it to be. Some teens may view it as a *go big or go home* project and want to make it as realistic as possible, while others are perfectly happy with a much more simplified version. Take into consideration how much of a budget you will have, how many volunteers might be available to help create the game elements, how large of a meeting room space the library has, how much time you have to put into prep work before the event, and the audience you are aiming to serve with the event. As many of my life-sized games were funded by grants, I usually ended up with about one month in which to prep and run the program to meet grant deadlines. If expecting a large crowd of teens, I suggest holding the program on a weekend, when you can often acquire more library time. I have found that ten to fifteen teens is a nice number of participants for our The Game of Life program. If expecting more, it may be a good idea to host groups during certain time slots throughout the day.

NECESSARY EQUIPMENT AND MATERIALS

- A copy of the physical board game The Game of Life. There have been many versions throughout the years, so keep that in mind when determining which game you want to make life-sized. My teens chose a classic version, circa 1970s.
- Your game board layout will require various colors of printer paper to match the spaces on the game board (primarily pale yellow, white, and

dark orange/red if doing the classic version) and a machine to laminate the spaces (if saving for future re-use).
- Paper money and insurance tickets will need to be enlarged and printed on corresponding colored paper (white, pale blue, gold, pale yellow, pink, purple, and pale green).
- Props that reflect the contents of the space a player may land on (i.e., *A son is born. Collect presents.* could have a boy doll or a wrapped present as the prop). Ideally, the more props you can buy, borrow, or make, the more detailed your game will become.
- Buildings will require five to six pieces of white foamboard (four for the sides and one board for a flat roof or two to make an arched roof). Utilize creative and artistic teens to draw details on the buildings with Sharpies and/or paint.
- Peg children and spouses can be made from wrapping paper tubes and round hand-sized balls spray-painted pink and blue. Vehicles are optional (see the Program Instructions section for a related program suggestion).
- If crafty and brave, you can make a life-sized spinner to add to the game. The materials needed include a clear storage box, various PVC piping, wooden skewers, colored poster board, white foamboard, plastic buckets, zip ties, and scenery props (to match the forest scenery on the board around the spinner).

STEP-BY-STEP INSTRUCTIONS

Preparation

- The most important step in creating a life-sized game is to first acquire a physical copy of the game you plan to enlarge.
- I highly recommend getting teens involved in all steps of preparation for your game. This is a great way to give them a meaningful and memorable experience while they earn volunteer hours. I have had many teens say the acts of brainstorming, preparing, and seeing their creation come to life was more awesome than playing the life-sized game! My teens went full-out in our creations, and the average teen who worked on the project earned anywhere from twenty to fifty volunteer hours during the month of preparation we had for our games (based on nearly three hundred to four hundred volunteer hours total for a group of ten to fifteen teens).

- Once your group has decided which version of The Game of Life they want to make life-sized, hold a brainstorming meeting (don't forget snacks). Give yourself one to two hours with your helpers to really analyze the board game and make a list of all the components you will need to make it life-sized. This is the point at which your budget will determine how in-depth you want to make your game! However, don't forget to see what you can make and what you can borrow before cutting any ideas, and don't forget to reach out to friends' groups to see if they can provide some extra funds to make your event really amazing!

Board Spaces and Board Backgrounds
- There are nearly 170 spaces on the board of the 1977 version of The Game of Life. Determine, based on how large the meeting room is, how many spaces your game will contain, and if you'll need to cut anything.
- The spaces are the easiest things to construct and can be done either by staff or a teen volunteer if they have access to a computer. Start with making a list of the spaces that have white, pale yellow, and dark orange/red backgrounds. Create the text on each of those background colors in a Word document and then print out each group on corresponding colored paper. For some of the spaces that have arrows in the background behind the text, teens can draw orange Sharpie arrow outlines on the pages in the corresponding directions.
- If planning to offer the program again in the future, laminating the spaces is a must. This allows for teens to step on the space pieces while playing without destroying them. Another bonus of laminating is that the spaces will have some heft to them and can be laid out on the floor without needing to tape them into place to secure them.
- If going for a detailed life-sized version, pay close attention to all the creative things in the background *dead* space of the game board. A favorite is the jungle safari scene by the Day of Reckoning House or the whale swimming off the coast of the beach. Feel free to brainstorm ideas for props that can be placed in these spaces to add more detail.

Game Tokens
- The primary game tokens (besides children and spouses) are the money and insurance papers. A simple way to incorporate these into the game is to just use those tokens that come with the physical game, as they are technically life-sized (a little smaller than a normal dollar bill). If you

want more detail, take a photo of each denomination/insurance paper, enlarge them, and print them onto corresponding colored paper.

Buildings and Bridges
- Preparation in this area is ideal for creative and artistic volunteers who want to help create! There are seven buildings in The Game of Life (University, Church, Farm, Large House, Industrial Building, Day of Reckoning House, and Mansion). An inexpensive way to make buildings is to use white foamboard from a dollar store (especially because the buildings are white) and tape them together into square shapes. I recommend five to six pieces for each building (four for the sides and one to two for the roof). If you have artistic teens, have them use Sharpies or paint to decorate the buildings. They can add windows or outside details such as shrubs. If they really get into it, allow them to paint scenes inside the windows to add a fun kind of Where's Waldo? element. For example, my teens added everything from a TARDIS to a chimney with stockings to stained glass windows for the church to a dance party to a murderer sneaking up on an unaware victim!
- There are three white bridges and two mountain passes in the game. This one is tricky, so get ideas from your volunteers. My teens used five short story-time tables and draped them with white and green plastic tablecloths from the dollar store to create the effect of elevation off the floor, where the rest of the game spaces were placed.

Props
- What props you decide to purchase, make, or borrow depends on your budget for the event and how detailed you want the life-sized game board to appear. For a super-detailed experience, try and have one prop for every space on the game board. Again, the creativity of your volunteers will help you brainstorm what will work best for your event. Here are some examples to help get you started:
    - *Career Spaces*: Use dollar store toys for these sections such as a doctor's kit for becoming a doctor, a fake apple for becoming a teacher, etc.
    - *A Son/Daughter Is Born*: Use stuffed dolls from the dollar store.
    - *Gambling Loss*: Use a spinner set of poker chips and cards.
    - *Buy Car Insurance*: Include a picture of Flo from Progressive on the space.
    - *Buy Furniture*: Use doll house furniture such as a couch.

- *Car Accident*: Carefully take a hammer to a Hot Wheels car to make it appear as if it were in an accident.
- *Aunt Leaves You Fifty Cats*: Place a bunch of borrowed Beanie Baby cats in the space.
- *Need False Teeth*: Use a toothbrush and a variety of denture products.
- *Payday*: Have a bowl of PayDay candy bars available; each time a player lands on a Payday space, toss one at them!

Children and Spouses
- The children and spouse peg people can be made with wrapping paper tubes and large hand-sized balls (from a dollar store) that are spray-painted pale blue and pink.
- For a fun, interactive moment, when players get married, have them stop at the church and fill out a fake marriage license and take a picture with their peg spouse. For each child born, have the parents fill out a birth certificate.
- For a more detailed version, actual wooden peg people can be purchased (I recommend shopping for these items at Woodworks, Ltd.) in bulk. Peg people come in adult and baby sizes. Volunteers could then decorate the peg people to look like diverse family members.

Vehicles
- Vehicles made life-sized can make playing the game a bit cumbersome. Depending on the size of the space, you can opt to not include vehicles. A fun spin-off program is to invite teens to come the week before and make cardboard boxcars they can wear to the event but easily take off to make game play easier.

Spinner
- If budget and space prevent making a life-sized spinner, just use the spinner that comes with the game. Teens will be happy and impressed enough just getting to walk through a life-sized version; they won't mind if a really big spinner is missing from the game play.
- If adventurous, you can build a life-sized spinner. My spinner was four feet wide. I built a circle frame using PVC piping purchased from a local building supply store. For the numbers, I used colored poster board for the wedges and cut the numbers from white foamboard and glued them

CHAPTER 35 | **How to Create a Life-Sized Game of Life**

FIGURE 35.1
The four-foot-wide spinner

on. You can also cut holes into the wedges and attach them in intervals around the circle with zip ties. Using white tape, attach wooden skewers cut in half (get rid of the pointy bit) and secure them around the circle to be the plonks that eventually stop the spinner. The rest of the rigging can be made from more PVC angles, two buckets, and a clear storage box. The buckets go inside the middle of the constructed circle frame to give it stability. The piping is used to create an arm—which is attached to the stopper—that comes up from under the wheel. The storage box is what the buckets and the stopper arm connect to, which help add the height the wheel needs to lift off the floor and allow it to spin. Place the constructed spinner on top of a white tree skirt and add fake trees and green confetti grass to mimic the forest that surrounds the wheel on the classic board.

Program Instructions

We recommend setting up the life-sized game board the day before the event to ensure you have enough time to get everything laid out and address any concerns that may arise.

Setup Tips
- Begin by placing the spinner wheel in the middle of the room, if using a life-sized wheel. Based on the size of the room, estimate the placement of the buildings, bridges, and mountain passes and then place them where you believe they should go. Next, lay down the spaces in the same order they appear on the game board. It's helpful to have multiple assistants for this step; that way, you aren't constantly trying to relocate nearly 170 spaces by yourself! If you're about halfway through the placement of the spaces, and it looks like you're going to run out of room or have more than enough room, pause to realign the spaces by putting them closer together or spacing them a little farther apart.
- Once the physical layout of the game board is ready, begin the prop placement. Add the props made, borrowed, or purchased to their correct spots on the game board.
- On a table off to the side, place the miscellaneous gaming tokens (money, insurance paperwork, marriage certificates, birth certificates, etc.) for easy access. Also place any life-sized peg people here.

Running the Program
- Depending on space and time restrictions, registration may be required for the program to inform you of how many people/groups will be attending. If you wish your playgroups to consist of separate sections of groups of teens, make sure you allow, at a minimum, fifteen minutes between each game to reset anything.
- Give each player a number so they know their player order, based on how many teens will be playing at once. They can also use their player number as a physical reminder of where they were standing on the game board if they need to step away to spin a life-sized spinner.
- If using a life-sized spinner, let teens spin the wheel—because it is a lot of fun! Warn them to be gentle, though—don't grab it like the wheel on *The Price Is Right*! If using the spinner from the game, have the librarian act as Game Master and spin for everyone. This will allow the game to

- move quicker and avoid any confusion caused by people forgetting their order or where they were standing.
- Start the game and start cycling everyone through their turns. Your game play should mirror that of the regular board game.
- If teens get antsy and distracted (depending on how many are playing at once), don't be discouraged. Ultimately, they will have fun, even if they don't finish a game!
- At the end of the day, ask for volunteers to help clean up the room. Find a suitable box to store the laminated game spaces and the tokens for future use, put any made or purchased props in a moving box for easy storage, and make sure all borrowed items get returned to their proper owners. For the buildings, label the pieces "right roof" before taping them together with book tape. This allows you to easily cut through the tape with scissors in order to collapse the buildings for future re-use.

RECOMMENDED NEXT PROJECTS

- The Game of Life is a medium-difficulty project primarily due to the amount of game spaces and props required to make the game really shine. There is no shame in starting smaller with an easier life-sized game project, such as Candy Land, which is always a great introduction to making life-sized games. However, once teens get to enjoy a life-sized gaming program, expect them to ask when they can do another one!
- Keep an eye out for local and national grants that may assist with creating future life-sized board games. You can always use grant funds to make one large, spectacular game or create a variety of smaller games that can be held during the same event.

Always try to get teens involved in the process as much as possible as volunteers! Life-sized games are a great way for them to earn volunteer hours, and teens are amazing sources of knowledge you can tap as you brainstorm how to turn a board game into an epic, life-sized version of itself. The more heads and hands you have to help make your game a reality, the better!

How to Organize an Escape Room for Faculty

MAYA BERRY
Digital Librarian

MELISSA WRIGHT
Director of the Learning Resource Center

R. C. Pugh Library, Northwest Mississippi Community College

FACULTY WILL PARTICIPATE in a librarian-designed escape room using print and electronic library resources as the basis for solving clues in order to *escape* from a room in the library.

The benefits of creating an escape room event for faculty include increasing their awareness of library resources, such as its print and electronic resources and the services librarians provide, and providing them with a fun break from traditional classroom settings or staff meetings. This event also gives faculty members the opportunity to learn how to plan their own escape room event for their students.

Age Range	Type of Library Best Suited For	Cost Estimate
Adults	Academic Libraries School Libraries	$0–$100

Cost Considerations

You may have many things in your library already that you can use as clues or hiding spots for clues. You also may need to purchase items to enhance the experience such as a fake dictionary safe and other props.

OVERVIEW

In our Mystery of the Missing Student escape room program, we wanted to highlight resources that were new to us (ArtStor) and existing databases that may not have been used frequently (ChiltonLibrary, ProQuest Global Newsstream, and our Subject Guides). Your library may not subscribe to these databases or have these resources; therefore, we'll provide suggestions for alternative resources that may be used in their place.

In our Scientific Christmas Carol escape room, we wanted to give our science and math faculty an opportunity to participate in a short escape room after our presentation on how escape rooms have been used in the library and classroom.

The escape room's duration should be limited to thirty to forty minutes because one hour can be too long for faculty members who need to prepare for class or go to meetings. Any extra time after the escape room has been completed can also be used for feedback, announcements of upcoming library programs, and networking.

It is also best to limit your group to no more than ten participants. If there are more than ten participants, it is better to do multiple sessions so that participants will be better able to use the resources to locate clues.

NECESSARY EQUIPMENT AND MATERIALS

- locks—mostly four-digit combination ones with one or two three-digit locks as well
- timer (phone app or online countdown clock)
- items that can be locked such as toolboxes or double-zippered bags
- computer or tablet if the clues and resources are available electronically
- clues and the backstory to the escape room
- puzzle pieces that participants will find throughout the escape room—they will put the puzzle pieces together to solve the mystery and escape. You can either create puzzle pieces on the computer and cut them out or purchase blank puzzle pieces and write the clues on them.
- props such as photographs, letters, puzzle pieces, and other items that correspond to the theme of your escape room
- Breakout.edu account if needed for an online escape room or other websites that you create and add escape room clues to such as a Google Site

CHAPTER 36 | **How to Organize an Escape Room for Faculty**

STEP-BY-STEP INSTRUCTIONS

Preparation

- Identify library resources to be used in the clues (print or electronic resources). Resources may be targeted toward one department (science, math, English, etc.) or more generalized toward all faculty departments.
- Create a scenario in which the chosen resources could be used logically as part of the answers to the clues. Have a mystery for participants to solve in order to *escape* from the room. Invite faculty to participate. Remember, if more than ten sign up to participate, you may want to run multiple sessions.
- Create clues to go with the storyline. The answers to the clues may be found in the chosen library resources. The clues should build upon each other, with each one leading participants toward the final puzzle.
- *Very important*: Have someone test the clues beforehand to make sure that everything works or reads as it should. This gives facilitators the opportunity to make any needed corrections or changes to the clues prior to the activity.

Sample Faculty Escape Rooms

Mystery of the Missing Student
This escape room is meant to be solved in thirty minutes or less. The library clues may seem obvious to library staff, but the faculty may not be aware of the breadth of the library's resources. You may wish to have a *ringer* participant in the escape room—a library staff member who has not been exposed to the clues or puzzle but can play along with the faculty and assist them if they have difficulty in determining which resource to use. If you use a ringer, ask them to step in only if the faculty are truly struggling to find the correct resources to solve a clue. Let the faculty try to search independently as much as possible. The goal of this is to have fun and expose the faculty to your library's resources: electronic, print, or a combination of both.

Backstory
The scenario is as follows: You've noticed that one of your students has been missing from class. After asking around, you confirm that no one has seen this student anywhere. You've even taken the trouble to question your

student's twin brother, who is in some of your other classes at school. In response, he says that he thinks that the pressure of school has gotten to him and that his brother has run away. You've read many mystery novels, so instead of calling campus police to investigate, you've decided to crack the case with a team of your faculty friends. You've located his last known location—the library's meeting room. Some of his belongings are still in the room. Can you solve the mystery of the missing student? We created a video for our scenario, but you can read it aloud instead.

Setup
The setup for the room would be a table with the missing student's backpack on it. We put locks on several of the backpack's double-zippered compartments to hide clues. You could have miscellaneous papers, books, and textbooks in and around the backpack—we used flyers for upcoming library programs. You may wish to use other props that students commonly have such as water bottles, pens, a calculator, etc. You will also need to have several lockboxes or toolboxes with locks stashed around the room to contain additional clues. We also had a lockbox that opened with a key that was disguised as a dictionary and had iPads and laptops around the room that faculty members could use to search the library's electronic resources. In addition to clues, puzzle pieces were placed in the lockboxes and around the room. Participants collected the pieces and put them together to solve the final clue.

Clues
- Although we do not intend for you to label each clue as clue 1, clue 2, etc., during the actual escape room, we have labeled the following clues here to make it easy to keep track of them.
- The first clue for the Mystery of the Missing Student was a typical student's research paper with a works cited page that was marked with an instructor's red pen. If you utilize this clue in your game, you can ask student workers if you can use their work for the basis of the paper, but have the works cited page be entirely made up by you. In our game, this research paper was sticking out of the student's backpack in the library's viewing room and is the first clue the faculty needed to find. The works cited page had one citation that was incomplete, and the note written in the instructor's red pen stated: "Clue 1: This citation is incomplete. Remember, you need the journal volume and the rest of the

CHAPTER 36 | How to Organize an Escape Room for Faculty

page numbers! Find this article again in Academic Search Premier to get the numbers you need!"
- The faculty can then search the database using the information from the incomplete citation to find the two-digit volume number and two-digit page number. The two-digit volume number and two-digit page number will open a four-digit lock on the backpack.
- If you do not have access to Academic Search Premier, use another database that contains journal articles and citations.
- After opening a lock on the backpack, the faculty can find a picture from the database ArtStor. Our picture obscured four digits of the ArtStor accession number. Make sure that there is a clue written on the picture. Ours was "Clue 2: Help me! Find out where the Art is Stor-ed in the library."
- The picture we used was of a very familiar local landmark. The faculty located ArtStor on our webpage and did a search for this landmark in order to find the picture with the missing accession numbers.
- If you don't have a subscription to ArtStor, choose another database that has pictures and find an accession number or other number that corresponds to the picture within the database.
- The four digits missing from the accession number can lead your group to open a four-digit combination lock on a toolbox.
- The toolbox can contain a few pieces of a puzzle; ours was a paper copy of a fake texted dialogue between the student asking for help due to car trouble and a friend responding with a mechanic's name and a receipt for car maintenance at a local car shop. The receipt had a note from the mechanic, which stated, "Clue 3: For future reference, check Chilton's to diagnose the issue with the brakes." A printout of a Chilton's recall notice was attached to this receipt. The recall notice number happened to be a four-digit number, but in the printout the faculty received, it was obscured and circled. The faculty then had to find the four-digit recall number for the particular make and model of car listed in the printout to open the next four-digit lock located on the backpack.
- If you do not have a subscription to Chilton's database, you could use a printed car repair guide.
- Once opened, the backpack pocket can have more puzzle pieces and a small paperback book. Our book was an old library discard of a travel guidebook with a note stuck in it. The note read, "Clue 4: Is this where I could be found in the future? I need the most recent edition—it is key."

- The faculty then had to use the library catalog to see where the most recent edition of the travel guidebook was located in the library stacks. The book in the stacks was sitting on top of a key. If your library stacks are not accessible from your escape room space, you could roll in several carts of books and hide the key there, but you risk players discovering the key before they have opened the other locks. If this is the case, you may want to switch one of the earlier clues with the key; that way, if they find it independently of the clues, they will not get to skip ahead too far. Or, you could hide the key on the book cart when they are searching Chilton's database (just make sure they don't see you do it!).
- The faculty can then find the key, and, if they haven't already found it, can search for a lock that opens with that key. The key will open a lockbox dictionary. You could camouflage it amongst a pile of other dictionaries and reference books. If they find it early, that would be okay, as they will be unable to open it until they have the key. Inside our dictionary were more puzzle pieces and a typewritten note: "Clue 5: Is this SUBJECT of finding me too difficult for you, instructors? Do you need a GUIDE? I'd check on your HISTORY. Publication dates are very important!" If you have subject guides on your website, put a fake link in your history subject guide just for the escape room. In our program, the link directed players to a website that we'd designed. That site contained a link to ProQuest Global Newsstream as well as information next to the link to use a citation. We removed part of the title, part of the author's name, and the publication date information within the citation to challenge players. Our citation: Redmond, Lisa. "Fake Twin Alibi no Good, Man Gets 3 to 5 Years for Robbery." McClatchy-Tribune Business News, Aug. 31, 2006, pp. 1. ProQuest. The faculty can then search for the citation and find the two-digit month and two-digit day that the article was published. They can then use that information to open the four-digit lock combination on the final toolbox. Our combination: 0831.
- If you do not have Subject Guides, make a fake website that contains your clue and link to the database. If you cannot make a fake website, you can create a Word document with the same information.
- The rest of the puzzle pieces and a congratulations message can be found in the final box. When fully assembled, the puzzle can state that the missing student is not really missing but is actually the *brother* of the student who is in your other classes, and he doesn't have a twin. He just loved taking your classes so much, he knew if he had a *brother*, he could

take them twice! Now that his secret is out, he is going to transfer to another school to avoid embarrassment, but he will always think of you as his favorite professor!
- Make sure that the puzzle pieces that tell the main part of the final message (fake twin, not really missing, etc.) are only in the final lockbox. You do not want to give away the solution to the mystery too soon by having key pieces discovered in the earlier boxes!

A Scientific Christmas Carol

We hosted a group of science and math faculty members at our library just before the holiday break in between semesters. We created an escape room very loosely based on *A Christmas Carol*, by Charles Dickens. Our scenario was displayed in a video, but you could read it aloud as well.

Backstory

Dr. Screamy McMeany dislikes the holiday season and has decided to blow up the world by setting off an atomic bomb. Sir Isaac Newton visits him as the ghost of our scientific past and tells him that he and his group of ghosts from the scientific present and future will help thwart him, along with a group of very smart and talented faculty members. Dr. McMeany is displeased and starts the sequence to detonate the bomb, which will conveniently take thirty minutes. Sir Isaac Newton says that he and his other ghosts will help the faculty by leaving clues that will help them figure out how to stop the diabolical McMeany.

Setup

We used our computer lab, as it was a large enough space to hold our faculty participants. We used our Anatomy & Physiolog (A&P) skeleton, dressed in a lab coat with a name tag, to represent McMeany. We also had locked toolboxes around the room, along with other props. For the Sir Isaac Newton clue, we used a variety of apple products such as a bag of apples, a box of Apple Jacks cereal, apple cookies, and an Apple iPad box. We created a Google Site that had an embedded Google Form with one validated input box. We also used a lockbox disguised as a dictionary. You can also print out a copy of the periodic table or ask faculty to look one up online as part of the escape room. Puzzle pieces were also included in the locked toolboxes and around the room. The puzzle pieces were assembled to reveal the final clue.

Although we said the escape room could take thirty minutes, we really intended for the game to be very short, such as fifteen minutes long, as we gave a presentation to the faculty members on escape rooms and how to incorporate them into their classrooms before they started our escape room program.

Clues
- Although we do not intend for you to label each clue as clue 1, clue 2, etc., during the actual escape room, we have labeled the following clues here to make it easy to keep track of them.
- In our program, Sir Isaac Newton leaves players a message to look for what he is known for. We hid a key in a box of Apple Jacks. "Clue 1: I am Sir Isaac Newton. The clue you seek can be found in that which I am best known. Take a peek!" The clue, a key, was in the box of Apple Jacks.
- The key goes to the lockbox dictionary, which has a clue with a URL.
- The URL goes to a Google Site that we created with a clue from the ghost of science present. The website contained a picture of the band Queen; the following clue; and a form with one input box. The clue (Clue 2 of our game) on our website was: "I am Tim Berners-Lee and, not to brag, but I created the Internet. Name the band in this picture (Queen), input the name of a famous scientist in one of their songs, and you'll be all set." The answer was Galileo. When the answer is correctly inputted, they will receive a number to a four-digit lock on a toolbox. The toolbox contains a number of puzzle pieces and a clue.
- This third clue is from Mariah Curie, Marie Curie's great-granddaughter, the ghost of Christmas future. She describes a horrible future if the atomic bomb goes off; so, she gives a clue to help you stop McMeany. "Clue 3: McMeany is a nasty one. You can't helium and you can't curium, so you might as well barium. Add the elements together, and McMeany is as good as done." This will lead faculty to the periodic table (either online or a print copy), where they can add the element numbers of curium, helium, and barium together to get a three-digit combination for a lock on a toolbox.
- Our toolbox contains puzzle pieces that have the final four-digit lock combination.
- Make sure that the most important puzzle pieces with the actual combination lock numbers are only in the box with the final combination lock. Draw pictures, make designs, or add in fake combination lock numbers

on the rest of the puzzle pieces and then put those portions of the puzzle in the earlier toolboxes.
- After they open the final combination lock, they will read a note indicating that they have defused the bomb and saved the world! Holiday candy for participants may also be included in the toolbox.

Program Instructions

- Set up at least two hours before the program to allow for any last-minute changes to clues or design of the room.
- Explain the concept of an escape room for those who may not be familiar with it.
- Read or play a recording of the backstory and answer any questions about what participants are to do.
- Set the timer.
- Allow participants to begin searching for clues.
- Facilitators can provide assistance when asked.
- At the end, talk about the idea of creating an escape room event in their classrooms and how it could work.
- Offer to help faculty members develop an escape room for their courses.

RECOMMENDED NEXT PROJECTS

- Use your first escape room as a launchpad to design additional games for different courses.
- Ask participants what other library resources they would like to know more about so that future escape room events may be planned.

Live Video Games
Library Battle Royale

SARAH AMAZING
Teen Services Supervisor

Warren-Trumbull County Public Library

THE BATTLE ROYALE video game genre continues to dominate the industry with games such as Fortnite, PlayerUnknown's Battlegrounds (PUBG), Apex Legends, and Blackout remaining popular among gamers. However, it can be difficult for a library to host an event showcasing a battle royale game, as their massive multiplayer format and constant updates require more than most branches are able to provide. Alternatively, hosting a live Library Battle Royale is a fun and active way to get fans away from their personal computers at home and into a space where they can interact socially and meaningfully. Oh, and they get to run and scream in the library too!

Age Range	Type of Library Best Suited For	Cost Estimate
Kids (ages 3-7) Tweens (ages 8-12) Young Adults (ages 13-18) Adults	Public Libraries Academic Libraries School Libraries	$20-$200

Cost Considerations

This program can be done with minimal money for snacks and a few rolls of masking tape, if relying on patrons to bring toy weapons.

OVERVIEW

If you're familiar with the battle royale genre, you'll know the games involved are fairly simple: land in a battlefield, find weapons, eliminate enemies, and survive to the end. A Library Battle Royale is played throughout a single floor of a library the same way, only your participants will use toy guns to eliminate players from the battlefield. Boxes are provided as defensive shields as well as to build forts.

FIGURE 37.1
The final few survivors of a round of library battle royale! Those eliminated look on from the sidelines.

Many libraries have found success asking for participants to bring toy guns; however, Nerf guns can be purchased in bulk from shop.hasbro.com for under $5 per toy.

Some rounds will last fifteen minutes or more; others may be over faster. Your participants will have ideas for modes, such as duo, quad, or solo—or even choosing a mode with weapons or one that requires them to scramble to find them. Plan at least ninety minutes for this program.

Staff act as referees, blowing a whistle to alert a player that they are out or if an infraction has occurred. One to two other staff members on hand, depending on the size of your battlefield, should be sufficient.

NECESSARY EQUIPMENT AND MATERIALS

- toy guns and ammunition such as Nerf guns—approximately one toy gun and three darts per participant
- drop zone signs
- masking tape in at least three different colors
- whistles
- snacks
- water/other beverages
- small prizes such as candy, buttons, etc. (optional)

STEP-BY-STEP INSTRUCTIONS

Preparation

- Familiarize yourself with the battle royale genre if needed by searching online for videos of people playing. Check out a variety of games to get a feel for what differentiates PUBG from Fortnite, etc.
- Decide a prize, if any.
- Collect cardboard boxes (check with your materials processing department).
- Create signs denoting drop zones and post in their respective places.
- Create a way for players to choose drop zones such as writing them on a popsicle stick for them to choose randomly.
- Lay down at least three different colors of masking tape in circles of descending size.
- Place caution tape or other barrier blocking areas that are *out-of-bounds*.
- Place toy guns, ammunition, and boxes throughout the playing field.
- Denote an area for eliminated players to go throughout the rounds.

PROGRAM INSTRUCTIONS

- After the battlefield is set up, bring all participants to the middle of the field.
- Break up participants into teams of four.
- Read aloud the rules. An example set of rules follows.
    - Throughout the library are your drop zones. Every team will draw their drop zone, and at the sound of the whistle you will proceed there to find weapons and building materials.
    - All weapons, ammo, and materials are in plain sight—nothing is hidden behind books, shelves, desks, etc. *Do not* enter any area that is blocked off, and *do not* go behind any desk. If you are discovered in any out-of-zone area, you will be eliminated.
    - If you are hit, you are down and must be revived by a team member. You must immediately drop to your knees, although you may move away from the action and take cover. In order to be revived, one of your team members must tap you on the back.
    - If, however, you are hit again before a team member revives you, you are eliminated. When eliminated, please report to the elimination zone until the round is over.

- Staff members will act as referees. A whistle blow means a violation has occurred, at which time you must do as the referee says, whether you are told to go down, that you were eliminated, etc.
- As time goes on, the arena will begin to shrink. Pay attention to the announcements to learn which color circle to report to.
- Anyone outside of the circle when the clock winds down will be eliminated.
- There are building materials throughout the arena. You may use these as shields or to build a fort to defend your team.
- Alliances are permitted; however, there can be only one winning team.
- The game will be played multiple times, invoking variations of single-player, squad play, and other fun surprises.
- Ask if there are any questions.
- Have teams draw their drop zones.
- Blow the whistle to start the first round!
- After the first few minutes, begin making announcements to alert players that the playing field will begin to shrink; that is, "In two minutes all players must be inside the *red* circle!" Continue until final players are within the final circle.
- All members of the winning team receive a small prize (candy, a button, etc.).
- Begin a new round!

RECOMMENDED NEXT PROJECT

- Try out a Survival Challenge program based on *The Hunger Games* in the next chapter in this book.

Hunger Games Survival Challenge

SARAH AMAZING
Teen Services Supervisor

Warren-Trumbull County Public Library

THE HUNGER GAMES Survival Challenge encourages players to work together in groups to complete a series of tasks (similar to a scavenger hunt) that entail a variety of survival skills such as foraging, animal identification, first aid, and weapon-making.

Age Range	Type of Library Best Suited For	Cost Estimate
Tweens (ages 8–12) Young Adults (ages 13–18) Adults	Public Libraries Academic Libraries School Libraries	$0–$75

Cost Considerations

This program can be done for as little as nothing, but the addition of drawstring backpacks ($15–$25 for twelve), toy bows ($25–$50), and snacks make for a more memorable experience.

PART III | **Live Action Game Programs**

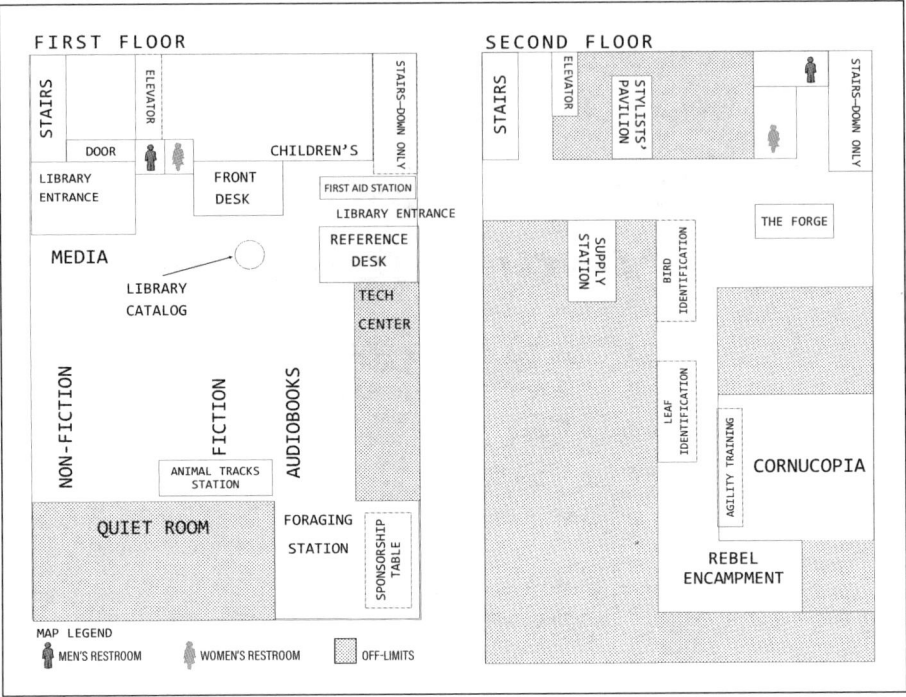

FIGURE 38.1
Map of the W-TCPL Arena

OVERVIEW

While this program can be done by anyone, we recommend it be overseen by someone familiar with Suzanne Collins's series, *The Hunger Games*. If you are not familiar, check out the first book or watch the first movie to get a feel for the survival aspects of the story. Katniss, the heroine of this story, uses a variety of skills throughout the series—hunting, foraging, archery, insect identification, and simply observing her surroundings. This is what this program hopes to emulate.

The bulk of this program is in the preparation, which involves creating the tasks and setting up the *arena*. The number of tasks created should correspond to how long you'd like the program to last. Ten tasks will allow for about forty-five minutes of total program time (including instructions and grading), while fifteen to twenty tasks will allow for about an hour's worth of fun, with fifteen minutes before and after for instructions and grading for a time total of ninety minutes.

This program can be done with one staff member, but we recommend having one to two other staff members on hand to help.

NECESSARY EQUIPMENT AND MATERIALS

- up to twelve bags
- at least ten tasks
- station signs and instructions
- timer/hourglass/stopwatch
- prize(s), if any
- snacks
- research materials as determined by the tasks created such as laptops, iPads, animal identification books, foraging books, etc.
- other equipment as determined by the tasks created such as toilet paper and masking tape, toy bows, craft supplies, etc.

STEP-BY-STEP INSTRUCTIONS

Preparation

- Decide how many teams there will be, with a maximum of twelve (for the twelve districts, as in the story).
- Create at least ten tasks. These can be narrative in format, such as a picture of a common snake with the caption, "You've been bitten by this snake! Head to the Animal Identification Station on your map to determine if you'll survive!" Don't be afraid to get creative! Some ideas:
  - *Foraging*: Find images of berries, mushrooms, and other wild plants and ask players to determine which are edible. If they are wrong, they must sit out (for a predetermined amount of time) until the effects of the toxins wear off. A small hourglass timer is helpful for this task.
  - *Bird identification*: Find images of ten birds, asking players to name them.
  - *Tree identification*: Find leaves from ten trees, asking players to identify which trees they came from.
  - *Snake/spider identification*: Find images of harmless and poisonous animals and ask players to identify which animals are deadly.

- *First aid*: Each team member must construct an arm, leg, or head bandage with toilet paper and masking tape that lasts until the end of the challenge.
- *Fashion design*: Set out materials and ask teams to create unique costumes for their districts.
- *Weapon creation*: Create fuse bead swords, origami shuriken, or pencil arrows.
- *Animal track identification*: Find tracks of common animals and ask players to identify which animals they belong to.
- *Decoding*: Uncover a message using Morse code or a running cypher.
- *Map reading*: In addition to using the map throughout the program, have players use the hint uncovered during the decoding task to find something on the provided map.
- *Trivia*: Ask teams to answer questions from the book/movie.
- *Agility*: Players must successfully finish a level of Just Dance or Dance Revolution, play hopscotch, or complete some other dancing/agility task.
- *Archery*: Tributes must hit a target using a toy bow.

- Print out enough tasks so that every team gets a copy of each.
- Fold the printed task sheets.
- Create a map of the *arena* using areas of the library that are in play. Mark areas that are off-limits and where the various supply stations are located.
- Place a map, pencils, and copy of each task inside each bag.
- Create a grading rubric in order to quickly determine points for each team.
- Set up stations with appropriate materials and instructions to help players complete tasks.
- Place bags in the location on the map that you have labeled as the Cornucopia.

Program Instructions

- Begin the program by welcoming all tributes and split them into teams.
- Go over all the instructions, which should include reminding players not to run in the library, to work as a team on each task, and what (if any) the prize is. Be sure to let them know what time they must return to the Cornucopia for grading.

- Have one member of each team surround the Cornucopia. At the signal, your Hunger Games Survival Challenge can begin!
- Throughout the program, walk throughout the arena to advise struggling teams and/or alleviate confusion.
- When the time is up, announce that all tributes must return to the Cornucopia. Retrieve all tasks from your teams and grade them.
- Have snacks ready for participants to enjoy while they await the results.
- Announce the winning district!

RECOMMENDED NEXT PROJECT

If you haven't already, check out the previous chapter and run the program Live Video Games: Library Battle Royale.

How to Create a Live Clue Game

JONATHAN DOLCE
Branch Supervisor

Astor and Paisley County Libraries

HAVE YOU EVER wanted to host a whodunit mystery event at the library, but you didn't know where to begin? Live Clue may be the solution. Live Clue is a life-sized adaptation of the hit board game, Clue. Participants become the characters and navigate a life-sized board, while a non-playable character (NPC), usually a butler or host, ensures proper game play. The game board comes alive with life-sized props, weapons, and even furniture that denotes the theme of each room in the mansion.

Game play is simple. Three to six players try to figure out the three main facts of a murder that has been committed in the library: the murder weapon, the room the murder occurred in, and the identity of the murderer. To solve the game, players move throughout the mansion and gather evidence. By discussing possible solutions and what process of elimination to use with each other, players get closer to solving the crime.

Younger participants will love dressing up as the characters, while older tweens and teens can practice improvisational (improv) theater. Teen advisory boards can be utilized to help design, create, and implement this program. What's more, this program is highly adaptable—you can incorporate your own theme! Imagine a Harry Potter– or Star Wars–themed Clue game. Plus, it's life-sized! The possibilities are endless!

PART III | **Live Action Game Programs**

Age Range	Type of Library Best Suited For	Cost Estimate
Tweens (ages 8–12) Young Adults (ages 13–18)	Public Libraries School Libraries	$0–$40

Cost Considerations

For Live Clue, the sky is really the limit in terms of the props, costumes, and sets. In terms of costuming, the best strategy is to head to your local charity shop and purchase jackets or blazers that match the colors of the characters. You could buy just the blazers for about $5 each and make everything else from things around the house or library. In terms of the sets, make it as simple or elaborate as you like. For example, if your library has a mini kitchen for children, consider using that for your Live Clue kitchen. No idea what goes in a ballroom? How about a bowl full of tennis balls? Why not? Make it fun! For the billiards room, just use a table and a printout of the balls. A dowel rod makes a good billiard cue. For the study? How about a table, a chair, and some books? Even a simple set is still effective.

OVERVIEW

The game of Live Clue takes about half an hour to complete, so if you have younger children, consider speeding up game play by using two dice or allowing participants to move at diagonals. Younger children can have people help them with tasks such as carrying the clipboard or keeping track of evidence.

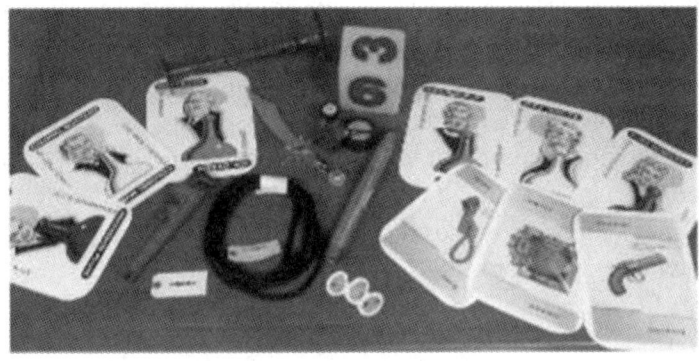

FIGURE 39.1
Some suggested props, cards, and size of dice; note the weapons have evidence tags on them—cool, right?

Because there are only six players possible at a time, consider letting characters have assistants, thereby making a maximum of twelve people on the board at one time. Also, for spectators, have snacks or some board games to play while they wait their turn at Live Clue. In terms of staff, an NPC—a butler or host—is needed to make sure game play is adhered to accurately and that order is maintained. Beyond this, you may need only one other staff member to keep spectators behaving.

NECESSARY EQUIPMENT AND MATERIALS

- a room or space large enough to create the mansion, comprised of nine rooms and space for hallways
- one-inch masking tape, any color
- 8.5" × 11" cardstock—approximately thirty sheets
- 8.5" × 11" detective notebook sheets
- large manila envelope
- life-sized prop weapons
    - wrench
    - gun (toy gun)
    - rope
    - dagger
    - lead pipe
    - candlestick holder
- life-sized furniture
- clipboards with pencils or pens
- costumes
- large dice

STEP-BY-STEP INSTRUCTIONS

Preparation

There are three key areas to plan for:
- the game board or mansion
- costumes
- props

Game Board

The game board does not necessarily have to match the actual Clue board game. Think of the elements of the game as suggestions. If you have the desire, then go for everything. If not, a big square divided up into the nine rooms and hallways is all you really need. If you don't have twelve-inch tile on the floor, or if you have indoor/outdoor-type carpet, determine how many rolls of the die it will take to move from one room to another. See the sets section on the following page for suggestions on making your *rooms* come to life. The secret passages need only be small triangles of black paper for the corners of four rooms.

Make sure you have small, colored discs representing characters in case someone needs to step away or otherwise leave the game. Having a chair in each *room* is good too, so characters can take a rest if needed while other players complete their turns.

Place a table in the center of your mansion with the manila envelope containing the solution. Maybe add some props to this table too, such as a feather duster, graphite, and/or a magnifying glass.

Costumes

Costumes can be as elaborate or simple as you like. Mrs. White's costume could be just a white lab coat. Professor Plum's costume could be a purple blazer. But consider adding more props, like some cool glasses, gloves, or other accessories—things that participants can use to customize their experience. Try not to have many or any props that need to be carried in people's hand(s), as this interferes with holding a clipboard and pen/pencil.

Props

The props for this game are simply the six weapons. You can choose to just print them out on cardstock, or maybe you want to make it the real thing, with a real rope, a real piece of pipe (PVC or otherwise), a real wrench, a plastic knife, a candlestick holder, and a toy gun.

The cards for the game should be made on cardstock. You will need one for each of the nine rooms, six weapons, and six suspects. Traditionally, they are:

- rooms:
    - study
    - hall
    - lounge

- library
- conservatory
- dining room
- billiards room
- ball room
- kitchen

• weapons:
  - knife
  - gun
  - rope
  - lead pipe
  - candlestick
  - wrench

• suspects:
  - Professor Plum
  - Ms. Scarlet
  - Colonel Mustard
  - Mr. Green
  - Mrs. White
  - Mrs. Peacock

• sets—some suggestions for how to *fill* your rooms:
  - study:
    » chair
    » table
    » book
    » desk set (pens, stapler, magnifying glass, etc.)
  - hall:
    » potted plant
    » area rug
    » hat or umbrella stand
    » chair or two
  - lounge:
    » ideally, comfy furniture, but failing that, just about any table or chair combination

- » magazine(s)
- » television/radio
- » prop snacks
- library:
    - » a cart of books, possibly
    - » table
    - » chair
    - » lamp
- conservatory:
    - » lounge-type furniture, but consider plastic outdoor furniture
    - » potted plant
    - » fan
- dining room:
    - » table
    - » chairs
    - » tablecloth
    - » table setting (You can use paper plates and plastic forks/spoons. Take this as far as you like!)
- billiards room:
    - » Use a table and lay green paper on it. Mark the pockets with a black magic marker.
    - » Print out the triangular arrangement of the billiard balls.
    - » Get a dowel rod and make it look like a billiard cue.
    - » Consider using stools.
- ballroom:
    - » chairs for the border of the room (It is, after all, mostly a dance floor!)
    - » Consider adding a big bowl of tennis balls for fun!
- kitchen:
    - » If you have a children's play kitchen, use it!
    - » No play kitchen? Use a table and put some fake fruit/veggies on it—maybe a plate and a plastic knife. Print out a picture of a sink or some groceries. Make it as elaborate or simple as you like!

- Book your room with plenty of time to set up your mansion—include both setup and cleanup times.
- Prepare your mansion the day before so you can just jump into game play on the day of your program. You may need extra hands to help set up, so consider utilizing your volunteers or teen advisory group for setup and cleanup.
- Make your flyers/posters, but also consider making smaller ads in the form of invitations.
- Purchase or otherwise gather your props and costumes and determine what you will use for the sets. You may need a staging area.
- Lay out your props and costumes beforehand and ensure that you have an equal amount for everyone. Arranging them on the day of game play is good too, so attendees can grab what they need quickly.
- Make all your character, weapon, and room cards ahead of time, and gather all your other equipment.
- Consider having prizes for winners. Grand-prize winners could get a copy of the game or one of the movies. Other participants could get a small goodie bag.

Program Instructions

Determine where you can feasibly hold your event and how you will divide it up into nine rooms with space for hallways. If you are going to use multiple props for your sets, you will likely need a staging area.

Setting Up the Mansion
- Use one-inch masking tape to delineate the board.
  - If you don't have one-foot tiles or have carpet, determine what roll of the dice could get a player from one room to another.
  - You can make just a large rectangle to demonstrate where the mansion is, or you can copy the game board exactly—it's up to you and your imagination!
- Determine what props/sets you are going to create. Try to balance how much you put into each room, so you don't have one grandiose room and nothing in another.
- Don't forget to put in some black triangular (paper or cardstock) corners to represent the four secret passages.

- Use colored construction paper to indicate where each character starts using corresponding colors.
- Don't forget to determine where the doors should be for your rooms! Do this by leaving gaps in the masking tape lines of your rooms. Look at the traditional Clue board for ideas based on how many doors there are and where they are located in the game.

Gather Your Costumes
- Using blazers, jackets, or large shirts with colors that reflect the characters' names is probably the easiest costume design for this game. Younger or smaller players can roll up their sleeves if too long. Charity shops tend to have jackets and blazers in every conceivable color.
- Consider a few extra props for players but try not to get props that must be carried. Balance the number of props you have so one character doesn't have more *cool stuff* than another. Accessories could be glasses (try not to get sunglasses), gloves, ties, or hats.
- Don't forget the host/butler! The host or butler for the program is really the person who keeps the game moving along, so a costume is essential for this NPC. You could also make this character a detective. Have fun with it!

Gather Your Weapons
- Determine if you want just cardstock with printed weapons on them or physical (real) weapons.
- Strongly consider using actual *weapons*, as this heightens the authenticity of the experience.
- Weapons:
    - Rope is safe enough, but please don't use string; that would just look silly.
    - Lead pipe—consider using a real one, but PVC pipe works too.
    - Knife—do not use a real knife. Plastic knives are available at local discount dollar-type stores.
    - Wrench—consider using a real one or a toy version.
    - Candlestick—charity shops frequently have large brass candlesticks at exceptionally low prices.
    - Pistol—a toy gun should do the trick but make the tip a bright color.

- Make your deck of cards, ideally from cardstock. I recommend that you make them *life-sized* or oversized, so that they have to be put onto your players' clipboards.
- Art for the cards:
  - Scan and enlarge existing cards from a set you already own or have purchased.
  - Print some out from the internet, adhering to all requisite copyright laws.
  - Make up some of your own using clip art.
- Make *police report* pads for players so they can keep track of the evidence they have found. Use MS Excel or MS Publisher to make a gridded piece of paper with headings for the rooms and for suspects and weapons that can be easily marked off.
- Get a large manila envelope and label it "Case File." This will be used to hold the solution to the crime.
- Make or purchase two large, oversized dice from your favorite retailer.

Setting Up

- Once your mansion is set up, ensure that characters' starting positions are clearly marked. If you have fewer than six players, use those placeholders mentioned earlier to indicate suspects when suggestions are made.
- Lay out the weapons in the various rooms.
- Place your Case File prominently on a table in the center of the mansion.
- Divide your cards into their respective piles of rooms, suspects, and weapons facedown. Place one from each pile into the Case File envelope. Shuffle and divide the remaining cards amongst your players.
- Ensure that players mark off their evidence sheets to reflect the cards they already have in their possession.
- Traditionally, Ms. Scarlet goes first and then, subsequently, the player on her left.

Playing the Game

- Players move around the mansion and try to enter a different room at each turn. Have them roll the dice and then move those number of spaces. If you want faster game play, allow diagonal movement; otherwise, just have players move horizontally and vertically, like a rook in chess. Just don't backtrack.
- Two players can't be on the same square at one time.

- If a player is in a room with a secret passage, at the start of their turn, they can choose to use the secret passage instead of rolling the dice. Players must announce their intention before moving through the passage.
- To enter a room, simply roll a number high enough to make it one space past the entryway to the room.
- You can't re-enter the same room in one turn. Sorry.
- Make sure players are aware that if they wish, they can block other players in a room by standing in front of the room's doorway(s). Trapped players have to wait for a doorway to be vacated before they can exit.

Suggesting a Solution
- Once a player enters a room, they should suggest a solution to the crime, including the room they are currently in, the weapon, and the suspect. The host/butler moves the weapon into the suggested room.
- Once the suggested solution has been made, the other players, in turn, prove the crime false *if they can*, starting with the player to their left. They do this by showing the player whose turn it is a card that shows one of the suggested weapons, rooms, or suspects. If they cannot disprove the crime, the next player is asked to disprove the suggestion. Of course, if no one can disprove the crime, the current player can announce a final accusation or attempt to gather more evidence in a later turn. Only one suggestion can be made in a turn, and you cannot forfeit a turn. To use the same room again, a player must exit and re-enter the room in a subsequent turn.
- *Pro tip*: Let players know that they can make suggestions from their own cards. This helps narrow down suspects, rooms, and weapons and may also mislead other players.

Solving the Case
- If a player is ready to solve the case, they may make a final accusation during their turn. Players can make only one final accusation in an entire game.
- If the player making a final accusation is correct, they are the winner.
- If the player making the final accusation is incorrect, they are out of the game, and game play continues without them. Additionally, their cards cannot be viewed by anyone once they are eliminated.

RECOMMENDED NEXT PROJECTS

So, that was a lot of work. What next?
- Consider using this game for a number of age groups—you can make game play faster for younger participants by allowing for diagonal movement.
- Don't limit this game to just the traditional characters, weapons, or even setting. You can adapt it to dozens of other possible settings and characters, from any form of literature or pop culture. For example:
  - *The Lord of the Rings*: Use the setting of Middle-earth (for example, there's Mordor, the Shire, the Kingdom of Rohan, and more! Plus, this world offers lots of characters. There could be an orc raid during game play, causing players to lose cards! Maybe the objective of the game isn't to solve a murder but to discover who has the *one ring*?
  - *Star Wars*: So many planets to choose from, and so many characters and cool weapons! You could incorporate blasters, ion cannons, light sabers, or thermal detonators into the game. Wouldn't it be neat if there were spy drones who could sneak peeks at other players' cards? Or maybe there could be *Star Wars*-themed traps involved, like a good old-fashioned trash compactor! Wow!
  - *Harry Potter*: Lots of characters to choose from, and—whoa—how about some spellcasting? Maybe a spell could make another player lose a turn? Or, maybe someone has a time turner and can be in two rooms at once? And there's the possibility of monsters!
- For an even greater twist, have teens do improvisational theater, giving their characters unique voices, personalities, dialogue, and character idiosyncrasies such as a twitch or secret crush on another character. There could be a crime within the crime! Like a double homicide! Or, even better, how about throwing in some forensic science?

One last suggestion before I let you go: Maybe one or more rooms is an escape room? [Mind blows.]

Scavenger Hunt
Zombie Tag

KARLENE TURA CLARK
Coordinator, Peer Research Consultant Reference Service

Chester Fritz Library, University of North Dakota

ZOMBIE TAG IS an event that can be run after hours or later in the evening with a soft close, so you can make others aware that the building will be noisy due to the event. It indirectly introduces information literacy by having students find physical *resources* (cards such as housing, food, weapons, etc.) given to them by a librarian. The students need to avoid *zombies* while they seek out computers throughout the building designated as Centers for Disease Control (CDC) stations, where someone is on hand to help them use the information literacy system (ILS) to become aware of and find different types of items including books, maps, encyclopedias, journals, and other physical materials. With the call number in hand, they then retrieve the item and return it to the reference desk without being *bitten*. Each successful item turned in earns them an *inoculation* against one future bite. This event was put together by the author with assistance from Zeineb Yousif (digital initiatives librarian) and Kristen Borysewicz (information literacy coordinator).

Age Range	Type of Library Best Suited For	Cost Estimate
Young Adults (ages 13–18) Adults	Public Libraries Academic Libraries	$0–$50

PART III | Live Action Game Programs

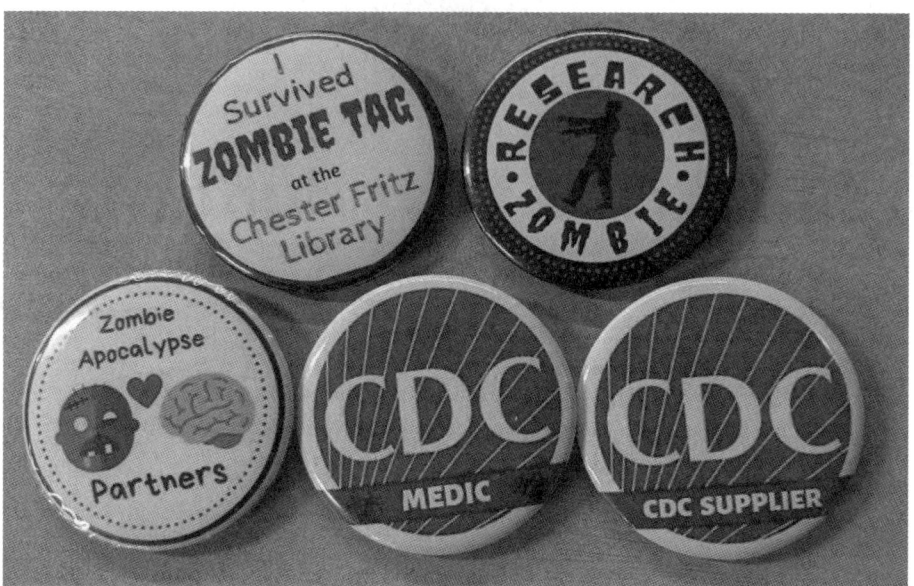

FIGURE 40.1
CDC buttons

OVERVIEW

On the night of the program, plan on having players assemble half an hour before the start in order to go over the rules. Actual game play will be one hour, followed by half an hour to wrap up and award prizes. The staffing listed is reflective of a university library with four floors. We allowed a total of sixty students to sign up for the event:
- two staff members at the Reference Desk to hand out resource and inoculation cards
- one staff member at the Reference Desk to accept materials brought back and to sort/verify the resources
- one staff member roaming the building to monitor for running and fair play
- one staff member, designated as the *United Nations*, to roam the building with special supply drops announced during the game (At our library, we had someone dressed as one of the doctors from the British television series *Dr. Who*, making him stand out—if he could be found!)
- four total student employees for each CDC Supply Warehouse (one on each floor on the opposite side of the building from the Reference Desk)

- They are at the Reference Desk while rules are given out and are introduced as CDC Supply Zone operators.
- We provided student employees with walkie-talkies from the Circulation Department for ease of communication if they had questions.
- Staff members were trained ahead of time to show students how to research but *not* to look up the information for the *living*.
• two student employee *zombies*
  - Once they have each *braaaained* one person, they can become monitors and just walk around to ensure others are playing fairly.
• two theater students for makeup (optional, but most players enjoyed this)

NECESSARY EQUIPMENT AND MATERIALS

• signage
  - *Example*: "The library is open, but a building-wide game is in play. Expect noise and library-wide announcements between 8 and 9 p.m."
  - *Bathroom door signs*: "In a zombie apocalypse, the sewer system is the first thing to go. Don't hide in the bathroom."
• two and a half yards of fabric—make a few extra of each
  - 60 zombie armbands (two will go to the zombie employees)
  - 60 living armbands
• four Supply Warehouse tags for the computer stations
• paper hospital masks
• signifiers for United Nations supply relief
• Halloween makeup for zombies
• a bag of makeup sponges
• notecards for resources
• if possible, lab coats to provide authenticity (we partnered with medical school librarians, who allowed us to borrow coats)
• prizes
  - Besides bragging rights, all students received one of two buttons at the end of the game. You can make buttons in-house if you have a button maker at your library. Some button pronouncement suggestions include:
    » "I survived Zombie Tag at the Chester Fritz Library."
    » "Zombie Researcher" (If they were "*turned*," this was handed out at the end of the game.)

» "Zombie Apocalypse Partners" (for the theater people, those assisting with floor walking, and those monitoring the snack station)
» CDC Medic (for those sitting at the reference desk)
» CDC Supplier (for those at the computer locations)
- You could also print out "Certificate of Literacy Zombification" (living or dead).
- You could also try to get gift certificates from local game stores for free game rentals.
- walkie-talkies or two-way radios, if possible
- snacks and drinks

STEP-BY-STEP INSTRUCTIONS

Preparation

- Clear the event with building administrators and, if applicable, with your campus Events Office.
- Waiver forms will be needed for each person participating.
- Pick a team to oversee the planning. This can be all librarians or a mix of librarians and staff members working on an outreach committee. Three to five people will be required to organize all preparatory materials.
  - Write out each of the cards.
    » Verify that you have sufficient materials from each category such as maps; government documents, such as a CDC sanitation publication; books; DVDs; etc.
    » Some cards can be general: a movie title that features zombies, shelter, food, water, protection, etc.
    » Some cards can have specific instructions: "Find a sanitation publication about X using a database," or, "Find the address to a senator's office—they need to know we won't stand for this!"
    » Our list, Resource Topics, is included at the end of the chapter and is based on materials available in our library.
    » Write "Inoculation" on a separate stack of cards.
  - Create the armbands.
- Pick a team to oversee the event.

- Talk to a local theater company about doing makeup for those who become zombies.
  - Our game provided great practice for UND's theater department!
- Promotion (before and after) avenues may include:
  - campus tour representatives
  - social media
    » example: www.facebook.com/watch/?v=2682228428669398
    » example: http://blogs.und.edu/und-today/2018/10/zombie-apocalypse-at-the-library
  - university newsletter
  - flyers
  - bookmarks
- pre-sign-up sheet to gain an estimate of interest
  - Walk-ins should still be welcome, provided it does not go over the limit approved by your Events Office. New participants could just add their name to the list that night.
- Have the student CDC operators participate in a half-hour reference training session before the event with a librarian to find out how to properly find (and teach others to find) the specific resources on the computer (in case *the living* have trouble).

Program Instructions

- Make sure waivers are signed.
- Have all students verify or add their name to the numbered sign-up list.
  - Tell them to remember the number by their name. This will be used to organize their resources.
- Tell students:
  - "The CDC has no idea what happened. A mysterious affliction has hit the country hard. Zombies are on the rise! To survive, you need to find the resources before the zombies find you."
- Provide *living* armbands to all players. Instruct them to only tie a half-knot.
- Introduce the two *zombies*, the CDC operators, and the *United Nations ambassador*, then let these three groups go off to their chosen locations.
- Hand each person (or team) one resource card.

Resource Topics

Food
- cookbooks (cooking game)
- native animals to the state for hunting
- native fruits/vegetables
- how to purify water

Clothing
- how to sew
- homemade armor
- protective clothing

State Weather
- weather patterns
- current weather

Shelter
- types of plants (trees)
- how to build a shelter
- tools for building
- Boy Scouts 101
- how to start a fire

Weapons
- common types of weapons for hunting
- survival tactics
- basic info on guns/bows and arrows
- knives
- how to acquire the weapons

Health
- nutrients you need to survive
- first aid
- common injuries and how to treat them
- infectious diseases
- the CDC—what is it?
- bug repellants

Maps
- Orienteering 101
- how to read a map (topography)
- map of the state
- map of the university
- map of the library

Zombies
- CDC Zombie Preparedness (online only—the CDC actually has this document!)
- movies on zombies
- famous zombies
- zombie encyclopedia
- Staff members (designated by their lab coats) should move throughout the building to ensure no one is running.
- While the above items are set into place, either hand out a sheet with the rules of play or have a digital screen where they can be shown.
  - Players may start as teams, but just like any apocalypse scenario, they are sure to lose members.

Rules (for the zombies):
- no running (Zombies can only shamble, after all!)
- no attempts to snipe other players at elevator or stairwell doors or at computers
  - Zombies keep moving!
- Players can *bite* the living by gently tugging on their armband. (Having players say "braaaains" while they do it might make this feel more authentic!)
- If a player hands you an inoculation card, let that player go. Take the card and turn it in to one of the roaming staff members.
- If played while the library building is open to everyone: If a person is without an armband, they are not playing! (This helps library patrons who are not involved in the game avoid an unwanted zombie *bite*.)
- If a person is at the snack table, they are in timeout and not playing.

Rules (for the living):
- no running (We'd rather not have accidents cause *real zombies*!)

- Research your supply item before you are bitten.
    - Bring one item from the area—there is no extra credit for bringing two or more of your resources.
- If you are bitten, report immediately to the Reference Desk to be revived and obtain a new zombie armband.
    - Players could also get *zombified* by the theater department's makeup experts!
- no hiding in the bathrooms
- Have a snack and take a quick rest at the snack station but remember you can only remain there temporarily. To survive, you need to keep moving!
- If played while the library building is open to everyone: Only a zombie can remove your armband. If your armband is otherwise removed, you will be asked to report back to the Reference Desk.

Can you gain an inoculation?
- yes—by finding a necessary resource and taking it back to the Reference Desk
- How this works:
    - You are given a supply item (food, clothing, shelter, weapons, etc.).
    - Once you are away from the Reference Desk, find a computer to look up books on that topic.
    - Take the call number and make your way to the location of your supply source!
    - With the item in hand, navigate around the zombies and head back to the Reference Desk.
    - You will gain a card that says "inoculation"—this is good against one bite. After that, sorry, buddy. It's a new world out there! (But if you make it back with your resource without needing it, we'll give you another resource to go find, giving you a chance to get more!)

How do I win?
- Game play will go to a specified time or until only a few remain *alive*. Those left alive win. But zombies are cool. So, we all win.
- Everyone reports back to the Reference Desk when the announcement to do so is made on the PA system.

Additional instructions
- announcements every fifteen minutes

- Assign each of the CDC operators a codeword ahead of time. This can be a color, an animal, etc., but not the computer terminal number or floor number. Using the radios, announce one of the assigned codewords every fifteen minutes so the appropriate operator is kept apprised.
- Over the PA system, announce: "A Supply Station has been overrun! There are no resources available there now.... Good luck, survivors!"
    » This slowly makes it harder for the players to gain supplies as the hour goes on. It also starts moving play toward the end of the game.
    » Just like in a *real* zombie apocalypse, the survivors need to use word of mouth to let each other know which stations have shut down. This means some people will still be going to the *overrun* stations for a few minutes after a shutdown occurs.
- Announce at random intervals:
    - "There has been a supply drop from the United Nations. They have provided two resources. . . . Here's hoping it's what you need, survivors."
        » These resources still need to be the type of item(s) players are looking for to be of benefit to them.
        » The United Nations person can either carry a sign and the two resources or stand next to the location of the items on the shelf.
- Announce five minutes before the end of the game: "The United Nations has been able to organize extraction of all survivors. Their transport will arrive at the Reference Desk in five minutes. Start making your way toward freedom, and good luck reaching us!"
- While the game is being played, organize the resources (cards) brought in by the number assigned on the sign-up sheet.
    - Stack all the resources into a numerically ordered pile, tucking a resource card into each book.
    - If not a good resource, the item is out of play and placed to the side.
- Announce the Ultimate Survivor (grand prize).
- Hand out buttons or other fun swag.

What about prizes?

Everyone should have something to walk away with. However, the big prize should be more substantial and can be a gift certificate to the local game store for a free board game rental. Choose the option that works best for your library when setting your reward parameters:

Option 1:
- At the beginning of the game, everyone can put their name in the bowl.
- Each time a survivor returns to the desk with a resource, you can add your name one more time.
  - If you come as a group, only one of the team members may put a name in the bowl.
- A name will be pulled after everyone reassembles at the end of the game.

Option 2:
- Resources you turn in will be stacked by your sign-up number (to maintain anonymity) with the card tucked inside.
- The person or people with the most items that best fit the resources will win the prize!
- Take pictures!

RECOMMENDED NEXT PROJECTS

- You might revise or adapt this scenario for your next game to incorporate a holiday theme. Instead of zombies, perhaps rogue elves are attempting to break into Santa's workshop and must be stopped.
- Alternatively for a springtime game, you could use a Monty Python theme from the movie Monty Python and Holy Grail in which players must avoid killer rabbits.

How to Create a Mini-Golf Mini-Tour

KAITLYN MAY
Access Services Librarian, Hood College

MARY ATWELL
Archivist/Collection Development Services Librarian, Hood College

EMILY HAMPTON HAYNES
Public Services Librarian, Carroll Community College

TWEENS AND YOUNG adults explore the library while putting around a course designed to highlight library resources and services targeted toward them. They will golf the course, moving through the service areas you want them to know about: group study rooms, information desks, graphic novel collections, or anything else you want to feature. This program can also be given a theme with decorations and signs to inform golfers about things going on at the library, including upcoming events or changes such as a library remodel. The golf course you create can be made more difficult by adding curves and hazards to suit a higher age group of golfers. You can get as creative as you want with this program: add flags at each hole, offer food at the beginning or end, hand out prizes for the most holes-in-one and so on.

Age Range	Type of Library Best Suited For	Cost Estimate
Tweens (ages 8–12) Young Adults (ages 13–18)	Academic Libraries School Libraries	$10–$200

LIBRARY MINI-GOLF										SCORECARD
Name	1	2	3	4	5	6	7	8	9	Total

FIGURE 41.1
Mini-golf scorecard

Cost Considerations

For office supplies, $10 to $20 is required. Program costs increase with the purchase of practice holes, golf balls, and any add-ons,

If your school has a golf team or club, the best option is to partner with them and ask for a loan of their golf equipment, including putters and practice putting cups. A local mini-golf course may also be willing to loan equipment, especially in the off-season, or your local thrift store probably has inexpensive equipment.

If costs or materials are limited, there is the option to designate one putter per hole so that the players would circulate but the putters would remain at their assigned holes.

OVERVIEW

The Mini-Golf Mini-Tour is designed to showcase the best and most important services and resources your library has to offer whatever age group you are targeting. You may want to be sure tweens see the library's graphic novel collection or remind them they can check out a guitar from your Library of Things. Academic libraries can highlight a newly installed meditation room; or, if you have an upcoming renovation, take people around a course of existing service points and include signage that explains changes to come, complete with architectural renderings. School libraries can showcase specific books and materials for upcoming projects, highlight nonfiction versus fiction, and so on. Think of the golf course as a self-guided tour of the library.

NECESSARY EQUIPMENT AND MATERIALS

- a theme
- golf putters
- nine practice putting cups
- approximately thirty-six golf balls
- scorecards and pencils
- numbered signs to designate holes, as well as sign holders or tape to display them
- the floor between rows of shelves to act as a course with barrier walls
- thick-spine books to build additional course walls
- brightly colored masking tape to mark the tee (starting point) of each hole
- miscellaneous materials to construct hazards on the various holes
  - cardboard ramps
  - potted plants
  - bookends

STEP-BY-STEP INSTRUCTIONS

Preparation

- Create and print scorecards. Using Microsoft Word or Publisher, create a 5" × 11" table and label the left-top box "Hole Number." Label the remaining top row of boxes with the numbers one through nine. Print scorecards on cardstock for easy writing.
- Gather your course-building supplies (tape, miscellaneous hazard materials, thick-spine books) and identify areas where you want to construct holes. Each hole should ideally be in sight of the next hole so that people can clearly see the path they are to follow.
- Build your course. Use the natural barrier of bookshelves as much as possible when creating holes. Place a putting cup at the end of each hole and be sure to create a barrier behind the hole for the ball to rebound if your hole doesn't end against a shelf or wall.
- Get creative: Place potted plants on the course holes to act as hazards, create ramps out of cardboard, or prop books up on their covers with the pages open to let people shoot the ball through the middle like a tunnel. Use tape or other materials to mark a tee-off spot at the beginning of each hole from which patrons should take their first shot.

Program Instructions

- If possible, have a staff member or volunteer posted at the beginning of the course to help people get started. Participants will need a ball, putter, scorecard, and pencil.
- Most of the work for this program is in the planning; the participants should be largely self-guided, although younger age groups may benefit from staff members or volunteer supervisors posted along or roaming the course to direct them.
- Be prepared for some noise; consider making an announcement if the library is open to patrons during the event.

RECOMMENDED NEXT PROJECT

If your participants enjoyed being active and moving around the library, consider creating a scavenger hunt with more library discoveries.

Spy Hunt
A Library Research Scavenger Hunt

KRISTEN CINAR
Instructor, Library Services

Suffolk County Community College

IN THIS PROJECT students will assume the role of secret agents in General Washington's Culper Spy Ring as they complete a scavenger hunt designed for researchers. They will race to solve a series of historically inspired coded clues for which library information and various research skills are required to complete. This spin on the traditional scavenger hunt activity will engage students as they learn more about accessing resources in the collection and utilizing other helpful library tools and services available to them. The inclusion of handheld puzzles and a competitive point system adds incentive for participants to find the correct answers and focus on the hunt's desired learning outcomes. The project not only offers students practice performing basic library research but also requires them to build on skills such as teamwork, problem-solving, effective communication, and creativity—all of which will help prepare them for academic success and the working world.

Age Range	Type of Library Best Suited For	Cost Estimate
Adults	Academic Libraries	$0–$50

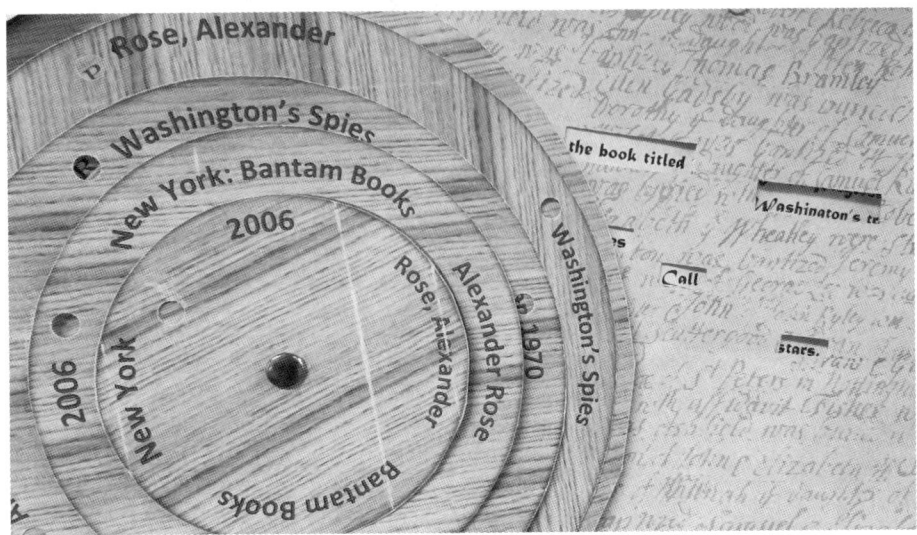

FIGURE 42.1
Handmade puzzles inspired by historical spy techniques

Cost Considerations

Little or no cost is involved. You may wish to create text *masks* or *screens*, decoder wheels, or other tricky-to-solve yet easy-to-make tools out of everyday office supplies. They may consist merely of materials, such as paper and brass paper fasteners, to achieve the desired effect.

For libraries with access to a 3D printer, sites such as thingiverse.com and other free online file repositories can provide access to a printable cryptex, puzzles boxes, and more, which can take your hunt to the next level!

For clues that involve invisible ink, consider purchasing a set of pens online that both write in disappearing ink and reveal the message with a UV light on one end. Sets of such pens can be had for less than $10.

OVERVIEW

In this project, students will learn about performing the basics of library research by solving a series of clues that require finding and utilizing information in the library's physical and virtual spaces. Basic information covered may include finding various branches and key areas, locating a book on the shelf, accessing an article through a database, finding an online subject guide, using proper citation, and performing searches using Boolean operators. Teams should consist of two to five students so there are enough players to communicate and solve clues together but not so many that more timid members shy away and lose interest. Each team will receive a packet of numbered clues that require them to find a piece of information that the library deems helpful or essential for their research. A clue for utilizing a database could be written as follows:

> Welcome, agents! You have now entered Rowe's Tavern. In an empty office in the back, you see a wooden desk with three small jars of bromine, gum arabic, and cobalt. Also noteworthy are some stacks of old American newspapers on the floor and a fireplace whose flames are almost extinguished. What database do the old newspapers inspire you to consult? Once there, enter all three names on the vials in one search to see if they lead to anything that might help reveal your secret message!

To answer a clue like this, players would require a smartphone or computer. They should access America's Historical Newspapers or a similar newspaper archive database that your library subscribes to. You might even specify one in the clue. Performing an advanced search using the names of the materials and the word "and" should reveal one or more articles about invisible ink. All the tools necessary to solve the clues should be provided in the initial clue envelopes at the beginning of the game. For this problem, players would choose the included pen that has a discreet UV light at one end. Shining a light on their clue sheet would reveal a secret word or message that provides players with the hidden answer.

Information gathered at each location will be required to complete the clue's riddle or puzzle. Feel free to modify historically inspired methods to suit your needs. For instance, a great take on the traditional cipher wheel might be requesting players to align the various layers of the wheel in proper citation order for a book they must find to reveal the letters or numbers that the clue requires them to identify.

Timing is an issue that can be problematic in an academic setting due to conflicting class schedules. For this reason, it may be helpful to offer an extended block of time in which the scavenger hunt is live, allowing groups to play at a time during which members are free. While some schools do have a common hour in which no classes are offered, clubs and departments often fight to take advantage of this time, leaving students with the difficult task of choosing which event to forgo.

Decide if any help should be offered, even if it comes with a point deduction. Players should not feel stuck or discouraged. Consider offering hints via virtual chat, if that service is offered at your library. While this may be frowned upon for more than one clue, it could be beneficial to market the service and allow players to experience using the electronic reference tool.

NECESSARY EQUIPMENT AND MATERIALS

Materials are dependent on the puzzles you wish to use. Online searches can help find an assortment of puzzles you might want to try with instructions on how to create them economically. Supplies that are essential:
- paper for clues, answer sheets, and, if you desire, an optional survey for the end
- writing utensils in the clue packets
- envelopes for each clue
- a large envelope to contain the clue envelopes, puzzles, and answer sheet
- certificates or prizes for the winners
- *Optional puzzle supplies*: brass paper fasteners, colored cellophane for *red filter* clues, invisible ink paint or pens, or UV lights or pens

STEP-BY-STEP INSTRUCTIONS

Preparation

- Backward plan to determine what educational information you wish players to take away from the activity. It may be helpful to approach some teaching faculty members during this process if you wish to include content relevant to courses being taught or enlighten instructors about an upcoming event they may wish to promote to their students.
- Consider what puzzles you might wish to include. Online research can help spark some ideas. I've assembled a few of my personal favorites at https://sites.google.com/view/kristenspuzzles. If you have a gaming program in your library, make use of some of the game pieces. Although not a historical decoding technique, spelling out a word or title using Scrabble pieces could be a stealthy way to reveal the numbers you need

for the next puzzle or clue! Assembling tiles in the proper order could reveal the digits to a missing phone number of a branch so players know where to head next.
- Invite staff to test out your clues and puzzles to iron out any kinks and identify areas of confusion. A staff run-through can also be a good time and difficulty indicator.
- Promote the project to departments and campus organizations. Social media marketing is a must! Performing all the prep work involved is quite a process. You'll want plenty of participants to enjoy the finished product, so get the word out to spark interest.

Program Instructions

- Require registration or collect interested parties' e-mail addresses so you can send a reminder beforehand as well as game-day instructions. If individual participants require a team, you may assign one during the days before the event so they can make plans to meet at a set time and location.
- Inform staff of the times that the event will be live so they can prepare for players to be wandering about their floor.
- As teams arrive, provide them with their packets and verbally reiterate the instructions and rules. Record each team's name and members.
- Record the end time if it's a timed event.
- Consider having one or more staff members walk around and take photographs of the event in progress for publicity purposes.
- Ask staff to monitor the state of each clue as teams leave the area.
- At the end of the activity, collect all the clue packets and answer sheets. Remind participants that they should complete and submit any optional surveys at the determined submission deadline.
- If the event is timed, tally points when all members have returned and announce the winner. If a larger window of time is planned, inform players that the winner will be announced via e-mail and social media by the end of the day.
- Post a summary of the event on your library's homepage and on social media to share your success and spread interest in the activities offered by your library.

RECOMMENDED NEXT PROJECT

Offer an online scavenger hunt so the clues need not be location-based. Use free programs, such as Google Forms, that allow you to make an entertaining quiz or choose-your-own-adventure-style scavenger hunt online. Going digital with your project could also be beneficial if you wish to offer an educational game for distance learners.

How to Run a Fandom LARP

ELIZABETH R. STRAUSS
Teen/Outreach Services Manager

Dover Public Library

ADVENTURERS, ASSEMBLE! PLAYERS will explore the library while facing enemies from multiple fandom universes in this highly customizable live action roleplaying (LARP) experience. Each team will consist of four participants, each with their own role to play within the team, complete with special powers and responsibilities. An additional Game Leader assigned to each group will ensure fair play throughout the experience. The Game Leader will be responsible for the team as they venture through the library on the hunt for their enemies and clues. Let the best team win!

Age Range	Type of Library Best Suited For	Cost Estimate
Tweens (ages 8–12) Young Adults (ages 13–18)	Public Libraries School Libraries	$0–$50

OVERVIEW

This program requires a large room or set of rooms for adventuring. Setup includes hiding enemies throughout the space and printing out cards and printables. The program itself will run approximately an hour, with time

FIGURE 43.1
Customize your game to feature any fandom, including Harry Potter.

added for larger-scale or more complicated adventures. The individual teams are designed to consist of four players and a Game Leader. Ideally, Game Leaders should be staff, volunteers, or trusted players. Staffing needs will depend on attendance. For this reason preregistration will be needed, but plan for flexibility regarding accepting players to the game.

Many options are included in this guide to make your Fandom LARP more or less complicated to fit the needs of your space and your group. Pick any fandom or create your own characters. Add clues and challenges to make the game last longer or to keep it simple. Above all, have fun.

NECESSARY EQUIPMENT AND MATERIALS

- per team:
  - six dice
  - one set of hit point (HP) tokens*
  - one set of HP cards*
  - one set of character ID cards*

- one set of Attack Damage Cards*
- one set of Custom Enemies (hidden in the library)*
- two Ziploc bags (for the Game Leader to keep the dice and HP tokens)
- scrap paper and a pencil (math)
• blank character IDs for flexibility*

Optional Substitutes or Additions

- non-standard dice
- collectibles (such as coins) hidden throughout the library
- one set of Bonus Cards* (to win in the battle) per team
- one set of Challenges* (one per enemy) per team
- optional prizes

STEP-BY-STEP INSTRUCTIONS
Preparation

- list your fandoms (*Harry Potter* elements are used in the example preparation below)
- for each fandom, pick out five characters to fulfill the following roles:
  - Game Leader (Dumbledore)
    » responsible for their team playing fairly, not destroying the library, and for taking on the role of the monster in the game
  - Scholar (Hermione)
    » Roll an odd number to learn the enemy's weakness(es)—the roll still counts for damage.
  - Rogue (Harry)
    » If a player rolls a five, they dodge the attack from the monster.
  - Knight (Ron)
    » one extra dice for the attack (six dice max)
  - Healer (Ginny)
    » can heal up to ten HP per teammate per turn* *or* revive one teammate per turn to max health if they have *died* (Healing/reviving counts as your turn. If you do not heal, you can roll.)

- For each Fandom, pick out at least five enemies for the team to battle, each with a weakness and with varying total HP and attack damage. More HP and uncommon weaknesses make for a more difficult enemy or a Boss.
    - Level 1 Enemy (Troll)
        » HP: 50
        » Attack Damage: 4
        » Weakness: Roll an odd number to double your total attack damage.
    - Level 2 Enemy (Pixie)
        » HP: 100
        » Attack Damage: 4
        » Weakness: If your roll total is an even number, add five to your total attack damage.
    - Level 3 Enemy (Dragon)
        » HP: 100
        » Attack Damage: 5
        » Weakness: Roll a six to do an extra two damage points (per six rolled).
    - Level 4 Enemy (Nagini)
        » HP: 150
        » Attack Damage: 5
        » Weakness: If you roll exactly two ones in your set, you automatically win.
    - Level 5 Enemy (Voldemort)
        » HP: 200
        » Attack Damage: 6
        » Weakness: None
    - Add additional enemies for a longer game.
- Customize and print your game pieces.
- Create optional challenges* to go with each monster (see Revival Options).

CHAPTER 43 | **How to Run a Fandom LARP**

Program Instructions

Game Setup
- Teams of four characters and a Game Leader pick their theme.
- Each team member randomly draws their max HP card and takes that amount of tokens.
- Each team member randomly draws their Damage Card and will roll that many dice when it is their turn to attack.

Game Play
- Teams find a monster with their insignia to fight (such as a lightning bolt).
- The first team member rolls to attack the monster. The total number rolled is the damage inflicted on the monster. The Game Leader subtracts this damage from the monster's HP.
- The Game Leader rolls the number of dice listed as the monster's attack damage. The total number they roll is the damage inflicted on the first team member.
- The second team member takes their turn.
- Play continues until the monster is defeated or the whole team is out of HP.

Revival Options
- If playing the game just for fun, the team is simply Revived if everyone perishes, with the Game Leader noting how many times the team lost a battle.
- If playing the game as a race, the team suffers a timeout of thirty seconds in case of death, as timed by the Game Leader.
- If you're a fan of trivia and puzzles, add more challenges to the monster battles.
  - Each monster comes with a challenge such as a riddle or puzzle to solve.
  - If players solve the challenge before the team runs out of HP, the Game Leader can revive the whole team and send them to the next battle.
  - If playing without bonuses, the revival can only be used if the team is out of HP.
  - If playing with bonuses, the revival can be used at any time in the battle but using the Revive forfeits the bonus.

Optional Bonuses
- After defeating a monster, the player who strikes the final blow receives a bonus (cards can be attached to each monster with a paperclip).
- The player can share the loot with their team, but they do not have to.
- Bonuses are not revealed until the monster dies.

Winning Options
- Race: The first team to defeat all their enemies is the winner.
- Points: Assign positive points for winning and negative points for losing battles, along with bonus points for finding collectibles or solving clues. The team with the highest score wins.
- Everyone wins: If the team defeated their enemies, they won!

RECOMMENDED NEXT PROJECTS

Check out chapter 1: "Beyond Dungeons & Dragons: Building a Roleplaying Program" by Robert Taylor and Danielle Costello, chapter 2: "How To Start Tabletop Gaming Programs at Your Library, for Absolute Beginners" by Mark Halvorsen and James Tyner, and chapter 7: "Dewey and Dragons: Dungeons & Dragons at the Library" by Jamey Rorie.

*Download examples and templates at https://toomanyhobbies18.blogspot.com/p/downloads.html.

Anything Bingo

ELIZABETH R. STRAUSS
Teen/Outreach Services Manager

Dover Public Library

MAKE A FUN game of Bingo with limited preparation and unlimited possibilities using this easy tutorial. You can use Anything Bingo as a craft or a game and fit it to any theme, age, group size, or budget. Make Superhero Bingo, Color Bingo, or even Spanish Bingo. The program could also be used as part of a longer event, such as a lock-in or summer reading kickoff. You can do anything with Anything Bingo!

Age Range	Type of Library Best Suited For	Cost Estimate
Kids (ages 3–7) Tweens (ages 8–12) Young Adults (ages 13–18) Adults	Public Libraries School Libraries	$0–$50

OVERVIEW

This program is highly adaptable. One staff person should be sufficient to run the program for teens and adults. For younger audiences, parents or extra staff should be on hand to help, depending on the attendance. The program should take an hour to an hour and a half. Group size is only limited by the space that you have and the prizes you want to provide. Some preparation is involved, but the process can be as simple as finding pictures and making enough copies for attendees.

In the technique outlined in this chapter, participants make their own Bingo cards with the materials mentioned below. This technique ensures that each Bingo card will be unique without a lot of effort from the program organizer: you.

FIGURE 44.1
Alice in Wonderland gets the Anything Bingo treatment.

NECESSARY EQUIPMENT AND MATERIALS

- Bingo card templates (at least one per participant)*
- Bingo pictures (one-and-a-half-inch squares, twenty-four to a sheet, and one sheet per Bingo card, plus one set for the caller)*
- bowl or basket (to put the caller's set of pictures in)
- scissors
- glue sticks
- Bingo markers (e.g., squares of colored paper, candy pieces, plastic discs)
- prizes

STEP-BY-STEP INSTRUCTIONS

Preparation

Pick Your Theme
- Find twenty-four pictures to fit that theme and resize them to one-and-a-half-inch squares on a sheet.
- free graphic resources:
  - https://pixabay.com
  - https://canva.com

Make a Sample Board
- Print out one Bingo board template and one set of pictures.
- Cut out the pictures.
- Arrange the pictures on your board any way you want.
- Glue the pictures down.

Make Your Caller Set
- Print out one set of pictures, preferably on cardstock, to distinguish them from your other sheets.
- Put them in a bowl, bucket, or basket for your caller.

For Younger Audiences or a Faster Game
- Cut out the pictures and place them in their own bags or bowls.
- Use stickers instead of pictures for an even easier cardmaking process.

For a Longer Game
- Use more than twenty-four pictures to create more variations of boards.

To Limit Printing Costs
- Print in black and white, using colored paper if desired.
- Print two boards to a page and two picture sets to a page to save paper.

Program Instructions
- Give each participant one Bingo card template, one set of pictures, and one set of Bingo markers.
- Have participants cut out the pictures and glue them on the board in whatever configuration they like.
- Randomly draw pictures from your bowl and start calling them out.
- For a faster game, have players keep their markers on their boards even after someone calls Bingo.

RECOMMENDED NEXT PROJECTS
- Make your own custom version of Monopoly.
- Customize a LARP game using a fandom LARP.

*Templates are available at https://toomanyhobbies18.blogspot.com/p/downloads.html.

Stop the Mad Librarian
A Library Orientation Escape Room

SUSAN M. HANSEN
Director of Library Services

Hoffman Family Library, Goodwin College

PARTICIPANTS WILL BE introduced to the library's collections, physical space, and online resources and services by participating in an interactive escape room experience. This program is an engaging way to highlight both the unique qualities of your library and the creative talents of your staff. The escape room can be modified for your target age groups and can be easily tweaked to serve as an after-hours fundraising activity for a Friends of the Library group. Participants will learn team-building skills, problem-solving skills, critical-thinking skills, and basic information literacy skills to keep them on the path toward lifelong learning—all while having fun!

Age Range	Type of Library Best Suited For	Cost Estimate
Tweens (ages 8–12) Young Adults (ages 13–18) Adults	Public Libraries Academic Libraries School Libraries	$10–$50+ (depending on supplies used)

PART III | Live Action Game Programs

FIGURE 45.1
Four successful groups from an English 101 class thwarted the mad librarian's plan and trapped her (back row in hat) in her office.

OVERVIEW

Typical escape rooms use dedicated rooms for game play. This project uses portable *clue stations* to guide participants throughout the library. The stations are easy to break down and store, and the escape room experience can be set up in a matter of minutes. It can be used during the hours of library operation with little interruption to other library users. The experience should be timed; an hour is an ideal amount of time, but you can customize every aspect of this activity.

The escape room activity needs a storyline to pique interest and present the primary set of instructions. Storylines can be linked to a staff member, a local history legend, an item in a special collection, a mascot, or anything of interest to your patrons.

Participants will navigate the library, following numbered clue stations, to solve a variety of tasks in search of clues that will lead to success. Groups of four to six people work well, as everyone will have a chance to help with problem-solving. Tasks should have multiple parts and include a variety of challenges. Tasks should not require additional instructions, although hints can be given if a group is having trouble with a problem.

Tasks can be as easy or as complicated as you make them. A library staff member, or other volunteer, should accompany each group through the escape room activity to give an occasional hint and monitor group behavior—if one group member has been *taking over,* the guide can encourage everyone to participate.

NECESSARY EQUIPMENT AND MATERIALS

- endless imagination
- four small, numbered signs (one through four)
- five mason jars
- two hollow fake books—one with a three-digit combination lock compartment
- three nesting boxes
- a blacklight flashlight
- a four-digit *realtor* (key storage) combination lock that fits over a door handle
- one 8" × 10" (approximate) three-digit combination lockbox (or locking money box)
- jigsaw puzzle, six pieces (created on a computer and cut out)
- riddles, photos, and *diary page* clues (created on the computer)
- iPad or other media device to play a music video clue
- red, yellow, and blue markers
- a printed copy of a color wheel showing primary and secondary colors
- clipboards
- six rocks of various shapes and sizes and one fake rock (the type intended to hide a key inside)
- *invisible ink* (fluorescent blacklight) marker
- two packages of colored origami paper; one 5⅞" × 5⅞" and one 9¾" × 9¾"
- a chess (or checkers) board that opens to store your playing pieces
- a small basket
- skeleton key (from a craft store) or any unused key
- Before you purchase any materials, ask staff members to bring in unused items from home. Anything destined for a tag sale is a perfect candidate for a clue! Old locks and keys, unused children's toys (a Rubik's cube, slide puzzles, brain teasers, matching games, word find puzzles, etc.) can be easily incorporated. This is a very inexpensive project to bring to fruition—and that's a librarian's favorite kind!

STEP-BY-STEP INSTRUCTIONS

Preparation

Mad Librarian Escape Room Details (Clue pictures are online at http://bit.ly/MadLibrarian)

- I advise spending several weeks creating the clues and riddles and designing tasks. Clues and props can be largely handmade and very low-tech. Find volunteers to test the escape room when you think it is ready and ask for feedback.
- *Storyline*: The Mad Librarian discovered a rare, single-volume edition of J. R. R. Tolkien's *The Lord of the Rings* in the library's collection, a book she had coveted for years. She has planned for weeks to devise a successful way to steal the book and make it her own. Unbeknownst to her, pages from her diary (where she has been detailing her scheme) slipped out in the library, where they could provide clues to her devious plot if anyone came across them. She left the rare book locked in her office and plans to return in an hour to take it from the library forever.
- *Challenge*: Find the combination to the lock on the Mad Librarian's office door and save the book. Visit all four of the clue stations and solve a series of puzzles and tasks. At the completion of each clue station, you will uncover one of the numbers needed to open the final box.

Program Instructions

Prepare all four stations, then guide your groups to the numbered stations in order.

Station One: The Table with the Hollow Book and Lockbox
Preparation
- Take the yellow, red, and blue markers and use a Sharpie to write numbers on their sides, as follows: "red = 5," "blue = 2," "yellow = 4."
- Take three photographs of the Mad Librarian (have a staff member play the part!) in this order: 1) touching a book on a shelf, 2) carrying the book through the library, and then 3) holding the book as she stands in her office doorway.
- On a computer, tint the first picture purple, the second picture orange, and the third picture green. Print the pictures and place them in the hollow fake book along with the three colored markers, the printed color wheel, and the following printed *diary page* clue:

CHAPTER 45 | **Stop the Mad Librarian**

- "At last, the special book I have wanted for so long is in my reach! It was never my *primary* purpose here to steal it, but it became a *secondary* obsession that colored my judgment."
- Close the hollow book and place it on a table.
- Set the combination on the metal lockbox to seven-nine-six. Write a clue on a slip of paper that will lead the group to any book in your collection that you want to use. A unique title works best. For example, to lead people to the book, *The Black Belt Librarian* (a book you placed on display somewhere in the library), the clue would say, "To find the next puzzle on your way, find this book that is on display: An individual who certainly knows how to fight, all while researching books throughout the night. . . ." Place this clue and the blacklight flashlight in the lockbox, close and lock the box, and then place it on the table next to the hollow book.
- Use the invisible ink marker to write a large number "7" on page 54 of *The Black Belt Librarian* (or any other title you choose to use).
- Write the following clue on a slip of paper to tuck inside the cover of that book that will lead to the page with the invisible ink number: "To retrieve the book as rare as a jewel, find the page number that follows this rule: higher than 15, lower than 65; even number, digits add up to 9." (Both pages 36 and 54 fit this rule; page 36 is a red herring.)

Doing the Activity

- Give each group of participants a clipboard, pen, and piece of paper to write down clues as they find them.
- Read the *Storyline* and *Challenge* to the group.
- Walk the group to the first clue station. Allow the group to explore the two items on the table.
- The group needs to place the tinted pictures of the Mad Librarian in a logical sequence order (purple, orange, green, etc.).
- Then the group needs to use the numbers written on the three primary-colored markers to identify a corresponding number for the secondary-colored pictures:
    - purple picture = red (5) + blue (2) = 7
    - orange picture = red (5) + yellow (4) = 9
    - green picture = blue (2) + yellow (4) = 6

This is the most difficult clue. Prompt the group to examine everything from the hollow book and consider why it is part of the clue. Give hints about creating secondary colors if players seem lost.

- The group needs to use the numbers from the color clue in order (7-9-6) to open the lockbox. Prompt the group to carry the blacklight flashlight from the box with them while they follow the rhyming riddle in the lockbox to locate the book on display.
- Using the clue inside the book's cover, the group needs to shine the blacklight on the correct page (54) to reveal invisible number "7."
- The group should write this number on their clipboards as the first digit of the final lock.
- The group can then proceed to station two.

Station Two: Nesting Boxes
Preparation
- Have staff members create a brief book record for the title *Keepsakes*. Assign a call number to the record. Search for this title in your catalog and make sure it is the only result—or the first result—the search retrieves.
- Write "Keepsakes" on all four sides of the largest nesting box, write "Memories" around the middle box, and write "Photos" on the smallest box.
- Place the two following clues in any two of the boxes:
  - Diary page: "I think the library staff is getting suspicious. They are watching my every move. To confuse them, I have brought in boxes of photographs and memories. I'm pretending to share my *keepsakes* while I plot to steal the ultimate treasure. . . ."
  - Written clue: "Help! The Mad Librarian has hidden a clue in a book. In order to find out which book, go to the library's online catalog and type in the correct word. . . . *Keep* your goal in mind and be quick, for your *sake*, or the precious volume she will take!"
- Stack or nest the boxes on a table or counter next to the sign for station two.
- Create a spine label for the fake book with the combination lock and assign it the call number for the *Keepsakes* record.
- Place a slip of paper with the number "4" in the fake book. This is the second number needed for the final lock.
- Set the combination for the fake book to 3-7-9.

- Close and lock the book and then shelve it in the correct place in your collection.
- Print a copy of the poem from the beginning of The Lord of the Rings. It begins, "Three rings for the Elven-Kings under the sky . . . "
- Place the printed poem in an acrylic display stand (or picture frame) and place it next to or above the shelf location of the fake book.

Doing the Activity
- Escort the group to station two and give them time to open all the boxes and find the printed clues.
- The group needs to find a library computer and look up the fake book title, Keepsakes, in the online catalog. (Note: if the record for the fake book is not the first one that comes up in your catalog search, you should prompt the group to look at the correct record where it appears in your result list.)
- The group should note the call number and then locate the fake book on the shelf.
- If the group does not notice the Tolkien poem after several minutes, let them know it is the final part of this clue station.
- The group needs to use the first word from each of the first three lines of the poem to correctly identify the combination that opens the fake book, 3-7-9, and retrieve the second number of the final lock (4), which should be noted on their clipboards.
- Proceed to station three.

Station Three: Library Special Collection and Database Search
Preparation
- Place the third numbered sign near your special collection (local history room, art gallery, etc.) and leave a written clue designed to simply direct the group to any other part of the library. For example: An academic library might have a special collection of Anatomy & Physiology (A&P) models that includes a small, standing skeleton. This station could begin with a note taped to the skeleton's hand that says, "Help me find the pieces of my friend," which would lead people to a box of bones in the A&P collection and the second clue. You can use the skeleton clue in your library by substituting a framed picture of a skeleton with the written

clue taped to the frame, and the "pieces of my friend" can be a second copy of the picture cut up and resting on a tray or in a shallow open box that also holds the second clue.
- The second clue is a *diary page* that says: "This is too easy! The other librarians pay no attention! I've used a database search on the library website 1,000 times, always typing 'Sadako Sasaki,' just daring them to stop me. If they did that same search and looked closely at the *second result*, they would have a hint of what I am up to." (*Note*: Test the search for "Sadako Sasaki" in your library's databases and look for a result that includes an image of a paper crane or the words "origami crane." Edit the diary page clue by replacing the word "second" with the correct number for your result list. This clue *must* point the group to the search for paper cranes.)
- Fold five small origami paper cranes in different colors and four large paper cranes in different colors—make sure one large crane is red. (Instructions are easily found online.) Write each number from 1 to 9 on one wing of each crane. Be sure to write the number 6 on the large red crane.
- Take a picture of the Mad Librarian holding a large red book; print and frame the picture.
- Stand the picture on a table and place the nine cranes around it. The big red book in the picture is the clue that points the group to using the number on the big red crane as the third digit in the final lock's combination.

Doing the Activity
- Walk the group to the third clue station. The written clue should be easily visible. The group will need a little time to discuss the clue and decide where it will lead them next in the library.
- When the group finds the second clue, they will need to go to a library computer to search for "Sadako Sasaki" in a database search.
- The search result provides the *paper crane* clue.
- The group needs to search the library to find the table with the paper cranes and the Mad Librarian photograph.
- Solving this clue provides the group with the third number of the final lock (6), which they then write on their clipboards.
- Proceed to station four.

CHAPTER 45 | Stop the Mad Librarian

Station Four: MediaScape (or any large monitor in the library)
Preparation
- Cut small shapes from colored paper: red hearts, yellow stars, yellow keys, orange crowns, and white flowers.
- Tape one red heart to the outside of a mason jar and then place the remaining hearts in the jar; repeat this process with each remaining shape and jar.
- Take a chess piece (or checkers piece) and hide it in the jar of hearts. Hide any other small object in each of the remaining four jars (examples: paperclip, file cabinet key, penny, flash drive, etc. It doesn't matter, as these four items are red herrings.)
- Create a six-piece jigsaw puzzle with an image of a basket and cut the pieces out. Place the pieces inside the chess/checkers board.
- Put the rocks in the basket. Write the number 4 on a slip of paper and hide it in the fake rock; add the fake rock to the basket.
- Place the basket in any library location you wish.
- Download the music video "Jar of Hearts" by Christina Perri to an iPad (or any other media device or laptop).
- Connect the iPad to the large monitor on MediaScape.
- Set the music video to play repeatedly.
- Place the fourth-numbered sign and the filled mason jars on a table near the monitor playing the music video.

Doing the Activity
- Walk the group to the table with the mason jars.
- The group will need to notice the music video in order to select the correct jar. If several minutes pass, prompt them to consider the music video as part of the clue. (The phrase "Jar of Hearts" is repeated in the lyrics and shown as the song title.)
- After the group opens and examines the jar of hearts, they discover the chess or checkers piece that directs them to find the game board.
- Finding and opening the game board reveals the jigsaw puzzle.
- Completing the jigsaw puzzle leads to the search for a basket.
- When the group finds the basket, they need to examine the rocks to find the fake one and open it, revealing the final number (4) to be noted on students' clipboards.

Final Challenge: Unlocking the Mad Librarian's Office
Preparation
Set the four-digit realtor/key storage lock combination to 7-4-6-4 and hang the lock on a door in the library to represent the Mad Librarian's office. Hide a small ceremonial key inside the lock.

Doing the Activity
Guide the group to the door. They should have recorded the numbers on their clipboards over the course of the escape room activity. By successfully entering the numbers, opening the combination lock, and finding the hidden key, they are declared winners and congratulated for stopping the Mad Librarian. Take a *victory picture* of the group to post on library social media as further promotion of the escape room. If you want, you can make small signs for the group members to hold up in this photo op, with declarations such as: "We stopped the Mad Librarian," "The One Book is safe," "We did it!" or anything else fun.

RECOMMENDED NEXT PROJECT

If your escape room is a success, start planning a new one so people come back for more.
- Make a note of what type of clues people liked best. Hi-tech or no-tech? Puzzles or riddles? Add more clues like those to the next event.
- Design rooms just for fun! Possible themes could come from local legends, a popular book or movie, or an escape room version of the game Clue.

How to Run a Library Research Gamification Program

LISA NJOKU
Senior Strategic Legal Analyst

Greenberg Traurig, LLP

THIS LIBRARY RESEARCH gamification program is designed as a tournament-style game that pits multiple participant teams against each other in friendly competition. The game is intended to incentivize use of library research databases in an entertaining way and is customizable to different resource types, skill levels, team sizes, and timeframes. Participants compete for their teams in a single-elimination bracket and for individual points and prizes. Players are motivated to engage in the competition as part of a team that they feel accountable to, as well as for the individual and team rewards and recognition. This program leverages game-based learning to increase awareness of the targeted information platform, create a long-term learning opportunity, and improve research skills, thereby maximizing the value of the gamified resource.

Age Range	Type of Library Best Suited For	Cost Estimate
Young Adults (ages 13–18) Adults	Public Libraries Academic Libraries School Libraries Private Libraries	$0–$500

Cost Considerations

Costs are flexible and designated for prizes for participants. The research resource vendor may offer to sponsor prizes, or the library may provide simple swag. Rewards can be virtual such as recognition via badges or awards. The prizes are not required to be expensive, just creative.

OVERVIEW

During the selected timeframe, such as a four-week tournament, teams will be matched against a new team each week. The teams eliminated in their face-off will move to the loser's bracket, where members can still compete for individual prizes unrelated to team success. Losing teams continue to play for a place in the final standings.

Points are tallied after each matchup based on predetermined, measurable actions (e.g., in-resource activities or logins, clicks that designate an online viewing or action, viewing a training video, or other relevant resource activity). Consistent communication (one to two contacts per week) is recommended to keep players aware that the game is ongoing. For example, every week, during the competition, send an announcement listing the top users and team winners and a separate notice explaining a new feature or useful aspect of the tool. These tips can be related to the actions required to earn points to increase motivation and improve game engagement. At the end of the tournament, the team that has won all its matchups receives a grand prize such as lunch, massages, or team gifts. The top three individual winners each week receive a badge or small token award.

NECESSARY EQUIPMENT AND MATERIALS

- a computer with e-mail access

STEP-BY-STEP INSTRUCTIONS

Preparation

- Select the library research tool you would like to gamify based on criteria such as:

- the opportunity to positively change workflow
- how much learning potential is possible, especially if the research method is new to your library (e.g., artificial intelligence resources including analytics)
- how the increase in that tool's usage will result in an overall savings for the library
• Determine your target audience. Which users is this tool designed for? Do you have any preliminary usage data you can review? Scale the program up or down based on need.
• Consider your staff workload, your target audience, and which season(s) during the year the proposed game period could take place in so you can choose a timeframe that maximizes participation.
• Separate your target audience into even teams based on location, level, title, etc.
• Choose a theme that is familiar to a wide audience and that will hold players' interest (e.g., March Madness or Summer Olympics). Use free online images or ask your marketing team to design your online communications if they're available.
• Identify champion users of this tool in your library who can act as marketers and provide feedback.
• Introduce a management to gamification business proposal and project plan to garner support and enthusiasm from the top down.
• Determine the length of the game and the time allowed between the rounds (weekly rounds over a four-week period is typical).
• Determine how to use the metrics gathered after each event. Many libraries can track the use of research tools via internal tracking platforms or by requesting usage data from the research database vendor.
    - Depending on your source, metric data can vary. You can use login data, IP authentication, searches run by players, specific other actions taken with the research tool, downloads, printing records, etc.
• Create your bracket and leaderboards. These can be as simple as free online bracket templates and a list of leaders and team standings in an e-mail message or as advanced as designing a website or intranet page to house tournament brackets and a weekly leaderboard. Badges or accomplishment completion notifications can be sent to players via e-mail as an embedded image.

Program Instructions

Promotion
- Create and send theme-based promotional print information: flyers, posters for public areas, etc.
- Send research vendor swag if any is available.

E-touches to Users
- Send a pre-gamification launch communication to patrons announcing upcoming games, giving a brief description and timeline of the event.
- Send a launch communication with information about teams, rules, and prizes.
    - *Optional*: Include an extra-points opportunity in your launch e-mail to encourage immediate engagement.
- Send weekly winner communications at the end or start of each week based on your tally date for both top individual players in each measured research category and team winners and losers of the week. Announce next week's matchups as well.
- Send weekly research tip e-mails midweek that reference ways to gain points and provide more information about the resource.

Training Sessions
- Hold a kickoff training webinar; invite all participants to attend to learn how to use the research platform.
- Host additional webinars or in-person group training sessions where appropriate.
- Provide a recording of a training session for those unable to attend.
- Trainings sessions can be incentivized by counting your players' attendance toward overall game point totals.

Incentives
- Offer weekly awards such as gift cards for top users.
- Include a grand prize for the first-place team such as a chair masseuse service for team members and/or a catered lunch, etc.
- First-place individual awards for each category could be gift cards and first-place certificates.

Measurement

- Quantify user engagement levels by tracking percentage increases in the number of users and game usage over the program period.
- Gamification identifies new resource users. The top players amongst this group are always a source of fresh feedback and are champions amongst their peers in terms of gamification progress and postgame adoption.

RECOMMENDED NEXT PROJECTS

Take your gamification project to the next level by introducing a different style of game, finding ways to offer additional feedback points, or incorporating additional technology software such as e-learning authoring tools (Captivate, Elucidat, Articulate, etc.).

Laser Tag in the Stacks

STEVEN WADE
Instructional Services Librarian

JULIE HORNICK
Instructional Services Librarian

RANDALL M. MACDONALD
Library Director

MARINA MORGAN
Metadata Librarian

Florida Southern College Roux Library

IN THIS ENGAGING live action Laser Tag in the Stacks event, participants join teams and take on other participants to see who will be the first to complete their mission, all while avoiding elimination. Missions take participants on a search for the secret of time travel, hunting for clues to rescue and transport a VIP to a safe place, controlling essential resources for survival on a new planet, or recovering the lost diaries of Count Dracula. This event is fully adaptable for any audience—from teens to adults—and costs can be controlled using equipment suited to your budget.

Age Range	Type of Library Best Suited For	Cost Estimate
Young Adults (ages 13–18) Adults	Public Libraries Academic Libraries School Libraries	$150–$300 for purchased equipment

Cost Considerations

Kits with four laser tag blasters and vests range in price from $60 to $130. To supply two teams of four players, budget twice that amount for the equipment, plus the cost of rechargeable or disposable batteries and supplies.

Rental costs vary widely. Having equipment shipped to your site and scaled to your event or holding managed events staffed by gaming companies are all factors that can contribute to your overall expenses.

OVERVIEW

Laser Tag in the Stacks is an exciting group event for teen and adult patrons. Two teams of players will roam the stacks, completing missions and attempting to eliminate their rivals. The size of your teams will depend on the number of blasters and vests, as well as the amount of space in your library available to devote to your game. Teams of at least three players are recommended for the best results. Run this program after hours with the lights off for a truly immersive experience!

FIGURE 47.1
Poster developed by Donna Marie Alfano for Laser Tag in the Stacks at Roux Library, Florida Southern College

Missions should be designed to be completed in a twenty- to thirty-minute time period, depending on the complexity of the objectives. Common laser tag missions include last man standing, capture the flag, or a scavenger hunt. For examples of custom missions, see the link in the list of Necessary Equipment and Materials.

Participants should sign up in advance and arrive at least five minutes before their scheduled game. Have a plan in place for walk-ins and for participants who sign up but do not show. Allow at least fifteen minutes between each game to reset any props or objectives, to clean gear, and to provide a safety talk and training demonstration for new players.

Depending on the size and scope of the event, a staff of four to six people should be sufficient. One person should check in players as they arrive and manage a waitlist for walk-in participants. Another can demonstrate the equipment and deliver any rules or safety procedures. Each game should have at least one monitor on hand to answer questions about the missions and deal with equipment failures or other issues. Plan to have at least one floater who can move between stations and relieve other staff members as necessary. The team can also work together to reset the props between missions.

NECESSARY EQUIPMENT AND MATERIALS

- laser tag blasters and vests
- rechargeable or disposable batteries
- site-specific or generic game missions to facilitate interaction or learning
- game props
- disposable disinfecting wipes
- paper for flyers, signs, and posters
- laminating materials (optional)
- Supplemental material can include specialty lighting and objects to add ambiance.
- Sample missions and other materials can be found here: http://bit.ly/LaserTagRoux.

STEP-BY-STEP INSTRUCTIONS

Preparation

- Consider whether you may encounter sensitivity to the idea of holding a laser tag event or to marketing that features shooting imagery. Choose language appropriate to your users (e.g., blaster vs. gun; tagging vs. shooting). Secure supervisory permission, if necessary.
- Research laser tag kits or gaming vendors.
- Decide whether to purchase or rent equipment or to hire a gaming company to manage the activity.
- Secure equipment or schedule a vendor to obtain any necessary supplies.
- Define the playing field and establish game rules (e.g., no removing non-mission books from the shelves, no physical contact between players, etc.).
- Develop or adapt game missions; many examples exist online.
  - Create a menu of missions for participants.
  - Decide how the end of each mission will be defined (e.g., time-based or the completion of the mission objective).
- Develop a promotional strategy to reach your audience:
  - Create engagement with your patrons by posting on social media.
  - Add the event to your events calendar.
  - Design and distribute flyers.

- Develop a sign-in plan.
    - Consider having advance sign-up.
    - Predetermine how to accommodate walk-ins who have not preregistered.
    - Have a plan for accommodating late arrivals.
- Test equipment and run through each mission in advance.

Program Instructions

- On the day of the event during setup, manage access to the staging and playing areas if necessary.
- As participants check in, have pairs of teams select a mission from the menu.
- At the assigned time, gather team members in the staging area for safety, equipment, and game orientation.
    - Ask patrons not to put on or experiment with equipment until instructed.
    - Inform players about the game rules.
- Signal players when the game begins and ends.
- After each mission:
    - Reset your props.
    - Check equipment functionality.
    - Change batteries as necessary.
    - Clean equipment.
    - Verify that the next group is ready to begin.
- At the conclusion, assess the event with team members and other stakeholders.

RECOMMENDED NEXT PROJECTS

- Experienced gamers can be recruited to create new missions, instruct participants, and assist with staff events.
- Collaborate with local game clubs to promote their events and organizations.
- Tailor missions to other local events (e.g., homecoming, civic festivals, holidays) or use specific themes, etc.

Save Lewis the Librarian!
An Information Literacy Escape Room

RUTH CHO
Instruction and Outreach Librarian

Biola University Library

IN THIS ESCAPE room program, college freshmen will be tasked with the mission of rescuing Lewis the librarian from the clutches of scientist-turned-evil-mastermind Dr. Weston, who has kidnapped Lewis from the library, shrunk him to a tiny size, and hidden him somewhere in the Weston home with plans to perform brainwashing experiments on him. Students will need to work collaboratively, gather clues, solve puzzles, and exercise information literacy in order to find Lewis before Dr. Weston returns home from grocery shopping. This escape room should be a fun way to introduce freshmen (e.g., first-year seminars or freshmen experience courses) to your library services, reduce library anxiety, and provide students an opportunity to think critically about the information they use. You can easily modify the suggestions given in this chapter to better serve your own situation and students.

Age Range	Type of Library Best Suited For	Cost Estimate
Adults	Academic Libraries	$100–$300 (You may already have many of the materials and supplies needed for this program on hand.)

OVERVIEW

An escape room is essentially a room containing challenges that a team of players must overcome in order to accomplish a mission within a limited amount of time. A Game Master (GM) explains the rules to the players before they enter the room and observes the players while they play the game. The GM also gives players hints when they aren't sure how to proceed. In this escape room event, a room in your library will serve as Dr. Weston's home; a class of freshmen will be the players working together to find Lewis, who in our example is a LEGO figure; Lewis is locked away and hidden in the room; and a librarian will be the GM.

The room might be a computer lab, conference room, or meeting room. Whatever room you choose, make sure it is not so large that players will need to cover a huge amount of space to look for clues. On the other hand, make sure it is not so small that a class will be uncomfortably packed in the room. Students will need space to move, cluster in groups, and perhaps even have an outburst of excitement when a puzzle is solved. You may have space in your library to dedicate solely to the escape room for the, say, week or month you decide to offer it. In this best-case scenario, you can leave props and clues in the room. However, if your library does not have a room you can dedicate solely to the escape room for the duration you offer the program, you will need to remove the props and clues from the room each time a class is finished and bring the props back when needed.

Most, if not all, groups should be able to escape this room within thirty minutes. (You want students to leave feeling that they have accomplished a mission rather than feeling defeated and daunted by the library.) However, you will need a few minutes before students enter the room in order to give directions. You will also need time after the room is completed in order to debrief the students on their mission details and either clean up the room or set it up again for the next class. Therefore, do not schedule classes in thirty-minute increments; rather, allow at least one hour for each class.

A single librarian should be sufficient for setup and can act as GM during the game. Require professors to stay with their students so you do not wind up as a babysitter of sorts, taking care of their class for an hour. Most professors will find amusement in staying and observing their students during game play.

CHAPTER 48 | Save Lewis the Librarian!

This escape room requires considerable time and effort at both the preparation and execution stages; obtaining buy-in from your library management can make the process go more smoothly. There will almost certainly be students who don't enjoy it and don't see the value of the activity, but the majority of players will likely have fun and appreciate getting to team up with their classmates while learning about the library and using information literacy skills. The feedback my library received was overwhelmingly positive. Some student comments are listed below:

- "I felt way closer to my class and learned how to work with them."
- "It got me to talk to people in the class that I wouldn't normally talk to."
- "I feel like I'll come to [the] library now."
- "Please let me do this as a sophomore. I will be sad if I can't do this again."
- "Great, creative way to get acquainted with the library!"
- "I learned about resources within the library."
- "I loved every bit of it."

The primary criticism received was that too many students were in the room; we allowed classes of up to forty students to participate. I recommend limiting the class size to fifteen or twenty students. Large classes could break into small groups to minimize congestion.

NECESSARY EQUIPMENT AND MATERIALS

Links to specific supplies and documents you can print for this program are available in the Dropbox folder at tinyurl.com/please-help-lewis. Links for widely available and general items (e.g., sheet protectors, glue) are not included in this folder.

Miscellaneous Supplies

- a room with tables
- a laminator (I highly recommend laminating all your paper props for durability.)
- Scotch tape
- a sound system (if you want to play background music)
- a countdown clock
- a LEGO Series 7 Computer Programmer Minifigure

Toolboxes

- three Dollar Tree toolboxes
  - You might want to consider purchasing a few extra boxes in case one breaks. These toolboxes are well worth the $1 they cost, but they are a bit flimsy.
- two Hyper Tough sixteen-inch toolboxes from Walmart

Locks

- five-letter word lock
- Master Lock 1500iD
- Master Lock 4680
- Master Lock 4697D
- Master Lock 5900
- Wordlock LL-207-SL

Supplies for the Book Safe

- AmazonBasics Book Safe, Key Lock
- How to Identify Fake News in Ten Steps checklist
- three URLs that lead to a background information tutorial, fake news question, and video footage

Supplies for the "Cite Your Sources" Puzzle

- a "Cite your sources" sign
- cipher key
- an "All caps with spaces" sign

Supplies for the Library Spaces Puzzle

- printed floorplan(s) of your library
  - Depending on how many levels your library has and how many spaces you want to highlight, you might decide to print the floorplan of only one or multiple floors.
- transparency sheet(s)
  - The number of transparency sheets you need will depend on how many floorplans you print. If you print only one floorplan, you will need only one transparency sheet. If you print two floorplans, you will need two, and so on.

- "Notes on Lewis' Workday" document
  - You will need to modify this document to reflect the spaces in your library that you want students to know about.

Supplies Needed to Unlock Three-Number Lock

- "Scientists Develop Shrinking Solution" newspaper article
- pictures of Dr. Weston
- Dr. Weston's research binder
- sheet protectors
- "Is this source scholarly?" sheet

Supplies for the Canvas Puzzle

- a small art canvas (6" × 6" inches in size should be fine)
- a small hairdryer
- red thermochromic pigment
- red acrylic paint
- Elmer's school glue
- 3M Command Strips

Supplies for the Shadow Art Puzzle

- a wooden slab
- various random objects (cardboard, small wooden blocks, pieces of plastic, etc.)
- hot glue
- a small flashlight
- colored paper (two different colors)

Supplies for the Block Animal Puzzle

- a WEYFLY Traffic Block Animal Puzzle
- an invisible ink pen
- a blacklight
- several chads (the circles that are punched out when you holepunch paper)

STEP-BY-STEP INSTRUCTIONS

Preparation

Before Your Escape Room Goes Live

- If you have never tried an escape room yourself, consider attempting one. There is likely an escape room facility in your area. Conducting your own escape room exercise isn't necessary, but the experience will help you understand the concept of escape rooms if you are not sure how they work. Find an escape room facility on Yelp, make a reservation, and recruit a few of your friends to go with you; you are guaranteed to have a fun time.
- You will certainly need students to participate in the escape room; so, decide how you will promote your program. Promotion can be as simple as e-mailing a link to a Google Form to professors who teach first-year seminar courses. The form might ask professors for their name, e-mail, first- and second-choice time slots, and if they would like to compete for the leaderboard. In your e-mail, briefly explain what an escape room is and perhaps even include some student learning outcomes for the program. Sample student learning outcomes based on participation in this program are below.
    - In this escape room, your students will:
        » identify scholarly sources
        » differentiate real news from fake news
        » recognize that research requires strategic exploration
        » identify key spaces in the library building

- Consider whether you would like to have a leaderboard. Including a leaderboard featuring the fastest class's completion time (e.g., Team Professor's Name, 17:07) on a lightbox might engender a little friendly competition on campus. You can find a lightbox with letters for $10–$25 on Amazon or at Target. Consider featuring a photo of the winning team on the library's social media channels after all scheduled classes have had their turn in the escape room.
- Plan enough in advance so that you have time to test the room with library staff members prior to going live with students. Testers will give valuable feedback on possible improvements, and testing will ensure that puzzles work as intended.

CHAPTER 48 | Save Lewis the Librarian!

Preparing the Puzzles
- Please see the "making and understanding the puzzles" PowerPoint presentation in the Dropbox folder at tinyurl.com/please-help-lewis.

Understanding the Flow of the Room
- Please see the "flowchart" document in the Dropbox folder at tinyurl.com/please-help-lewis.

Setting Up the Room
- Please see the "setting up the room" PowerPoint presentation in the Dropbox folder at tinyurl.com/please-help-lewis.

Program Instructions

Before Students Enter the Room
- Welcome them and introduce yourself.
- Tell them this should be a fun activity that will allow them to work together as a team while learning about the library.
- Briefly explain what escape rooms are and how they work for those who have never experienced one before.
- Give them a few tips and guidelines.
  - Divide and conquer; don't move together as one huge mass.
  - Communicate—the best teams do this well. If you find something, someone on the other side of the room might need it, even though it seems useless to you. Keeping apprised of team members' progress and needs will help players advance in the game.
  - Everything is used only once; so, if someone has already used it, it can't be used again.
  - Don't use any excessive physical force. Things can break! If there is a box you want to open, make sure you've first unlocked the lock before you open the box (we had a student break open a toolbox).
  - Don't cheat by inching open a box and pulling its contents out if you haven't unlocked the lock first.
  - There are numbered hint cards in the room, and they look like this (show them a sample hint card as you mention this tip). Example: "If you are stuck and want me to give you a hint, just give me a hint card. But use your hint cards wisely because you have only [a specific number] of them. You will not be penalized for using your hint cards."

- Keep players apprised of everyone's status on the leaderboard. For example, "The current leader is Professor Polly's class, who had an unbelievable time of fifteen minutes and seventeen seconds (show them the leaderboard if you have one)! Just an FYI. No pressure."
- If you are in a room with computers, I recommend not allowing phones because students will be able to use the computers to access the internet. We had a student use a phone flashlight to solve the shadow art puzzle, even though the class hadn't found the flashlight in the game yet. Keep an eye out for sneaky students using phone flashlights or other apps.
- Give them their mission: "Dr. Weston, evil scientist, has kidnapped my coworker, Lewis, shrunk him to a tiny size, and hidden him somewhere in the Weston home with plans to perform brainwashing experiments on him. Thankfully, for all his evil genius, Dr. Weston is forgetful and forgot to lock his front door today, and you—the freshmen of Smart University—have come as Lewis's last hope. Will you be able to find Lewis and save him from Dr. Weston's diabolical plan? You must hurry! Dr. Weston is scheduled to return from grocery shopping at Trader Joe's in exactly thirty minutes! Students, your mission to find Lewis before Dr. Weston returns begins with this: your first clue. It's a key." (Hand a student the key to the book safe.)
  - Show pictures of Lewis and Dr. Weston when giving students their mission so that students know that they are looking for a LEGO figure and can recognize that the creepy man whose likeness appears in the room is Dr. Weston.

Once in the Room
- Start the clock and music.
- Observe students as they attempt to accomplish their mission.

After Students Have Finished the Room
- Ask them to sit down and hold a debriefing, discussing aspects of the room. Sample discussion questions include:
  - "Can the people who worked with the floorplans tell me where the reference desk is? How about group study rooms?" (Tell them about key library services and make it clear where students can go for research help. This is a great opportunity to allay library anxiety in freshmen.)
  - "Why should we cite our sources?"

- "Can the people who worked using Dr. Weston's research binder tell me what you learned about scholarly sources?" (Talk about the peer review process and its significance. How can students access scholarly sources?)
    - "What are some ways we can identify fake news? How about a satirical piece?"
    - "What sets many library resources apart from Wikipedia or Google search results?"
- Ask them to fill out a brief survey, either online or on paper. Possible survey questions include:
    - Did you gain or learn anything by doing the escape room? If so, then what?
    - Were there things about the escape room you particularly liked and/or disliked?
    - Do you think the library should offer the escape room for next year's freshmen?
    - Any other thoughts or comments?

RECOMMENDED NEXT PROJECTS

- Explore other ways you might gamify learning.
- Incorporate active learning and experiential or "learning by doing" elements into library instruction sessions.
- Also check out chapter 34: "How to Run an Instagram Scavenger Hunt for New Student Orientation" by Susan M. Hansen, chapter 36: "How to Organize an Escape Room for Faculty" by Maya Berry and Melissa Wright, and chapter 45: "Stop the Mad Librarian: A Library Orientation Escape Room" by Susan M. Hansen.

How to Run a History Mystery Program for Teens

RUTH COVINGTON
Publicity/Event Specialist

Orem Public Library

PARTICIPANTS WILL ROAM the library, looking for clues, facts, and quotes from historical characters to help them solve a history mystery, such as what became of the lost colony of Roanoke, who killed John F. Kennedy, the identity of Jack the Ripper, or the disappearance of Amelia Earhart. This program is geared toward teenagers and young adults, all of whom can enjoy interacting closely with historical characters and evidence while using critical-thinking and reading-comprehension skills to try to solve a mystery.

Age Range	Type of Library Best Suited For	Cost Estimate
Young Adults (ages 13–18)	Public Libraries School Libraries	$0–$1,000

Cost Considerations

The main costs for this program are associated with researching, compiling, designing, and printing the information for the historical characters played by volunteers or staff to share with participants. Costs can also increase depending on how elaborate your history mystery props and costumes are.

OVERVIEW

After an introductory letter or speech from a volunteer or staff member posing as a historical character, participants will be given a map of the library directing them to the locations of other characters, props, and information, and a worksheet of questions to ask each character. The locations in the library should correspond to historical locations that are of significance to the historical characters who will be interviewed. The number of characters and amount of information can vary widely depending on how long and involved you'd like the program to be; if you are short on actors, actors can play more than one character connected to their historical location.

FIGURE 49.1
History mystery program character

A live history mystery night is best done in small groups (three to five people) over the course of one night. Treats can be included, along with a solution party at the end during which participants can compare their conclusions and vote on which theory is their favorite. The program should last about two hours—one hour to visit all the locations and fill out the worksheet and another to analyze the evidence, come up with a solution, and compare/vote on the conclusions at the end. If you anticipate a large group (over fifty people) attending your live history mystery night, you may need to divide participants into larger groups, recruit more than one actor per location to interact with the groups as the different historical characters at that location, or create handouts for the actors to simply distribute to the teens rather than recite to them the information. Because this is an interactive and noisy program, it is especially fun to do after hours when the library is closed.

NECESSARY EQUIPMENT AND MATERIALS

- about two to three staff members to manage the program and six to eight staff members/volunteers to pose as different historical characters in different locations of the library that represent historical places
- costumes, name tags, and scripts for each actor describing each historical character's name and what each character said, did, or reported that is of significance to the mystery
- signs or other decorations denoting the historical locations and characters the groups will be searching for in the library
- any other relevant historical information actors might need to give to participants (such as maps, photographs, objects, or handouts) to examine as evidence
- a packet for each group that includes the following:
    - a worksheet of questions to ask each historical character
    - a map of the library with all the locations they need to visit
    - a space to write their proposed solution
    - writing utensils
- a space (a wall, whiteboard, etc.) for participants to display their proposed solutions

STEP-BY-STEP INSTRUCTIONS

Preparation

- Writing a history mystery program requires a lot of background research. What is the official explanation for the mystery? Why do people agree or disagree with this explanation? Are there any recent developments due to new technology or information? Look for evidence from books, websites, museums, and historical connections in your community.
- As you read about the mystery, make a list of the different theories you wish to explore and the evidence supporting or challenging them. Aim to have at least three theories and no more than five. For each theory, do the following:
    - Compile quotes from historical characters, whether in the form of written letters, phone calls, secondhand reports, official reports, or journal entries.

- Find historical photographs of people, places, and objects relevant to each theory.
- Organize the quotes, photographs, and other evidence so that it can be presented in different locations in the library by different historical characters.
- Enhance your evidence by adding as much detail as you like. Gather costumes, props, maps, and historical artifacts—or the closest substitutes you can find—to serve as tangible evidence. Play music appropriate to the era. You can even encourage teens to come in costumes befitting that time period.

Program Instructions

- Begin the program by having a significant historical character, or host character, greet teens and deliver an introduction. This introduction can be prerecorded and played for the teens or read/recited in person. It should introduce the basic facts of the mystery and the questions you are hoping to answer, as well as situate participants in the historical place and time period they will be exploring. Here is an example:

    Greetings from the White House.

    I am Eleanor Roosevelt, wife of Franklin Delano Roosevelt, president of the United States of America. I am also the friend of Amelia Earhart, the famous female pilot who was the first woman to fly solo across the Atlantic Ocean in 1932. We were both passionate about advancing educational and professional opportunities for women and we both loved to fly. Once Amelia and I even flew from the White House to Baltimore and back—just for fun.

    On May 20, 1937, Amelia made an attempt to fly around the world. She left from Oakland, California, and flew through South America, Africa, and Southeast Asia, finally arriving at Lae, New Guinea, on June 29. She had completed 22,000 miles of her journey and only had 7,000 miles and the Pacific Ocean to cross. On July 2, 1937, Amelia and her navigator, Fred Noonan, departed from Lae and headed for Howland Island, approximately 2,556 miles away. At 7:42 a.m., the *Itasca*, a U.S.

Coast Guard ship on station at Howland Island, picked up a message from Amelia: "We must be on you, but we cannot see you. Fuel is running low. Been unable to reach you by radio. We are flying at 1,000 feet." At 8:45 a.m., Amelia reported, "We are on the line 157 337. We are running north and south." Then—nothing. An hour later, the United States government began a rescue attempt by air and sea. On July 19, after scouring 250,000 square miles of ocean and spending over $4 million, nothing was found. The search was called off.

What happened to Amelia? What happened to her airplane? Please accept my patronage to fly around the world to learn the truth, or the closest thing you can to it. Take this worksheet with you and write down your theory of what you think happened, then post it on our History Mystery Solution Wall.

Eleanor Roosevelt
First Lady

- Divide participants into small groups of three to five and give them each a packet with a worksheet of questions to ask the historical characters, a map of the library, pens/pencils, and a page to fill out their solution.
- After giving the groups a return time and place (about fifteen to twenty minutes before the time you plan the program to end), send them off to roam the library. If you have a high number of people, you may need to stagger the groups, sending one out every five minutes or so.
- Check in on the different locations throughout the program, making sure the actors have plenty of water and handouts (if needed) and that the groups don't get lost.
- When the return time arrives, have the historical characters round up the groups and return to the designated location.
- Have your host character welcome back the groups and invite them to submit their solutions.
- The host character will read each of the proposed solutions out loud and group them together by theory as they post them on a wall or other display location with a title (i.e., Teen History Mystery Night: Whatever Happened to Amelia Earhart?). Afterward, the host character may announce all the different theories and how many groups voted for each one.

- End the program with treats and a handout of suggested books, movies, articles, and other resources for more information about the history mystery.
- The theories can remain on display for as long as you wish. You may want to add pictures of the event or other decorations to highlight this program to other patrons.

Program Variations

There are many ways to create a history mystery program that will work for a variety of library spaces and resources. If a live history mystery night is unfeasible for your library, consider one of these options:

History Mystery Passive Program

Rather than having actors reading quotes and showing participants objects/photographs, a history mystery passive program involves creating posters with all the information that participants need to examine. You will need a designated location in the library for patrons to pick up packets. Each packet should contain a map of the library with locations to visit, a worksheet of questions to fill out using the posters, and a paper to write their solution. You may also want to have a designated space for them to display their solutions. The advantage of a history mystery passive program is that the posters can be left up in the library for as long as necessary, and the mystery can be completed by individuals, groups, and other younger or older patrons whose interest is sparked by seeing the posters.

History Mystery-in-a-Box

A history mystery-in-a-box contains all the same information as the history mystery passive program, except for the map of the library because the program is completed in one location. The information may be organized by historical location, chronological timeframe, proposed theory, or any other method you prefer. The history mystery-in-a-box may be added to the library collection as a regular passive program that could be checked out and worked on either in the library or at home.

History Mystery Display

A simple yet engaging history mystery program can be put together by setting out library books about the mystery and creating a display that invites patrons to take a closer look and do some digging into the mystery on their own. The display can be enhanced by a handout with a list of questions, page numbers, and resources to look up to find answers, and a blank poster, whiteboard, or other space for patrons to write down their theories or vote on different theories. This activity can be easily re-stocked with books and handouts and left up as long as you wish.

RECOMMENDED NEXT PROJECT

If your teens love solving a mystery and interacting with characters from another time, try staging a Murder Mystery Night during which volunteers play the different roles of the characters in a murder mystery and teens have to interview them to figure out who is guilty.

How to Create Life-Sized Board Games

LINDSEY TOMSU
Teen/YA Librarian

Algonquin Area Public Library District

LIFE-SIZED GAMES CAN be one of the most rewarding events you can create and can be offered to patrons of all ages. Over the years, my teens and I have created life-sized versions of the following games: Candy Land, Arkham Horror, The Game of Life, Hi Ho! Cherry-O, Battleship, Let's Go Fishing, Pac-Man, Family Feud, and Hungry Hippos (among many more that were brainstormed but never executed). In this chapter, you will learn the basics of what goes into creating a life-sized game from scratch and get tips on how to choose your game, brainstorm how to create life-sized components, tips on budgeting and running the program, and much, much more.

Age Range	Type of Library Best Suited For	Cost Estimate
Tweens (ages 8–12) Young Adults (ages 13–18) Adults	Public Libraries	$100–$1,000

Cost Considerations

Some life-sized games can be made on a small scale, while some can become much larger, so the cost can vary per project. Brainstorm and budget for the ultimate cost such an event would entail and then edit down from there, if necessary, by finding alternatives to your *dream* options.

Remember that not everything needs to be bought new! Calculate your budget, and based on that, explore what items the library may already own, what items can be made by volunteers, and what items can be donated/borrowed by patrons.

For those items you must purchase, remember your local dollar store is your best friend!

OVERVIEW

Life-sized gaming events are unique and memorable programs libraries can offer patrons of all ages. They are also a creative way to offer teens volunteer hours that go beyond busy work tasks that aren't all that exciting. Getting teens involved in the behind-the-scenes steps of program creation can really bring out their individual skills, make them feel they have really accomplished something tangible (seeing their hard work in the final result), and allow them a chance to practice their social and teamwork skills with teens they may not normally hang out with outside the library environment.

A life-sized game program can be offered at various levels of difficulty and budget. Based on games I have created or seen made, small-scale introductory games ideal for the program include Hi-Ho! Cherry-O, Pac-Man, and Let's Go Fishing. More medium-scale game options would include life-sized versions of Candy Land, Clue, Monopoly, and Chutes and Ladders. The most difficult (but super-rewarding) games to make into life-sized versions would be ones based on complex board games, board games that have lots of physical components, or games that would require some creative ingenuity or maker/engineering skills to bring to life such as Arkham Horror, Battleship, The Game of Life, Mouse Trap, and Mall Madness.

Other considerations, such as your final budget, how many people can attend the event, and how long the event will run, will vary greatly based on the actual game you decide to create. The step-by-step instructions below will help walk you through every step of the process, from brainstorming to running the event. Remember, you're only limited by your imagination and the effort you want to put into making a life-sized game event a reality.

NECESSARY EQUIPMENT AND MATERIALS

- a physical copy of any game you plan to turn into a life-sized version for reference
- basic crafting supplies such as scissors, Sharpies, paint, etc.
- A lamination machine is highly recommended for any paper props/game components. If you can laminate your hard work, you can re-use the props in the future and make your life-sized game event a repeatable one, not just a one-off program.
- The rest of the equipment and materials you need will really depend on what game you choose and how detailed you want to make it.

STEP-BY-STEP INSTRUCTIONS

Preparation

Brainstorming

- Brainstorming your game can take place in one of two ways: If you are creating the life-sized game yourself or with your coworkers, the game you want to make life-sized, and the level of detail you want to put into the program, is completely up to you. If this is the case, I recommend you stick with a simple board game that everyone has probably played before and therefore knows the rules. If you have an active group of teen volunteers or a teen advisory board, make the life-sized event a program they can get involved in every step of the way. See what games they would be interested in turning into life-sized versions and make sure you listen to all their ideas. In this case, if you have a dedicated group you can count on, you can be a bit more adventurous and try a medium- or large-scale game or one that may be new and exciting to more players.
- Once you have determined what game you will be making life-sized, you'll want to make sure you have a physical copy of the board game on hand for reference. If working with a used copy, make sure your copy has all the pieces! If using a game that has been around for decades, take into account different versions of the game that might exist and pick which version you will be using. For example, Candy Land can be made life-sized using its old food-related locations (Gumdrop Mountains, Ice Cream Floats) or character locations (the realms of Princess Frostine and Lord Licorice).

Recruiting Volunteers

- Life-sized games are a great way to get teens to earn volunteer hours doing something meaningful for the library in the form of helping create an actual library event. Teens are an excellent resource and can assist in brainstorming the logistics of making a game life-sized and help make props for the event. Plus, they can provide items that can be borrowed for your program. There are many tasks to be completed (from simple cutting to artistic painting), so teens at any skill level can assist. Joining in on the brainstorming part of the program from beginning to end also gives teens a chance to work on their teamwork and leadership skills, and because participation in helping with such an event would likely encompass more than a one-time meeting, they could list their contributions on college and job applications as well.
- When your volunteers can meet to work on the game will depend upon your schedule, your teens' schedules, and the times in which other teen programs at your branch are expected to run. For example, I had regular teen programs every Tuesday and Thursday at 6 p.m. So, my teens did their volunteer hours for each game from 3:30 p.m. to 6 p.m. on those days, essentially coming to the library straight after school and working on the game until the regular program started. Whatever you decide on, just keep it consistent! Teens tend to be so overscheduled that if they have a set day and time that remains the same, it is easier for them to remember to come and volunteer!

Constructing the Game Board

- You have your game picked; so, now what? The next step in the brainstorming process is to really examine the physical board game. Consider this the foundation for your life-sized version.
- How are game spaces handled on the board? How do players move? How many game spaces are on the board, and can you replicate them all? For example, Candy Land is made up of colored squares and special locations spots (Molasses Swamp), The Game of Life has spots with written text/commands, Arkham Horror has location spots (Arkham Asylum) connected by streets, and Hi Ho! Cherry-O has trees with cherries.
- Once you are familiar with the kinds of spaces used in the game, brainstorm how you might make them life-sized. Is it as simple as laminating some colored paper? Will you need to type up the text and print them

CHAPTER 50 | **How to Create Life-Sized Board Games**

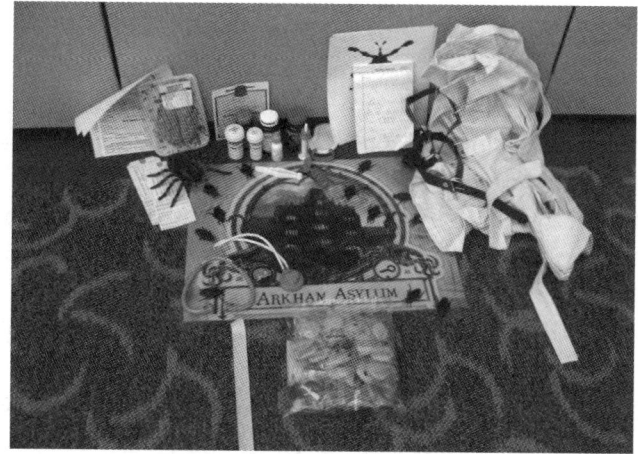

FIGURE 50.1
The scene for Arkham Horror's Arkham Asylum location on the game board

out on colored paper? Is it easier to take high-res photos of the spaces, blow up the photos, and print them out?

- If going for a detailed experience, don't forget to look at what is going on in the background of the game board! The Game of Life has many hidden jokes in places beyond the game spaces. For example, if making Hi Ho! Cherry-O, you could put fake vines around your game board to make it seem like you really have trees.
- Is your game more abstract? If so, it may require a bit more brainstorming to convert it into a life-sized version. For example, Let's Go Fishing isn't a board game—it is a plastic electronic game that runs off batteries that control little fish that open and shut their mouths while you try to catch them with fishing poles. How does one make that life-sized? You can construct the fish out of felt and place strong magnets where their mouths go. Then, use large flagpole-sized crafting dowels to create fishing poles with a magnet on the end of the line. The game board could then be made up of blue tissue paper and cellophane and confetti grass to resemble a small lake.
- If going for a more maker/engineering route for some game parts (see my chapter on The Game of Life and the four-foot spinner for an example), your local hardware store will be your best friend. Plastic piping and other similar home maintenance supplies might seem expensive, but the parts are relatively cheap and shouldn't scare you away from trying more hands-on crafting.

Constructing Game Tokens

- Once you have all your ideas brainstormed on how to make the game board life-sized, you want to move your attention to the tokens.
- For any paper tokens, such as money, you can easily recreate them in larger versions and print them out.
- If the game involves cards that are drawn, you can take high-res photos, enlarge and print them, and then laminate them for future re-use.
- If your game uses dice, make sure you acquire a set of fuzzy dice or larger inflatable dice, both of which players can literally toss when rolling for something.
- If your game has meeples or character pawns of any sort, you can decide to either bypass this step—because attendees will be physically moving around the game board themselves—and suggest players come dressed up for their roles, or you can have small props that will designate each player's role. For example, in Arkham Horror, players pick an investigator to play, and they each have their own identity and skills. Have a lab coat on hand for the scientist to wear, provide a jumbo-sized pencil for the reporter to carry, etc.
- All other game pieces are going to be very specific to your game, so brainstorm ideas of how to make life-sized versions and what will work for you. For example, there are monsters that players have to fight in Arkham Horror that are represented with monster tokens. My teens transformed dollar-store stuffed animals into monsters from the game. For Pac-Man, the food pellets were created with ball-pit balls.

Constructing Game Props

- All game props are going to depend upon the individual game. My biggest piece of advice is to consider what could be donated or borrowed from staff, patrons, or volunteers (a location in Arkham Horror is a train station; we borrowed a teen's dad's actual train set to put up and run at the location spot on the game board). What can't be borrowed can often be made from materials you can get relatively cheaply at your local dollar store! Listen to everyone's ideas. Teens will quickly let you know if they think something will work or if it is a stupid idea. Many patrons are just excited to be playing a board game in real-life size, so they probably won't care if the ships in your life-sized Battleship are floaty bathtub boats!

- Felt is your other best friend when it comes to making props from scratch. Whether you use felt to make fish for Let's Go Fishing or eight yards of felt to create the blue grid for Battleship, this material can be put to great use. I highly recommend purchasing felt by the yard in bulk from Blick Art Materials (www.dickblick.com). Blick has a wide assortment of colors to choose from, and the more you buy, the larger the discount you receive. Plus, you can never *not* use felt!
- The key to building props is to be creative! Your props can be as simple or as detailed as you want.

Program Instructions

Marketing
- Based on your meeting room space and how long you are planning for the event to last, you may need to require individual, group, or time slot preregistration. The benefit of this is you will know how many people to plan for, but the downside is often those who register take spots and then are no-shows.
- I recommend offering such programs on a weekend day (or a weekday and night if in the summer) when you can hopefully utilize your meeting room space from the time the library opens until its close, allowing time for a maximum number of participants to attend.

Pre-Event Prep
- It helps to make checklists of all the elements that go into your game, so when grabbing everything for setup, you can mark off sections as you go.
- Make sure your room is reserved and try to set up the day prior if possible (maximizing the time you have to offer the program). Set up for life-sized games always takes much longer than the cleanup time!
- If you can utilize teen helpers to help with setup, do so!
- Take lots of photos of the room and the game before anyone gets to play. I also suggest possibly taking a video walk-through as well if you want to include a fun commentary you'd like to remember.

Room Setup Tips
- Obviously, start with the layout of the actual game-board space itself. It will take a few attempts to get this perfect. You might put every item

into place and then see you have additional space to spread out; or, you may run out of space and need to condense some elements.
- If you have any props that you will be affixing to a wall, I suggest putting those up the day of the event. In life-sized Arkham Horror we had to hang eight six-foot-tall *portal* locations up on the wall. When I arrived the next day, they had all fallen and gotten tangled up! It was a mad rush to try and re-tape them in the thirty minutes left before the program was to start.
- If possible, have additional seating for those who are waiting their turn and offer light snacks/drinks if you can (nothing super-messy that could damage game items).

Running the Program
- How you run the program on the day of the event will depend on how you decide to accommodate your potential attendees.
- If dealing with a large group at once (because game play is simple and everyone is familiar with the rules), I suggest playing in rounds and having built-in breaks players can take.
- If dealing with a large group at once, it helps if you act as the Game Master and direct game play to make sure people don't get off track and waste time.
- If offering the program for teens, do not be discouraged if they seem to have fun for a few hours and then get distracted. Some of them just naturally won't be able to concentrate throughout a day-long program. They will have fun with it during whatever duration they can stay engaged in the program. Often, they may need to take a break, after which they can come back and start playing again.
- It is okay to skip players' turns if they are holding up the crowd.

Cleanup Tips
- If you can have your teen volunteers stay and help, cleanup time will breeze by!
- If you have limited time in which to clean up (say, the library is closing in thirty minutes and there is a program in the room the next day), it is okay to grab everything in like-sized piles and put stuff on carts or move to another room/place where you can organize more carefully later.
- Make sure you and any volunteers are aware of any borrowed items so you can return them to their owners at the end of the program.

Re-playability

- If you can laminate any paper-based items, do so! This will allow you to keep the elements for repeated use—one of the biggest steps in creating re-playable life-sized games.
- If you can, keep any props you made. Get some small-sized moving boxes to store all the items for future re-use.
- If you used borrowed items, make a list of what those borrowed items were, who loaned them, and why you borrowed them and keep this list with your notes. In the future, if you decide to redo the program, you will have a handy list of the items you are missing, which will make it much easier for you to request them again in the future or brainstorm other options for those items.

RECOMMENDED NEXT PROJECTS

- Don't be ashamed to start out small with a small-scale, life-sized game first to get an idea of how much preparation time might be needed and get a feel for if your patrons would enjoy the effort you might subsequently put into a larger-scale game.
- Don't be afraid of re-offering the event in the future and presenting a game that was originally marketed toward children to your tween, teen, and adult participants to play.
- Don't let your budget crush your dreams of bringing a game to life! Seek out local and national grants or ask your friends for assistance. Remind your potential financial supporters that some games may require a heftier than normal budget, but that figure can be an initial budget—all life-sized games are re-playable and can be more than a one-time event.

Share the wealth! If you created a life-sized Monopoly and your neighboring library created a life-sized Clue, share your games with each other!

Just Try to Escape Your Training!
Using Escape Rooms to Develop a Cohesive Student Worker Team

MELANIE BOPP
Librarian, Information Delivery and Access Services

Northeastern University Library

STUDENT WORKERS NEED to be trained. But why rely on boring checklists and quizzes when interactive learning is so much more fun and interesting for everyone? Student worker orientations should offer more than just a lecture or PowerPoint presentation. Pizza is always a good place to start, but it's not enough. Your orientation goals should be to make your student-worker team a unified front as they work to win the game while gaining job knowledge. So why not try an activity that will have them working together to solve a work-related mystery? By combining puzzles with library facts and activities, you can create an escape room that will not only keep your students engaged but also impart further library knowledge while reinforcing the team-based work they will be doing on the job.

Age Range	Type of Library Best Suited For	Cost Estimate
Young Adults (ages 13–18) Adults	Academic Libraries School Libraries	$50–$150

Cost Considerations

Costs may vary depending on whether you choose to purchase a kit or individual pieces for your room.

OVERVIEW

Using escape rooms for student-worker training fosters team building while also teaching essential job functions. Your trainees will learn to work together toward a common goal in a controlled setting while also becoming familiar with library functions. Maintaining employee engagement can be tricky. By using a game such as an escape room, you can get students moving while also encouraging their creative thinking.

FIGURE 51.1
Library staff testing (and trying to break) our newest student training escape room

Professional escape rooms last approximately an hour; however, your library escape room, which will incorporate training tools, should take around twenty minutes to complete—long enough for roughly three to five puzzles. Group size should be kept to around five people, if possible (accounting for physical-space limitations). I recommend making this program a part of whatever additional orientation or group training programs you already have in place. You will generally need one staff person per space (for example, if you have two simultaneous groups, you will need two staff members).

Also, keep in mind that escape rooms need to be reworked each time they are used with the same group of students, such as during yearly or semesterly orientations. While it is unlikely that student workers will remember the same clue/answer pairs, the escape room scenario may be familiar enough that the effect is lessened.

NECESSARY EQUIPMENT AND MATERIALS

- locks of varying types, including but not limited to:
  - directional locks
  - multi-locks (locks using interchangeable letters, colors, directions, etc.)
  - keyed padlocks
  - combination locks (of varying number lengths)
  - hasp locks (a claw-shaped piece with multiple holes on one side to attach multiple locks to one box)
  - a Cryptex device (a cylinder with rings that can line up to spell a word or code)
- countdown timer—a timer app that works on a tablet or computer screen is recommended (An app could also be used to provide ambient sounds!)
- a UV flashlight and an invisible ink marker
- lockboxes, lockers, or secondary spaces that need to be unlocked (depending on the size and scope of your room)

Note: These materials can be purchased as a bundle from a service such as BreakoutEDU or as individual pieces. Choose what works best for your library!

STEP-BY-STEP INSTRUCTIONS

Preparation

- Theme selection, such as: The Case of the Missing Mascot. "After a meeting in the library earlier today, staff discovered that the university mascot is missing! Use the clues in the room to find and release the mascot from its prison before time runs out!"
- Learning outcome: to focus on team building in a library setting and using information from their training and the job to figure out codes and combinations
  - This is also a good time to decide how large a group you want to work with. Take into consideration the size of the space you are using or the difficulty of the puzzles. Generally, a group of five to six is ideal—a high enough number to allow students to break up and work in small teams yet low enough that they can all work together as needed.
  - To personalize or change up the setup:

» consider the makeup of the team—look at the different positions student workers cover in your department and make sure your learning outcomes are not all geared toward one position—or even one area. For example, customer service skills are great but not as relevant to shelving students. Alternatively, the details of resource sharing are interesting but not something a desk student would necessarily need.
» Solicit learning outcome ideas from all staff members in your department, especially those who work directly with student workers. These can be as in-depth as *customer service skills* or as simple as: *Where in the building is this thing?* Incorporate these ideas into your checklist when you are putting together your clue/solution pairs.

- Clue/solution pairs—these pairs should be specific to your institution and student tasks, so take these as a starting point!
  - In the room there are:
    » a box with a hasp lock and three locks on it (one directional/one multi-lock, one three-digit lock, and one four-digit lock)
    » a twenty-four-piece puzzle with a "To Do" list written on the back in invisible ink (taken apart with the pieces spread around the space, including under things and inside things)
    » a binder labeled "Meeting Notes" with a fake agenda and an invitation list and with institutions attached
    » about a dozen DVDs, including five that use directions in their titles (we used *Downton Abbey, Up, East of Eden, South Park*, and *North by Northwest*)
    » a painting or picture (one of our staff brought in a small 8″ × 10″ canvas)
    » pull slips for interlibrary loans (or stacks maintenance)
    » some posters, clipboards, blank paper, pens, etc., for ambience

- The "To Do" list should have the tasks that must be completed to solve the three locks on the box:
  - sort DVDs
  - check the invite list for the meeting
  - bring the painting to ILL and pick up the items that must be searched

- The DVDs must be put in the proper Library of Congress (LC) call number order. After doing so, the directions are revealed as: down, down, up, right, up for the directional lock or multi-lock.
- In the binder labeled "Meeting Notes," include a fake agenda and an invite list. On the invite list, include a mix of institutions along with institution numbers that are three-digital codes that can be used to decode the lock.
- Behind the painting, leave four pull slips. When put in LC call number order, highlight four numbers using the UV light for the final four-digit code for the final lock.
- To personalize this program:
  - Each clue should be related to your goals in some way. If your student workers come from multiple positions (e.g., circulation students and stacks students), make sure your clue/solution pairs reflect the tasks they do and the knowledge they should have.
  - Consider how clues can connect for a solution to one lock. For example, if you are using a four-digit lock, your clue could refer to the call number of a specific book, and student workers would need to deduce the part they need.
  - Plan approximately two to five minutes per clue/solution pair, depending on their difficulty level—if your escape room is supposed to last twenty minutes, you'll want to have about three to five clue/solution pairs. Offering different levels of puzzle complexity is ideal—more complex puzzles are more satisfying overall but quicker puzzles keep up the excitement and momentum.

Things to Remember
- Each clue should only have one solution. For example, if the clue says the solution is in the Dickens book, you need to make sure you have only one Dickens book.
- Puzzles need to be fair and solvable! Clues shouldn't be heavily based in outside knowledge—you don't want to have a solution that requires students to know the author of a book if that information isn't in the room with them.
- If a clue and solution require tedious work, such as connecting coordinates, make sure the instructions are clear. Instructions that are more obvious than you think they should be usually translate into them being just about right for players.

- Make sure your clue and solution are linked. Some possible ways to link more ambiguous clues:
    - location
        » If a clue is found on a book cart, perhaps the lockbox is also on the book cart.
    - color/shape coding
        » If the directional lock is red, perhaps the answer is on a red chart or involves red book covers.
    - items used to find an answer or that require a task be performed
        » If there is a line that you need to draw, perhaps there is a written word puzzle that, when assembled, hints that you need to draw something.
    - Teams should not be able to destroy puzzles by accident. If someone moves a book, and that changes the solution to a puzzle, it's not a good puzzle. If your clue needs users to draw on, cut up, or otherwise wreck it, don't forget about replacements for follow-up groups!
    - Your clue/solution pairs will likely be too difficult on the first try. Make sure to give yourself time to test everything out, preferably with a group similar to the makeup you expect in the real thing.
    - Feedback for correct answers—even if it is as simple as a chime or a lock opening—is both useful to players (confirming they are on the right track) and encouraging!

Gather the Materials

Along with the materials listed above, what else do you need for your space? When looking at decor and other materials, you may want to include things such as:

- other mascots or related memorabilia (rival mascots, college banners for your institution, etc.)
- materials about the mascot (for example, if your mascot is a falcon, you could include books or movies involving the animal, the native location of the animal, etc.)
- Get your university archives involved. (Do they have yearbooks you could borrow? What about faculty publications?)
    - Decor can really help set the tone and theme of your room. Make sure, however, that the decor adds to the room and not the complexity of the puzzles! You don't want students trying to find a clue in an old banner when you just added it to the space for ambience.

- Depending on your technical abilities in the space, consider a soundtrack for the room—ambient noises further the immersive experience of your theme. They can also act as a bit of white noise if you have multiple-room activities going on at once!

Set Room Rules
Common escape room rules include:
- No force is needed to solve problems or open locks.
- Nothing will be above head height (approximately 5.5 feet).
- Nothing will be in the ceiling or under the flooring.
- Some things are not part of the puzzle such as light switches or certain wall décor elements.
  - Many rooms have "do not touch" stickers up or other appropriately placed labels to indicate what is not part of the room's puzzles.
- The room will be unlocked, and participants aren't actually trapped. (This may seem obvious to many but is definitely reassuring to hear!)
  - Some rooms include a warning indicating that if you leave, you cannot re-enter. This isn't recommended for training, but if there are concerns that students may try to leave to get the answers to puzzles, they should be addressed.
- Everything needed is in the room—no need for cell phones, tools, etc.
- Players can ask for clues, but all players must ask together.
  - Game builders can make a certain number of clues free or have them all cost a certain amount of time to obtain. For example, a room may offer three free clues, or one free clue with additional clues costing two minutes each, or have every clue request cost three minutes, etc.
  - Consider making a certain task the way to ask for a clue. For example, you could instruct everyone to dance or say the set codeword or phrase. Students who participated at my library had to say the name of the library together to get their clue.
  - Consider making a hint script for any staff members supervising the game so that they have a place to start for each puzzle. These hints can always be adlibbed, of course, but you want to make sure you're not just telling them the solution to the puzzle!
    » For example, instead of saying, "Use the UV light on the pull slips," you could try, "I wonder if something I already have can help me find something new?"

Additional Rules to Consider
- no climbing on the furniture
  - The head height listed in your program may still be a little high for some people. When working with students, it may not hurt to remind them not to climb on the furniture to try to reach something!
- A staff member will be present for the entire game but can only help when specifically asked for a hint by the group.
  - Because most libraries cannot afford to set up cameras to keep an eye on the group, having a staff member present to facilitate is necessary. Remind students that the game facilitator is not there as part of the actual game.

Build Your Room
- Confirm the space (or spaces) you will be using and then get to work! You already have the materials, so now you can:
  - Place a decor item.
  - Set up locks, lockboxes, etc., as well as clues. Consider the order in which students are most likely to find materials and place them in your space accordingly. Don't forget about the links between the clues and solutions!
- Accessibility issues to consider: What sort of limitations are there for people with accessibility issues? While our student group was relatively able-bodied, yours may not be, so consider things such as:
  - the needs of people in wheelchairs or with crutches, amputees, individuals without the use of a limb, etc. If you expect any special-needs participants, evaluate how the mechanics of game play may need to be adjusted. (How reachable are things? Does a puzzle involved in the program require the use of both hands?)
  - the needs of deaf people (Does your room have any audio clues?)
  - the needs of people who cannot bend/kneel/reach easily (Do your students need to crawl to find things or get to places?)
  - the needs of people with color-blindness (Are things color-coded? Are there other indicators, such as shapes, to make things clear?)
  - the needs of individuals with epilepsy or other disorders (Does your game have potential triggers such as strobing lights?)

Run a Test Game!

- Running a test game is highly recommended to catch the most likely hiccups before your student workers have their go.
- Gather a group of volunteers (staff groups usually work well) to run through the room as if they were student workers in a training session:
  - Use the space (or as close as you can replicate) you are planning on for the real deal.
  - Set up the space with the clue/solution pairs, as well as any red herrings, additional decorations, etc., that you have planned.
- This is a great time to see what clue/solution pairs are too difficult and need to be adjusted.
- Consider running the game without a time limit, but make sure to time your group. Did they complete the game in the time you expected? Did they finish too quickly? Why?
- Check your clue/solution pairs against your learning outcomes—consider making a quick feedback form or sheet for test players to see what worked well and what didn't.
- See how long it takes you to both set up in advance and reset after your group plays; if you need to run back-to-back student groups, you'll need to know how much time you should plan for a room reset.

Fine-tune Your Game

- Adjust your clue/solution pairs for difficulty.
  - If they are too easy, you can add another puzzle or two.
    - » Add an additional lock such as a dial (consider nesting boxes, and put your mascot stand-in inside a box that fits inside the initial box).
    - » On the agenda, add a note about a recommendation from an attendee. That recommendation could be one of the DVDs you've added to the space already; or, you could add additional materials such as a few books or reference materials.
    - » Set the dial lock to be the call number from the material you have chosen (e.g., the call number is PR6116A84T11; so, the lock code is 6–11–6).
  - If your tasks are too difficult, see if you can narrow down why—don't forget to check on how your puzzles are linked for the players.
- Double-check the decor to make sure you aren't inadvertently adding any red herrings into the room.

Program Instructions

The Day of the Game, Before Game Play Starts
- Run through your setup:
    - Are the room and decor ready to go?
    - Is there anything you need to add?
- Set up your puzzles:
    - Hopefully you will have time in advance to set everything up, but you will want to make sure everything is in place—you don't want clues to be found out of order or a lock left unlocked!
- Prep the timer, the hint scripts for your staff members (if you chose to use them), and any other materials the Game Master (played by you or any other supervising staff members) plans to bring into the space with them.

During the Game
- Sit back and let them go!
- Keep an eye on the timer and the players and an ear out for hint requests.
    - For other staff members pitching in during the game, this may be the time to give them those hint scripts.
    - Consider giving time warnings (i.e., fifteen minutes remaining, three minutes remaining, etc.).
- If they stumble, resist the urge to help if they haven't asked for a hint. That said, if they seem to have given up, you can always ask players if they want to use one of their hints.
- Wait for the time to run out or the group to escape!

After They've Escaped (or Time Has Run Out)
- Congratulate them on what they finished if possible; pick out one or two clues that were particularly tricky but that your students still solved or all worked together well on. Even if they didn't escape, they still accomplished something significant.
- Reflecting on what they just did, whether right or not, is important. Build in time to:
    - explain any puzzles not solved
    - answer any questions your players have
    - reflect on actions taken (or not taken):
        » What worked well within your group?
        » What do you think you personally contributed?

- » Consider making an online feedback form for students to fill out after the fact—just make sure it isn't too long after! The longer you wait, the fewer responses you are likely to get.
- Don't forget to reset the room if you have another group coming in!

RECOMMENDED NEXT PROJECTS

- Escape rooms also make great student outreach programs!
- You can also create online quizzes with an escape room feel—just make sure you use conditional logic (different responses lead to different outcomes).
- A roleplaying campaign (similar to Dungeons & Dragons) could also give the game a similar feel without the physical space interaction.
- Escape rooms can be expanded to include the entire library space, combined with scavenger hunt elements for student workers or student users.

The Amazing Race
STEAM to the Finish Line

SANDRA CALEMME MCCARTHY
Faculty Librarian

MAUREEN PERAULT
Faculty Librarian

Washtenaw Community College Bailey Library

THE AMAZING RACE program challenges STEAM students to learn key concepts of information literacy in the format of a race. The contestants complete each leg of the competition by answering a set of questions based on research process videos. The race comprises four challenges designed to test the participants' understanding of how to formulate a research question, distinguish between popular and scholarly sources, dissect a scholarly article, and evaluate online information. The race can be adapted to include other college students as well as encompass other components of information literacy.

Age Range	Type of Library Best Suited For	Cost Estimate
Young Adults (ages 13–18) Adults	Public Libraries Academic Libraries School Libraries	$0–$800

Cost Considerations

The overall cost for this program could be as low as $20 if you already have a subscription to LibGuides and plan to use it as the platform for your challenge.

OVERVIEW

The Amazing Race was designed to gamify the research experience in a way that is relevant to college STEAM students. Although you can apply the Amazing Race program to any level of library research, our STEAM Program focused on having students learn to properly write a research question and on helping them understand the difference between popular and scholarly sources. Our program also helped students identify and examine a scholarly article and evaluate website content. Each challenge constitutes one leg of the race. A student team cannot move on to the next leg without completing each challenge in the previous one correctly. Each challenge is presented to the team in an envelope that contains a form with questions that must be answered correctly. Students use the Amazing Race LibGuide to complete the challenge by watching the instructional videos. Once the team completes the first challenge, it presents its results to a librarian to check for accuracy. If correct, the team advances to the next challenge presented in the next envelope. This is repeated four times by each team. The first team to cross the finish line is declared the winner.

The Amazing Race takes fifty to sixty minutes to complete, based on the team dynamics. There should be at least two librarians as part of the Amazing Race to help teams check in as they complete a leg of the race and proceed to the next challenge. To manage the race, it might be best to limit the number of participants to less than thirty, with two to three students per team.

NECESSARY EQUIPMENT AND MATERIALS

- LibGuides or another instructional site with access to videos for viewing
- four envelopes for each team
    - four different-colored envelopes for each leg of the race
    - one set of 9" × 12" envelopes
- paper for printed questions
- a set of scholarly journals and a set of magazines
- a pack of green 4" × 4" cards and a pack of blue 4" × 4" cards
- small magnets (if using magnetic whiteboards)
- magnetic whiteboards (optional—you can use cards instead)
- a room or dedicated space, with a table and chairs for each team
- pens or pencils for each team
- a laptop computer for each team (you can use desktop computers)
- a prize for the winning team (optional)

STEP-BY-STEP INSTRUCTIONS

Preparation

Four Weeks Before the Amazing Race
- Identify the four videos for the four challenges, which are:
  - Understanding of How to Formulate a Research Question, Distinguishing Popular and Scholarly Sources, Dissecting a Scholarly Article, and Evaluating Online Information
- Create the questions for each video.
- If using a LibGuide, create an Amazing Race LibGuide.
  - Create a page for your videos.

Two Weeks Before the Amazing Race
- Determine how many teams will be participating based on your number of contestants.
- Number each envelope one through four for each team.
- Print copies of the Writing a Research Question challenge for leg one of the game.
- Stuff a copy of this challenge for leg one into envelope one.
- Print a copy of the Popular vs. Scholarly Question challenge for leg two.
- Grab health and JAMA periodicals—be sure to take enough issues for each team.
- Stuff envelope two with a copy of the Popular vs. Scholarly Question.
- Print the Anatomy of a Scholarly Article Question challenge for leg three.
- Use the 4" × 4" cards for the scholarly article components and definitions for each component.
  - Use one set of green cards for your scholarly article terms.
  - Use one set of blue cards for your definitions.
  - Add two-sided magnets to each card—this is optional if using cards and a tabletop.
- Stuff envelope three with a copy of the Anatomy of a Scholarly Article Question.
- Print out a copy of the Web Evaluation Question challenge for leg four.
- Stuff envelope four with the copy of this question.
- *Optional*: Give prizes to the winner and runner-up teams.
- *Optional*: Create an assessment of the end of your Amazing Race assessment based on the ACRL Project Outcome Instruction form.

- *Note*: Each challenge is given to each team in an envelope of a different color.

Day of the Amazing Race
- Grab the stuffed envelopes.
- Prepare your room or open area for the race.
- Separate the tables far enough away from each other to offer teams some privacy as they discuss the game.
- Break contestants into teams of two to three per table.
- Have players open their laptops and access the STEAM LibGuide Amazing Race.
- Have prizes ready.

Program Instructions
- Begin with a seven-minute introduction by the librarians explaining the Amazing Race format.
- Form teams that consist of two to three contestants.
- Hand out the first envelope to each team.
- Begin the race.
- Give students fifty to sixty minutes to complete the entire Amazing Race.
- After solving challenge one, teams then check in with the librarian. If the challenge has been correctly solved, the librarian hands the team the next envelope, which contains challenge two.
- If the team does not solve the challenge correctly, they are sent back to their table to re-attempt that challenge.
- The first team to solve all four challenges with the correct answers wins!

RECOMMENDED NEXT PROJECTS
- Consider what else your students can do after they've mastered your program.
- Check out chapter 48: "Save Lewis the Librarian! An Information Literacy Escape Room" by Ruth Cho.

INDEX

f denotes figures; *t* denotes tables

A

academic libraries
  circulating game collections at, 55–58
  clubs at, 127–132, 159–162
  donations and grants to, 97–101
  faculty programs at, 235–243
  library research programs for, 70, 179–182, 267–276, 281–286, 307–311, 357–360
  orientation programs for, 73–77, 79–84, 133–136, 137–145, 221–224, 297–306, 345–355
  science-themed programs for, 59–63, 127–132
  Sources card game for, 93–96
  study break programs at, 121–125
  tournaments at, 183–187, 307–311
adults, programs for
  live action game programs, 215–219, 221–224, 235–243, 245–253, 267–276, 281–286, 293–311, 313–325, 335–343, 345–360
  tabletop game programs, 3–13, 15–19, 21–27, 29–41, 43–47, 49–63, 65–71, 73–77, 79–101, 103–118
  video game programs, 121–125, 127–145, 153–170, 179–187, 189–193, 195–200, 207–211
The Adventure Zone podcast, 54
AFFECTED: The Manor, 157
ALA International Games Week, 13, 101
ALA Roundtables, 13

Amazing, Sarah, 245–248, 249–253
"The Amazing Race" program, 357–360, 5*t*, 6
Apollo/Titanic, 158
arcade-style programs, 163–170
Atwell, Mary, 277–280
augmented reality (AR) programs, 133–136
awards, websites for, 13

B

battle royale games, 245–248
Beatties Ford Road Regional Library, 50*f*
beginners, programs for, 15–19, 43–47
Berry, Maya, 159–162, 235–243
"Beyond Dungeons & Dragons" program, 3–13
Bingo, 293–295
Blades in the Dark, 5*t*, 6
Block, Maggie, 115–118
board games
  circulating collections of, 55–58
  conventions for, 85–92
  creation of, 79–84
  the Landlord Game, 37–41
  large-scale events for, 73–77, 85–92
  life-sized versions of, 225–233, 255–266, 335–343

board games (cont'd)
 locally designed, 115–118
 for older adults, 32, 34
 science-themed, 59–63
BoardGameGeek.com, 34, 56
Bookwyrm Con, 85, 86f
Bopp, Melanie, 345–355
Borysewicz, Kristen, 267
brainstorming, 337–338
"Brush & Shield" program, 21–27
Bufton, Martha Attridge, 93–96
Bullinger, Delaney, 43–47
Burkot, Emily, 183–187, 189–193
businesses, donations from, 97–99
Bussmann, Christopher, 103–113

C

Call of Cthulhu, 65–71, 101, 105–106
Canner, Leah, 171–178
card games, 17, 34, 93–96
Casselberry, Brad, 121–125
catalog searches, as activity, 198, 199, 303
cataloging, of games, 56–57
Chaosium, 70, 101
character-design prompts, 108–110
children, programs for, 97–101, 115–118, 163–170, 189–193, 245–248, 293–295. *See also* tweens, programs for
Cho, Ruth, 317–325
choose-your-own-adventure activities, 179–182
Chutes and Ladders, 82–83
Cinar, Kristen, 79–84, 179–182, 281–286
Clark, Karlene Tura, 267–276
classic consoles, 166
clubs, gaming, 127–132, 159–162
Clue, 82, 255–266
clues, tips for, 349–350

Code Combat, 193
coding, 132, 157, 193, 199, 205
collection development
 of circulating board games, 55–58
 of video games, 189–193
Colville, Matthew, 53–54
commuter students, collections for, 55–58
Consent in Gaming (Reynolds and Germain), 7, 12
consoles, selecting, 165–167
conventions, gaming, 85–92
cooperative games, 18, 32
Costello, Danielle, 3–13
costumes, for Clue, 258, 262
Covington, Ruth, 327–333
crib sheets, 8
Critical Role, 52, 54
"Culper Spies" program, 179–182
cybersecurity, 207–211

D

database searches, 236, 239–240, 283, 303–304, 307–310
Dease, Nicholas, 163–170
design, prompts for, 103–113
designers, local, 115–118
"Dewey and Dragons" program, 49–54
dice games, 5t, 17, 32, 50–51
dice tests, 105–106
DNA model kits, 196–199
Dolce, Jonathan, 255–266
Dominoes, 32, 35
donations and grants, 97–101
Dread, 5t, 6
Dungeon Masters (DMs), 49–54, 104–105
Dungeons & Dragons, 49–54, 101, 105–106

INDEX

E

EA games, 192
Earhart, Amelia, 327, 328f, 330–331
escape rooms, 235–243, 297–306, 317–325, 345–355
event capacity, 17, 31
"Exam Cram" program, 121–125
The Extraordinary Adventures of Baron Munchausen, 5t, 6

F

Facebook Live, 203–205
faculty, escape rooms for, 235–243
fandom LARPs, 287–292
fighter games, 147–151, 168
Figure Paint & Take events, 21–27
Finch, Shea'la, 103–113
Five Nights at Freddy's: Help Wanted, 157
Forbidden Island, 18, 32
Ford-Baxter, Tiffanie, 55–58, 59–63
fort design, 208–211
Fortnite, 165, 168, 174, 245
Fresno County Library Bookwyrm Con, 85, 86f
Fruit Ninja, 157
Furlong, Michael, 65–71

G

game consoles, selecting, 165–167
Game Masters (GMs)
  beginner's program for, 43–47
  games that require, 4–5
  resources for, 12
  role of, 104–105, 108
  See also roleplaying games (RPGs)
game nights, starting up, 15–19

The Game of Life, 225–233, 338
game publishers
  donations from, 100–101
  rulebooks by, 5t
game systems, most common, 105–106
gamers clubs, 127–132, 159–162
games. *See* board games; roleplaying games (RPGs); video games
GameStop, 191
gamification, of research, 70, 179–182, 281–286, 307–311, 357–360
gaming conventions, 85–92
genres, selecting, 167–168, 174
golf games, 277–280
Google Cardboard, 202, 205
Google Forms, 57, 180–182, 286, 322
grants and donations, 97–101
Green Door Labs Edventure Builder, 137, 138, 140

H

Halvorsen, Mark, 15–19, 21–27, 29–36
Hansen, Susan M., 221–224, 297–306
Happy Salmon, 32
Harkness, Colin, 93–96
Harrison, Randal Sean, 37–41
Harry Potter games, 187, 265, 288f, 289–290
Haynes, Emily Hampton, 277–280
hearing limitations, 32, 33
"Hero's Handbook" program, 43–47
history mystery programs, 327–333
Honey Heist, 5t, 6
Hornick, Julie, 313–316
"Hunger Games Survival Challenge," 249–253

INDEX

I
information literacy, 70, 93–96, 267–276, 281–286, 297–306, 307–311, 317–325, 357–360
Instagram, 221–224
International Games Week, 13, 101
"It's Locked" program, 195–200

J
Jenga, 4, 8, 9
jerseys, 173, 174–175f, 176
Job Simulator, 158

K
Keep Talking and Nobody Explodes, 157
Keepers, role of, 66–71
Kerbal Space Program (KSP), 127–132
kids, programs for, 97–101, 115–118, 163–170, 189–193, 245–248, 293–295. *See also* tweens, programs for

L
Landlord Game, 37–41
large-scale events, 73–77, 85–92
LARPS (live action roleplays), 215–219, 287–292
"Laser Tag in the Stacks" program, 313–316
leagues
 in Pokémon GO, 184–186
 recreational, 171–178
Lee, Haley T., 153–158
"Level Up!" program, 137–145
LibGuides, 357–358

"Library Battle Royale" program, 245–248
library orientation programs, 73–77, 79–84, 133–136, 137–145, 221–224, 297–306
library research programs, 70, 179–182, 267–276, 281–286, 307–311, 357–360
life-sized games, 225–233, 255–266, 335–343
literacy
 information, 70, 93–96, 267–276, 281–286, 297–306, 307–311, 317–325, 357–360
 science, 59–63
 socioeconomic, 37–41
live action game programs
 battle royales, 245–248
 escape rooms, 235–243, 297–306, 317–325, 345–355
 history mysteries, 327–333
 LARPs, 215–219, 287–292
 laser tag, 313–316
 life-sized games, 225–233, 255–266, 335–343
 scavenger hunts, 221–224, 249–253, 267–276, 281–286
live action roleplays (LARPs), 215–219, 287–292
locally-designed games, 115–118
locks, for escape rooms, 236, 238–243, 299–304, 306, 320, 321, 347–354
Lockwood, Jacqueline, 127–132
Logan, Errol, 215–219
The Lord of the Rings games, 265, 300, 303
Lovecraft, H. P., 65–71

M
MacDonald, Randall M., 313–316
"Mad Librarian" program, 297–306
Makey-Makey, 197–199
maps, 198, 199, 273

Markman, Chris, 207–211
May, Kaitlyn, 277–280
McCarthy, Sandra Calemme, 357–360
Metaverse, 134–136
Microsoft, demos from, 208
Mind's Eye Society (MES), 217, 219
Minecraft, 207–211
miniature painting, 21–27
mini-golf, 277–280
mobility limitations, 32, 33
model-painting programs, 21–27
Monopoly, 38, 336
Monte Cook Games, 5t, 7, 12
Morgan, Marina, 313–316
Morrison, Matthew, 97–101
multiplayer setups, 165–166, 191
Mystery of the Missing Student room, 236, 237–241
mystery programs, 195–200, 235–243, 255–266, 327–333, 345–355

N

Nancy Drew games, 195–200
Neill, Kyle, 121–125
Nintendo Switch, 148, 164, 166
Njoku, Lisa, 307–311
non-playable characters (NPCs), 7, 10, 69, 255, 257
"Not So Trivial Pursuit" program, 79–84

O

Oculus Go, 201–205
Oculus Rift, 154, 205
older adults, programs for, 29–36
online subscriptions, 165, 192
orientation programs, 73–77, 79–84, 133–136, 137–145, 221–224, 297–306, 345–355

P

painting programs, 21–27
The Pale Codex, 49, 51–53
Palodichuk, Daniel, 55–58
Pathfinder, 43–47, 101
Paz, Selenia, 195–200
Perault, Maureen, 357–360
peripheral hardware, 166–167
phone-based games, 133–136, 137–145
piano keyboards, 196–199
planning spreadsheets, 142f, 143
players, resources for, 12
Playroom VR, 153–156
PlayStation, 153–158, 164, 165–167
playtesting, 115–118, 143–144
Pokémon GO, 183–187
Polfer, Tiffany, 85–92
prizes and swag, soliciting, 174
promotional videos, 59–63
Prosser, Sarah, 147–151
public libraries
  clubs at, 127–132, 159–162
  donations and grants to, 97–101
  gaming conventions at, 85–92
  library research programs for, 70, 267–276, 307–311, 357–360
  life-sized games at, 225–233, 255–266, 335–343
  older adult programming at, 29–36
  orientation programs for, 79–84, 137–145, 221–224, 297–306
  painting programs for, 21–27
  recreational leagues at, 171–178
  science-themed programs for, 127–132
  tournaments at, 147–151, 183–187, 307–311
publishers, 5t, 100–101
puzzle design, 284–285
puzzles, in escape rooms, 236–243, 320–323, 349–354
PVP tournaments, 183–187

INDEX

Q
QR codes, 136f, 142f

R
racing games, 167, 168
raffles, 74–77
Rand, Allison, 43–47
recreational leagues, 171–178
Reflector software, 184, 185, 186
research, programs that teach, 70, 179–182, 267–276, 281–286, 307–311, 357–360
resources, lists of, 12–13, 100–101
Return of the Lazy DM, 54
rhythm games, 167, 168
roleplaying games (RPGs), 3–13, 43–47, 49–54, 65–71, 101, 103–113
Roosevelt, Eleanor, 330–331
Rorie, Jamey, 49–54
rulebooks, for RPGs, 5t
Running the Game (YouTube series), 53–54

S
safety, resources for, 12
"Save Lewis the Librarian!" program, 317–325
scavenger hunts, 221–224, 249–253, 267–276, 281–286
scenario-development prompts, 110–113
school libraries
  clubs at, 127–132, 159–162
  donations and grants to, 97–101
  library research programs for, 307–311, 357–360
  orientation programs for, 79–84, 221–224, 297–306, 345–355
  science-themed programs for, 127–132

Sources card game for, 93–96
study break programs at, 121–125
tournaments at, 183–187, 307–311
science-themed programs, 59–63, 127–132
A Scientific Christmas Carol room, 236, 241–243
Scratch, 196–199, 205
selection tips, 165–168, 174, 190–192
Selga, Jennifer, 55–58
senior citizens, programs for, 29–36
shooters, 168, 174
Silberman, Ronna, 30f
Silent Memories, 4, 5t, 8, 9, 10–12
small businesses, donations from, 97–99
smartphone-based games, 133–136, 137–145
Smash Bros. tournaments, 147–151
Smite, 172f, 174
social media, 62–63, 69, 221–224, 271
socioeconomic literacy, 37–41
software selection, 167–168
Sources card game, 93–96
space travel games, 127–132
spinners, 227, 230–233
sports games, 192
spreadsheets, for planning, 142f, 143
spy games, 179–182, 281–286
Star Wars games, 265
Statik, 158
STEAM/STEM programs, 59–63, 127–132, 195–200, 201–205, 357–360
Stier, Zachary, 201–205
"Stop the Mad Librarian" program, 297–306
story creation, tips for, 7
Strauss, Elizabeth R., 287–292, 293–295
students
  circulating game collections for, 55–58
  orientation programs for, 73–77, 133–136, 137–145, 221–224, 297–306, 345–355

Sources card game for, 93–96
study break programs for, 121–125
worker training of, 345–355
subscription services, 165, 192
Super Smash Bros., 147–151, 168
SuperData, 183
swag, soliciting, 174

T

tabletop gaming programs
  conventions, 85–92
  large-scale, 73–77, 85–92
  life-sized, 225–233, 255–266, 335–343
  with locally-designed games, 115–118
  for older adults, 29–36
  science-themed, 59–63
  starting up, 15–19
  See also board games
Tang, Yingqi, 133–136
Taylor, Robert, 3–13
teens, programs for. *See* young adults, programs for
The Thing (movie), 6, 8
threat modeling, 207–210
Tinkercad, 208
Tomsu, Lindsey, 225–233, 335–343
Toren, Beth Jane, 137–145
tournaments, 147–151, 183–187, 307–311
training programs, 345–355
Trivial Pursuit, 79–84
Tucci, Ryan, 93–96
Tumble, 158
tweens, programs for
  live action game programs, 225–233, 245–253, 255–266, 277–280, 287–292, 293–295, 297–306, 335–343
  tabletop game programs, 3–13, 49–54, 79–84, 97–101, 115–118

video game programs, 127–132, 147–151, 153–158, 159–170, 183–187, 189–193, 201–205, 207–211
Twitch, 174, 192
Tyner, James, 15–19, 85–92

U

University of Wisconsin Stevens Point Library, 122*f*

V

Vadnais, Annette M., 73–77
Vampire: The Masquerade, 101, 215–219
Van Ross, Bryce, 59–63
Vann, Charlcie, 133–136
video games
  arcade-style programs for, 163–170
  clubs for, 127–132, 159–162
  collection development for, 189–193
  for final exam study breaks, 121–125
  for library orientation, 133–136, 137–145
  for library research, 179–182
  recreational leagues for, 171–178
  with STEAM/STEM focus, 127–132, 195–200, 201–205
  teaching cybersecurity through, 207–211
  tournaments for, 147–151, 183–187
videos, for promotion, 59–63
virtual reality (VR) programs, 63, 153–158, 167, 201–205
volunteers
  recruiting, 25, 88, 338
  thanking, 92
VR Worlds, 157

W

Wade, Steven, 313–316
Walsh, Andrew, 93
Warnings at Waverly Academy, 195–200
websites, for resources, 13, 34, 100–101
Williamson, Tanya, 93
worker training programs, 345–355
world-building prompts, 106–108
Wright, Melissa, 235–243
writing workshops, 103–113

X

Xbox, 164, 165, 166, 192

Y

young adults, programs for
  live action game programs, 221–233, 245–253, 255–280, 287–295, 297–311, 313–316, 327–333, 335–343, 345–355, 357–360
  tabletop game programs, 3–13, 21–27, 37–41, 43–47, 49–63, 65–71, 79–101, 103–113, 115–118
  video game programs, 121–125, 127–145, 147–151, 153–178, 183–187, 189–193, 195–205, 207–211
Yousif, Zeineb, 267
YouTube channels, 52, 53–54, 129

Z

"Zombie Tag" program, 267–276